Praise for *Absurdistan*

'*Absurdistan* is like Campbell himself; funny, intelligent, passionate' *Sydney Morning Herald*

'The standout feature of *Absurdistan* is that the story is about more than the craft of journalism – Campbell's vivid descriptions also serve as an empathetic survival guide for any person suffering a fish-out-of-water feeling' *Eureka Street*

'… tragedy and its aftermath bind this book together and make what would otherwise be an entertaining and intriguing memoir something more' Philip Clark, *Australian Book Review*

Eric Campbell is one of Australia's most experienced foreign correspondents, reporting from more than 100 countries and on every continent. From 1996 to 2000 he was the Australian Broadcasting Corporation's Moscow correspondent, covering the tumultuous changes across the former Soviet Union and Yugoslavia. A year later he was appointed China correspondent, dividing his time between the Middle Kingdom and the 'War on Terror' in Afghanistan. His posting was cut short in March 2003 when he was injured in the first suicide bombing of the Iraq War, which tragically killed his cameraman Paul Moran. Eric spent his recovery writing *Absurdistan*, an account of his travels across Eastern Europe and Asia. Since 2004 he has been a roving reporter on the ABC's international affairs television program *Foreign Correspondent* and is currently based in Spain.

SILLY ISLES
Eric Campbell

FOURTH ESTATE
An Imprint of HarperCollins*Publishers*

Fourth Estate

An imprint of HarperCollins*Publishers*

First published in Australia in 2017

by HarperCollins*Publishers* Australia Pty Limited

ABN 36 009 913 517

harpercollins.com.au

HarperCollins*Publishers*

Level 13, 201 Elizabeth Street, Sydney NSW 2000, Australia

Unit D1, 63 Apollo Drive, Rosedale, Auckland 0632, New Zealand

A 53, Sector 57, Noida, UP, India

1 London Bridge Street, London, SE1 9GF, United Kingdom

2 Bloor Street East, 20th floor, Toronto, Ontario M4W 1A8, Canada

195 Broadway, New York, NY 10007, USA

National Library of Australia Cataloguing-in-Publication entry:

Creator: Campbell, Eric James, 1960- author.

Title: Silly Isles / Eric Campbell.

ISBN: 978 0 7322 8594 4 (paperback)

ISBN: 978 1 4607 9487 5 (ebook)

Subjects: Reporters and reporting.

War Correspondents.

Foreign correspondents – Journeys.

Foreign news.

Cover design by Darren Holt, HarperCollins Design Studio

Author photograph by Dave Martin

Typeset in Bembo Std by Kirby Jones

Printed and bound in Australia by Griffin Press

The papers used by HarperCollins in the manufacture of this book are natural,
recyclable products made from wood grown in sustainable plantation forests.
The fibre source and manufacturing processes meet recognised international
environmental standards, and carry certification.

To Brietta,
My shelter in the storm

Prologue

No man is an island, entire of itself; every man is a piece of the continent, a part of the main; if a clod be washed away by the sea, Europe is the less.

John Donne

Gilligan's Island is wherever you want it to be in your mind.

Bob Denver

The Isles of Scilly lie just 45 kilometres from southwest Britain and by all accounts are quite sensible. This book is about islands that are far from sensible. Many verge on silly. Some are endearingly strange. A few are dangerously stupid. And a couple are both dangerously stupid and heavily armed (more on the Falkland Islands later).

As a reporter for an international television program, *Foreign Correspondent*, I spend half of each year travelling. Within reason and an ABC budget, I'm allowed to go almost anywhere I can find a story. But I've developed a habit of going to islands.

By definition, islands are self-contained worlds, usually with small communities, which makes storytelling easier. As mini versions of big communities they can also be wonderful symbols of humanity, microcosms of the vanities, ambitions and conflicts of great powers but with the folly laid bare, like local councils with tanks. But mostly they tend to have intriguingly weird sides. Isolate a community and add water and within a few generations strange things start to happen.

How many of us know, for example, that family fun in the Faroe Islands, north of Scotland, consists of Mum, Dad and the kids deliberately beaching whales then slaughtering them? Or that plumes of smoke rising over the environmental paradise of the Galápagos Islands usually means riot police are firing tear gas at fishermen trying to kill park rangers? Or why Icelanders found it perfectly sensible to try to make Reykjavik replace Wall Street as the global financial capital? (Many in that huge community of 119,000 people are still puzzled by why it ended so badly.)

Insularity tends to bring out the silly in people, and distance or sovereignty allows islanders to indulge it. Just look at Australia, an odd place indeed, even if technically it's not an island but a continent. (For reasons we'll see later, it can't be both.) Could we possibly have turned out the contradictory way we are – laid back and welcoming but terrified of boat people – if we weren't girt by sea? And let's not start on Tasmania.

The journey you're about to go on would never have been organised by a travel agent of sound mind. Tourists may soak up the sun in Zanzibar, but I'm yet to meet anyone who has ever booked a holiday in Yuzhno-Kurilsk. Hopefully it will convey something of the strange, addictive appeal of little-known communities in far-off places. And if World War Three really does kick off in Ayungin Shoal, as some predict, you can proudly boast you read it hear first.

Thanks to the many for the help in this journey, particularly Brietta Hague for putting up with me, Tracey Ellison for digging out tapes and transcripts to unjumble my memory, Geoff Lye, Wayne McAllister and Brett Ramsay for tracking down old photos. Special thanks for honest feedback from my father, Eric, and the wonderful women in my family, Juliana, Anna, Gwenda and Natasha. And my embarrassed and sheepish gratitude to the kind people at HarperCollins for endlessly gritting their teeth at missed deadlines as I kept travelling to ever more islands.

Barcelona, December 2016

1. Save the Whales (for Dinner)

The Faroe Islands, July 2007

> **There are people in this world who can wear whale masks and people who cannot, and the wise know to which group they belong.**
>
> Tom Robbins, *Jitterbug Perfume*

Let me say at the outset that I have never killed a fellow human, stolen a disabled person's crutches, pulled wings off butterflies or joined the Young Liberals. I am not knowingly a bad person.

However, I do enjoy the odd plate of whale meat.

Before I tried it, I felt the same Western middle-class horror of whale cuisine as the next middle-class Westerner. I was shocked when I first saw it on a menu in 1998, in a pub on the Norwegian island of Spitsbergen. High in the Arctic, downing pints of Nøgne Ø in 24-hour sunlight, I succumbed to peer pressure and ate a slice of whale pizza. The meat was tough, having been deep-frozen for some years due to International Whaling Commission troubles, but wickedly tasty: a cross between exotic fish and dark red meat.

I promised myself I wouldn't do it again but later I ordered an interesting-sounding pie, only to find the main ingredient was minke whale. It was even more delicious, with a frisson of forbidden fruit. On my next Nordic trip, to Iceland, I couldn't resist asking for lightly fried whale in a hipster restaurant in Reykjavik. After all, even installation artists with beards were eating it.

So I don't write this shamefully, just extremely defensively. Whales are of course magnificent creatures and their sheer scale humbles us as humans. But in Scandinavia, where most people eat cows and chickens, even nice people see whales as an acceptable free-range alternative. As long as the species isn't endangered and the dispatching is no worse than for other animals I eat, then I'm comfortable to tuck in, at least when I'm in Scandinavia. Being culturally sensitive I just wouldn't do it in Australia, even at a Young Liberals function.

Environmentalists have been known to make grudging concessions on cultural grounds if it involves indigenous people. The International Whaling Commission has never opposed what it calls 'aboriginal subsistence' whaling, provided it's not commercial and doesn't endanger populations. Arctic Inuit continue to hunt whales as they have for centuries (albeit now with outboard motors and high-powered rifles) and I'm not aware of greenies ever running blockades and telling them they're monsters.

The problems start when it's white folk doing the killing.

Føroyar, known in English as the Faroe Islands, is a prosperous Nordic nation of mainly blond people midway between Iceland and Scotland. Ever since their Viking ancestors settled there in the 9th century with shiploads of sheep (Føroyar is Norse for 'Sheep Islands'), the Faroese have also been slaughtering passing pilot whales with knives and clubs. Once it was necessary for survival. Now it's a cultural tradition.

Every summer, whenever a pod is spotted, boats rush out to drive the whales in to shore. As soon as they're beached, it's on for young and old. Mums and dads race out of their design studios and apartment lofts, kids put down their iPhone 6s and everyone picks up sharpened knives for some old-fashioned family fun. Within moments, they're down on the beach happily stabbing and slicing in a sea of blood. And it's whale for tea!

Outsiders tend to take an extremely dim view of this. The eco-warriors of *Sea Shepherd*, led by Paul Watson, tried to stop the 2014 season, driving whales away from shore with a Zodiac donated by the animal rights advocate and renowned Hollywood actor, Charlie Sheen (see *All Dogs Go to Heaven 2*). The Danish navy arrested 14 anti-whaling activists while locals happily chopped up 33 whales.

'The hunt is done because of the absurd belief by the Faeroese that God gave the whales to the people to be slaughtered,' *Sea Shepherd*'s website declared in disgust. Charlie Sheen was even blunter, accusing the navy of collusion with whale murderers.

'The 40-foot Zodiac called the BS *SHEEN* that I donated to Mr Watson's tireless and heroic efforts has been shamefully seized,' he said in a statement.

In further alliteration, suggesting he had made the statement early in the day, he added: 'This level of insidious and vicious corruption must be dealt with swiftly and harshly.'

I'd long been fascinated by the annual slaughter, known in Faroese as the *grind*, sadly pronounced with an 'ih' rather than an 'eye' which would be so much more appropriate. In 2007 I managed to persuade a sceptical executive producer that this nation of 50,000 had a Story That Must Be Told. Mainly, I just wanted to go there.

Getting there meant flying from the Danish capital, Copenhagen, some 1300 kilometres away. As with all Viking islands, sovereignty had passed between the kings of Denmark and Norway over centuries.

(The exceptions are Britain's Orkney and Shetland Islands, which Norway pawned to Scotland in the 14th century in lieu of a dowry. Shetlanders still celebrate their Viking heritage every year in a winter festival of mead drinking, longship burning and forehead splitting called 'Up Helly Aa'.)

Denmark took charge again in 1814, spurring the beginnings of an independence movement among islanders sick of being ruled by distant kings. But it wasn't until 1948 that Denmark agree to grant the islands autonomy.

To learn more about the islands' history, culture and politics, I opened the tourist brochure, written in the belief held by many tourist agencies that people travel to places to learn their exact measurements.

The archipelago is composed of 18 islands covering 1399 km² (545.3 sq miles) and is 113 km (70 miles) long and 75 km (47 miles) wide, roughly in the shape of an arrowhead. There are 1100 km (687 miles) of coastline and at no time is one more than 5 km (3 miles) away from the ocean. The highest mountain is 882 m (2883 ft) above sea level and the average height above sea level for the country is 300 m (982 ft).

Of more immediate interest as I sat in my 43-centimetre by 58-centimetre seat with its 69-centimetre high back was that the North Atlantic Ocean had whipped up some typically filthy weather for our arrival. The islands' rocky peaks (none higher than 882 metres) jutted ominously out of fog as the plane descended in high wind and heavy rain towards the runway. A cacophony of muttered expletives came from the cameraman, Dave Martin, as he tried to hold his 18-kilogram camera steady in front of the scratchy perspex window. Bouncing around beside him was our producer, Marianne Leitch, giving helpful advice on what to shoot as the plane flung the camera around.

I was happy to have a field producer in charge, particularly Marianne who had worked for our program *Foreign Correspondent* since it started. Like most of the program's producers over the years she was a middle-aged mother and saw complicated shoots even in war zones as a welcome relief from wrangling teenage boys. Sadly, in the changing media landscape field producers were becoming a rarity as scarce production funds were being redirected to important emerging digital areas, like multiple platform content development and innovation management. (Other key expansion areas include vertical integration implementation, priority marketing frameworks and executive car park allocation.) It was simply becoming too expensive to take a third person on overseas trips that could cost more than an entire weekend's management team-building workshop in the Hunter Valley. (Importantly, this has not made me bitter.)

Dave, on the other hand, tended to be happier without producers, seeing any third wheel as just another 'blowie', the generic camera crew term for journalists, short for blowfly: n. pest, insect, habitually hovers around head making annoying sounds.

I was thinking about none of this as I tried to hold down my in-flight meal as the plane rocked and shuddered its way towards the runway, Marianne asking Dave if he was getting enough good shots of the mountains.

We finally skidded to a halt and staggered into the terminal to meet the one person we could never do without on a TV shoot – the fixer. This is a local person who acts as our eyes and ears on the ground, usually a journalist who can both translate and guide us objectively through the political and social landscape. The Faroe Islands are too small to have professional television fixers, but I'd managed to persuade a local journalist to take time off work to help us. Bjørt Samuelsen, a blonde middle-aged mother of two, was waiting inside the terminal with disappointing news.

'You just missed a good *grind*,' she told us. 'A lot of whales were caught a few days ago. But if you're lucky there'll be another one before you leave.'

Bjørt's normal job was being press secretary to the prime minister. Despite having a smaller population than Wagga Wagga, Faroese take great pride in having a full-scale government, even though Denmark continues to control defence and foreign policy.

'We don't have any bad feeling to Denmark, my husband is Danish,' she explained as we drove away from the airport. 'But we just don't feel Danish. Our country is the Faroe Islands.'

As we drove towards the capital, Tórshavn, I couldn't help thinking the islands had done rather well out of Denmark. The road became a freeway which then descended into a giant undersea tunnel. Bjørt explained that most of the islands were now linked by tunnels so people no longer had to travel everywhere by boat.

'But that must have cost billions of dollars,' I said.

'Yes, why not? We pay the money for it ourselves. We have many industries. A lot of fishing. Denmark gives only 10 per cent of the budget. We can do without it.'

Like many Faroese, Bjørt wanted full independence from Denmark, even though her boss, the Prime Minister, was against it. It would be an unusual sovereign country. As the freeway emerged from the tunnel it seemed like we had entered an illustrated fairy tale. Giant waterfalls gushed down the steep green slopes as we passed improbably quaint villages of stone cottages with turf roofs. It was a design little changed from the days of Viking settlement, the turf insulating the houses and deadening the sound of wind and rain. But there were modern touches. Every now and then we passed men pushing lawn mowers across their roofs, trimming back the thick grass.

The design motif continued as we reached the suburbs of Tórshavn – turf-roof houses in neat rows next to shopping malls and internet cafes. But the big surprise was when we reached the centre of Tórshavn. Everybody was dressed like extras from *The Lord of the Rings.*

We had arrived in time for the national holiday of Ólavsøka, when almost the entire population wears traditional costume. For women it's long dresses with lace-up bodices, while the men wear breeches and elaborate waistcoats: the Hobbit-like clothes worn by farmers and gentry right up to the 20th century.

'We pass them down each generation,' Bjørt said, 'but we spend a lot of time making new ones. You start making your child's dress as soon as she is born.'

The three-day festival marks the anniversary of the death in battle in 1030 of the Norwegian king Olaf the Second who was credited with bringing Christianity to the Faroes. Interestingly, he'd become a Christian himself after visiting a seer on the Scilly Isles. His Scilly conversion led him on a spree of torturing and killing anyone who wouldn't open their heart to Jesus. Apparently it worked a treat. (In a probably unintended tribute, Islamic State is using Olaf's conversion method today.)

Faroese take their Viking ancestry very seriously and it's still written in their faces. Most people can trace their ancestry back to the first settlers. It remains one of the most homogenous societies in Europe. Everyone still speaks a variation of Old Norse, closely related to Icelandic, even though the Danes spent much of the 19th century trying to force everyone to speak only Danish. Being northern Europe, everybody also speaks perfect English.

Tórshavn was one of the first settlements in the Faroes and the harbour is still surrounded by narrow cobblestoned streets and medieval houses. Just behind these is the islands' parliament, claimed to be the world's oldest. When not raping and pillaging, Vikings established a kind of democracy where all men's voices could be heard. They called the meeting place a *ting*, which roughly translates as a 'thing'. As it passed law, known as *løg*, it became known as *løgting*. The Faroese insist their *løgting* has been there longer than any other *ting*, even though the Danish closed it down for several centuries. Now it was up and running again.

Faroese clearly didn't like 'outsiders' telling them what to do, and I had a sense that included foreign media crews. Even Bjørt had been suspicious at first about my interest in whaling, fearing I would portray the islanders as barbaric. But she'd agreed to get permission from the local police stations for us to film a *grind* if one happened during our visit. Whale hunts are never scheduled in the islands; they only occur when pilot whales are sighted close to shore and fishing boats manage to beach them.

Just in case luck was against us, our first stop was the local TV station to try to buy some archival footage of a *grind*. The news director refused to sell us any. 'That's our station policy,' he said. 'You might put music under it or something to make it look bad.' Presumably not adding music would make hacking up whales look good.

So as not to be totally unhelpful, he put us in touch with a local freelance cameraman whose hobby was shooting *grindir*. This proved to be all we'd need. The cameraman was a chubby, untidy man with a garage studio crammed with cameras, microphones, camera parts and tapes strewn across the benches and floor. He happily showed us hours of his best *grindir*. It was not just enough to make me never want to eat whale again. I momentarily contemplated becoming a vegan.

The hunts begin colourfully enough. Fishermen bang pots and toot horns to turn the pod towards shore, while hundreds of villagers gather excitedly at the water's edge. Sometimes the waves wash the whales onto the sand. Otherwise dozens of people wade in and stick hooks in the whales' blowholes to drag them up. Then the killing starts. A spike in the brain is supposed to kill them instantly. But in most of the footage some whales thrashed about as they were sliced up, their blood turning the sea a deep red. In most of the videos there was a strange carnival atmosphere to the slaughter. It usually took only 15 minutes for the entire pod to be carved into chunks of dark meat.

We took the tapes back to our rented apartment to dub what we needed, trying to hold down our lunch.

The next morning Bjørt announced she had good news. 'I've found a family you can eat whale with!'

Our hosts lived just outside Tórshavn on a farm called Kirkjubøur (pronounced Chish-choo-bur), one of the oldest in the Faroes. They had just received their share of meat from the latest *grind* and were busily preparing a whale banquet. A giant, ancient whale fin bone lay outside their house. The head of the family, Jóannes Patursson, met us at the front door, as his ancestors had been doing for 450 years.

'My family took over this farm in 1557,' he told me in slightly accented English. 'So today we are the 17th generation on the farm.'

Jóannes was a trim man in his thirties with greying fair hair and piercing blue eyes. I could easily imagine him wearing horns and sailing a longboat. (Important historical note: Vikings didn't actually wear horns into battle as they would have made excellent things for enemies to hold on to while slitting throats. The image comes solely from 19th century British opera costumes. But still.)

He took me inside the oldest room of the farmhouse to show how even the 17 generations of Paturssons were relative newcomers to the property. It was a dark and spare space with creaking timber floors and walls decorated with whaling tools.

'This here is what you call *roykstova*, translated it means the "smoke room". The name comes from the smoke rising from the fireplace. Originally there was an open fireplace here. The timber we're walking on today used to be a soil floor. The room goes back to the year 1000 maybe. The saga says it's 900 years old.'

I momentarily thought of telling him that my apartment in Sydney was in a heritage-listed building because the former warehouse was constructed in 1879. But it didn't feel appropriate.

Jóannes had modernised the interior of much of the rest of the house, building comfortable bedrooms for his three children and a state-of-the-art kitchen, where his heavily pregnant wife Guri was preparing lunch. A huge chunk of whale meat and blubber was simmering away in a large pot.

'It's best if you boil it for two hours,' she said, scooping out the blood as it rose to the surface. 'The meat's looking pretty good now. Not sure about the blubber. I used to eat a lot of blubber when I was a little girl and I'm not so fond of it any more. I probably ate too much,' she laughed.

I was surprised to see that Guri was planning to eat the meat. The Faroese government puts great stock in the nutritional value of whale and defends the *grindir* as a cultural rite, but in recent years it's been warning pregnant women not to eat it. The reason is marine pollution. Pilot whales are at the top of the food chain, eating mainly squid. That makes them the repository of every toxic chemical remnant consumed by lesser sea life. And these days that's a lot of toxins.

As remote as the islands are, they're in the middle of one of the world's most chemically polluted oceans. The North Atlantic enjoys the output of both Europe's and North America's factories, including chemicals like mercury, lead, PCBs and DDT derivatives. Doctors in Tórshavn found unusually high levels of mercury in children's blood, leading to attention, language and memory difficulties. It was not a great leap of logic to blame it on the whales they eat. Whales don't metabolise organochlorines. They concentrate them in their meat and blubber.

Guri had heard all the warnings about limiting the intake for children and abstaining during pregnancy. But with three months to go until her next child was born, she was prepared to take a chance.

'I'm, I'm a bit worried, yeah, I am, but I eat it as well although I'm pregnant. I eat it about four times a year.'

'Did you think about not eating whale at all?' I asked.

'No, no, I'm going to keep on eating. It's good for you too. It's food from the sea.'

I left her cooking to share a drink with Jóannes in his study, decorated with paintings of his ancestors. One of them was a stern portrait of his great-great-grandfather who had founded the independence movement in the 19th century. Jóannes was carrying on the family tradition.

'For me Denmark is a foreign country,' he told me. 'Just like Norway or Iceland or any other of our neighbouring countries. Just as they see us as a foreign country.'

As he rolled and smoked cigarettes, the smoke rising through the shafts of light from the latticed windows, he reeled off the calumnies Denmark had committed against the Faroese culture and language.

'Even in the church you were not allowed to speak Faroese,' he said. '"God didn't understand the Faroese language" was the claim. So all the church language, all the legislative language, all the administrative language was in Danish, a foreign language to us.'

Jóannes was friendly but rarely smiled. He told me how hard life had been on the storm-battered islands, with pastures so steep sheep had to be lowered by rope to feed. I could see how it would produce a dour, unsentimental people.

'You have living conditions here that you don't find anywhere else in the world,' he said. 'A lot of what made people being able to survive here was cooperative efforts.'

Guri announced the whale was ready.

I wasn't really in the mood for the ultimate politically incorrect meal. But I didn't want to be rude. Guri served up the boiled pilot whale and sliced off a thick wad of blubber to put on top.

As I played with the food, cutting and moving it around the plate, Jóannes told me of the customs that made whale meat a birthright.

'You don't even have to participate [in the *grind*],' he said. 'You will get your share anyway if the pod is large enough. The minute you are born you are put up on a list in the village and you won't be scratched off that list unless you die.'

I swallowed the meat and blubber and made appropriate 'Mmm, delicious!' noises. In truth, boiled whale meat wasn't nearly as tasty as the steaks and pizzas I'd had in the past and it was an effort to swallow the viscous blubber, which Jóannes explained was once the islanders' only source of Vitamin C.

Sensing my residual Anglo abhorrence, he asked me if I'd ever been inside a working abattoir. I nodded, remembering the smell of terror from the cows.

'Seeing it on TV the *grind* looks very cruel, I understand that of course,' he said. 'There's a lot of blood, but if you took the blood from the abattoirs and let them into Sydney Harbour it would look exactly the same. Your beef goes to McDonald's. Ours is a bit different.'

Thoughts of vegetarianism filled my mind as Guri continued to ply me with blubber.

But I was about to find, Australians could learn to love the *grind*. Bjørt had arranged an interview with the Faroe's chief international negotiator on whaling – a woman from Sydney.

Kate Sanderson had been studying Norse literature at Sydney University in the 1970s when she came to the Faroes to learn the language. She met and married the islands' most revered writer and had been there ever since.

She invited us round to supper, welcoming us in an Aussie drawl completely unaffected by spending most of the past 22 years speaking Faroese. 'What I like about here is that it's a small tight-knit community,' she said, 'but it's also a nation.'

To my relief, her family hadn't yet received its share of the *grind* so she was preparing a chicken salad. 'You know what they say,' she quipped as she sliced the lettuce. 'Save the whales – for dinner.'

Kate was contemptuous of the International Whaling Commission as a political group posing as a scientific body. She thought the anti-whaling brigade was 'full of shit'. Over supper she scoffed at suggestions that pilot whales were endangered.

'There are about 100,000 pilot whales in the Atlantic. We have records going back to 1600 almost unbroken and the long-term average of whales we take is 1000 a year. If you can do that for 400 years straight, I think that's evidence enough. But we also have modern methods to ensure or keep an eye on the level of the population. Two generations of media hype and campaigning against whaling have really warped people's view of what whaling today is all about. Those countries that continue to whale are all countries that have a very long tradition of eating whale.'

I nodded, enjoying the beer and the blubber-free chicken.

Outside we could hear the first chants of '*Góða Ólavsøka!*' meaning 'Good Olaf's Wake', a sign the celebrations were underway. We headed down to the harbour where a boat race was about to start between young Faroese dressed in hats with horns! Dave set up to film the action and studiously ignored Marianne's instructions for him to shoot the faces of young children in traditional dress.

Dave was the program's only dedicated cameraman and we had worked together on and off for more than 20 years, starting when he still had hair. On trips that could last months we had shared countless sunsets, fireside camps, small rooms and even small beds, which always left us deeply depressed about our personal lives. But we could work together instinctively, Dave always knowing the shot I wanted without me asking. I could even order Dave's dinners before he arrived at the table, knowing exactly what he felt like anywhere in the world (usually spaghetti bolognaise). He didn't like being told what to shoot by producers and Marianne didn't like being treated like an annoying mother. We were an island of stubborn individualism in a sea of Faroese cooperation. It's what we like to call creative tension. On a long shoot (this was our fourth story in seven weeks), it can also be a sign that it's time to go home.

The end of the shoot proved to be even more extraordinary than the sight of a *grind*. The Faroes are the last place in the world to still have mass chain dancing, a medieval tradition of linking arms and dancing all night while reciting epic poems. Dave set up his camera at the edge of the town square as it filled with thousands of Faroese in full traditional dress. A man next to him told us they had never stopped doing it because it was the traditional way to keep warm as they waited on the shore for *grindir*.

As one, the crowd began to sway together and sing. The sounds of Old Norse poems filled the cold summer night. And on the dancers went, chains forming within chains, arms linking with friends and strangers, people dropping out to drink and returning to fortify the chain. After an hour, Dave had filmed all he needed. But we stayed on past midnight, then 1 am, then 2 am as the exuberance and unsteadiness built higher and higher.

This was a strange, unique and magnificent place. I'd recommend a visit. Unless of course you're a whale.

2. Smoking Ruins

The Kuril Islands, August 2005

The strongest of all warriors are these – Time and Patience.

Leo Tolstoy, *War and Peace*

World War Two is widely believed to be over. It's not. Despite being utterly defeated in 1945, Japan refused to sign a peace treaty with the Soviet Union. Today, it is no closer to signing one with the USSR's successor, Russia.

Japan's continuing outrage is not over the Allies' destruction of its armed forces or the nuclear annihilation of two of its cities. It's because the Soviet Union pinched four of its islands after it surrendered. Tokyo continues to demand them back and Moscow continues to tell Tokyo to get stuffed. So both countries remain technically in a state of war.

This is not necessarily cause for alarm. Diplomatic spats aside, there's no suggestion that either country would resume armed hostilities. However, with both countries adopting more aggressive foreign policy, the spat has the potential to become serious. Moscow and Tokyo continue to make threatening noises about the islands, while nationalists on both sides continue to get unpleasant frothy bits on their lips every time they talk about them.

As in all such disputes, the two sides have entirely different names for the islands, which lie just off the coast of the northern Japanese island province of Hokkaido. Tokyo calls them Hoppō Ryōdo, meaning 'Northern Territories', insisting they're an integral part of the country. Moscow says they're just the fag end of a Russian chain of volcanic islands called Kuril, meaning 'Smoked'.

What's not in dispute is that Moscow invaded the Northern Territories/Southern Kurils, or as one Russian politician told me, 'liberated' them. The Red Army expelled all the Japanese who had been living on them for generations and moved in thousands of Soviet settlers. Grateful rocks, trees and sandbars have presumably been celebrating their liberation ever since.

What rankled Japan most was that Moscow mounted its invasion after it was all but defeated. Ignoring the urging of its Allies, the USSR had spent the entire war avoiding Japanese soldiers, choosing to concentrate on the Nazis. The Soviet Union didn't declare war on Japan until 8 August 1945, two days after the first atomic bomb was dropped on Hiroshima.

The Red Army had swept down the Pacific coast, reclaiming the giant island of Sakhalin that had been lost in the Russo-Japanese War 40 years earlier. (In 1905 Russia sailed its mighty Imperial fleet all the way to Japan where it was promptly sunk, creating a bitterness that passed seamlessly from the Tsars to the

Bolsheviks.) Between 18 August and 1 September the Soviet 16th Army occupied the four southern Kuril Islands, completing the invasion just 24 hours before Japan's formal surrender to the Allies.

The Soviet empire now stretched from the coast of Norway to a rowboat's ride from Japan. The ensuing Cold War kept the dispute frozen. But when the Soviet Union collapsed in 1991, it fired up again. Tokyo began screeching for the islands' return. Moscow cried *Nyet!*

None of this unpleasantness stopped the world celebrating the 60th anniversary of the end of World War Two in 2005. I persuaded the ABC to let me travel to the disputed islands to point out that the most destructive war in history hadn't actually finished.

*

The Japanese city of Nemuro, on the eastern coast of Hokkaido, is the official centre for banging on about Hoppō Ryōdo. The westernmost island of Habomai lies just on its horizon and most of the 17,000 islanders were settled in Nemuro after the Soviets expelled them. Nemuro's main visitor attraction is a huge propaganda museum with interactive displays on how Japan was robbed and high-powered telescopes to look at the lost land.

Like any Japanese city, it is a model of order. The streets are clean and well maintained, and though they were full of drunken *sararimen* the Friday night we arrived, the office workers were unfailingly polite even while paralytic.

Our budget hotel rooms were small but perfectly formed, with just enough space to fit a bed only 10 centimetres shorter than me and a moulded plastic bathroom capsule. Entertainment came in the form of a coin-operated TV showing Japanese blue movies with chequerboard effects over the rude bits.

Unusually, I was travelling with a full crew, meaning both a cameraman and a sound recordist. Geoff Lye, the shooter, had spent several years in the Tokyo bureau and was excited to be back. Nathan English, the sound recordist, was excited to be on one of his first overseas shoots, unaware it would also be one of his last. (Despite the importance of good audio for long-form television, sound recordists were going the way of VHS cassettes. They were deemed unnecessary in a digital world where cameras had their own microphones, albeit extremely crappy ones. The Sony camera's 'top mike' as it was known, was already being nicknamed 'the Japanese soundo'.)

We had timed our visit for Nemuro's annual outdoor rally to demand Russia return the islands. We arrived at a large park expecting fierce ultra-nationalists with rising sun headbands shouting, 'Death to Putin!' Instead, there was a crooner in a purple velvet suit entertaining families having picnics. Tears flowed down his pancake makeup as he belted out ballads for each island by name.

'Habomai, Shikotan, Etorofu, Kunashiri, I can see the islands close together in the old time,' he sang. 'You are ever in our dreams, you are ever in our dreams.'

A large crowd watched happily, many munching barbecued octopus. The city administration had thrown in free food to attract people, and several families with small children had come in anticipation of a promised Power Rangers show.

When the crooner was done, the sleekly dressed mayor, Hiroshi Fujiwara, took the microphone. 'The war hasn't ended for Nemuro,' he shouted. 'There's no such word as "post-war" here!' Many dropped their octopuses to applaud.

When I met the mayor later in his office, he was positively brimming with optimism for an early resolution to the half-century dispute. His hope rested on the apparent goodwill of an ex-KGB clerk, Vladimir Putin, then enjoying what was meant to be his second and last term as Russian president. 'President Putin's term is until 2008 and since Putin has great authority, I deeply hope he will solve this problem during his tenure in office,' he said.

Even back then, long before Putin started seizing former Soviet territory like Crimea (or as the Russian Foreign Ministry would put it, liberating it from CIA-backed fascists), the thought of Putin giving up anything seemed absurd. But the mayor was already drawing up redevelopment plans.

'If the four islands return, first of all we must develop the land as we protect the nature on the four islands. We will improve the social infrastructure such as harbours, roads and airports and then Japanese people will start to live there. The four islands belong to Japan. We will confirm our sovereignty and jurisdiction.'

There were still 8000 islanders living in Nemuro, though their numbers were thinning with age. Mayor Fujiwara put me in touch with a stooped, white-haired old man named Ken Takamoto who had lived on the island of Habomai. We met on a lookout he visited every day to try to catch a glimpse of his homeland. But we couldn't see it through the fog.

'I remember only the good memories,' he said. 'I was a first year student in elementary school, but when I lived there, I worked hard. We would go out in a boat every day to collect seaweed then dry it in the village. It was a hard life, there was no electricity, but it was a good life. We would go to Nemuro to see a movie, which I loved.'

Mr Takamoto was 68 but looked far older. He'd been eight years old when the Soviets invaded. 'We were very frightened. They took over everything. In one place, some people rowed out in the sea and drowned themselves in protest. After two years, they put us in boats and made us leave.'

He had only been back once, two years earlier. After months of negotiations, Russia had agreed to let him and a few score pensioners take a charter ship to one of the islands to visit a village that is no longer there. After 90 minutes on land, laying offerings to their ancestors, they were herded back on the boat by armed Russian soldiers.

'First, tears came out and I couldn't believe what I saw,' he said. 'Nothing, nothing was how it used to be. I investigated for about 30 minutes, but there was nothing I could remember from the time I was there. It was uninhabited. It was a wasteland. Why doesn't it return? It's a complete mystery for people like us who are not involved in politics or military. We want it back. After all, it's a fishing place and island where our ancestors farmed. Rather than sadness … it's indescribable. Why did this happen? How did it get so complicated?'

It's an article of faith in Japanese politics that every party must demand the return of the Northern Territories. Japan spends tens of millions of dollars a year trying to press its point. The museum outside Nemuro features hi-tech holograms of life in the fishing villages, medieval documents of Imperial references to settlements, and child-friendly touch displays of international law.

I watched a school student push a button and get the simplified version. 'Hello! You have chosen history of the Northern Territories,' a digital manga child cried. 'It's about the history of reclamation. It was never under Russia's control and it was Japan's native territory where only Japanese people lived permanently.'

But in fairness to Stalin (even noting that a genocidal monster ranks low on the entitled-to-fairness scale), it's not quite so clear-cut. The four islands are at least geologically part of the Kuril Islands chain that runs down from the Kamchatka Peninsula in northeast Russia. While the Japanese emperor administered the southernmost islands from the 17th century, tsarist fur traders and fishermen continued to move down from the Russian mainland, establishing their own outposts in the northern islands. Much unpleasantness and violence followed. After Russia won The Biggest Naval Loser contest in 1905, Japan forced it to cede any claim to the Kurils.

In February 1945 the Allies met in Yalta and agreed Stalin could reclaim the Kurils. It was an incentive for the Soviet Union to join the fight against Japan once it had finished with the Nazis. But Japan would later claim that the wording of that agreement was ambiguous, arguing it could not possibly include the southern Kurils, which were clearly part of Japanese territory. Despite resuming diplomatic relations with Moscow in 1956, it refused to sign a peace treaty.

This situation is not as unusual as it might sound. Some nations have remained technically at war for centuries simply for neglecting the paperwork. Bizarrely, the modern record is held by those (otherwise) sensible islands, the Scilly Isles. The Duchy of Cornwall, which administers Scilly, unwisely backed the Royalists in the English Civil War. The Netherlands, spotting the likely winner, backed the Parliament. In 1651, it declared war on Cornwall for allowing Royalist ships/pirates to use Scilly as a base to attack Dutch ships. There was no actual fighting in the war. After seeing the pathetic state of the all but defeated Royalist fleet, the Dutch commander decided not to waste any cannonballs on it and sailed away to more important matters. It wasn't until 1985 that the Dutch embassy in Britain realised it had never formally ended the war. The ambassador was promptly dispatched to Scilly to sign a peace treaty. The 335-year-old conflict/clerical oversight is now known as 'The Scilly War'. (Interestingly, the Scilly War was not the only notable event in Scilly maritime history. In 1707, four British navy ships sank in a storm off the islands, drowning 1700 sailors. The disaster was blamed on poor navigation under the Commander-in-Chief of the British Fleet, the impressively named Sir Cloudesley Shovell. It is now known in maritime circles as 'The Scilly Navy Disaster'.)

Unlike the Netherlands, Moscow is in no hurry to settle old wars. And that's why you can't hire a rowboat in Nemuro to get to the islands. You have to fly to Russia first.

*

Sakhalin is classed as part of the Russian mainland, even though it's actually an island, the largest on Russia's Pacific Coast. It's not renowned for being tourist friendly: its main claim to fame is for shooting down a Korean passenger jet that strayed into its airspace in 1983. But if it were desperate for a catchy slogan, it could always call itself 'Gateway to the Kurils'. Twice a week a ferry takes cars and passengers on an overnight run to Yuzhno-Kurilsk, the administrative capital on the island of Kunashiri.

We made a pale and sickly impression as we arrived at the ferry port. It was the first time my camera crew had been in Russia and they were not feeling well. Geoff Lye had spent the entire night at a nightclub marvelling at the number of beautiful Russian women with rich ugly men. Nathan had spent the night trying to find his way back to the hotel from the nightclub after someone stole his wallet. I'd stayed in with a dose of food poisoning and was now negotiating with a toothless, extortionate babushka at the port to gain entry to The Worst Toilet In Russia. '*Po bolshomu – desiat!*' she demanded. (For a big one, $10!)

The crossing took 18 hours on a boat that had seen better days, eating food that had seen better weeks. But the hardest part of the trip was getting off. The Russian Border Service remains the most unreconstructed remnant of Cold War stupidity. It still treats every border territory as a top-secret security area and every foreign visitor as a possible enemy agent.

We queued on a rickety gangplank, trying to hang on to six cases of camera gear and our personal luggage above the water, as officers inspected each person's documents, suspiciously comparing dates and faces, calling over more senior officers to double-check dates and faces. The sight of a foreign television crew spread a frisson of almost sexual excitement through their ranks. Reinforcements came racing across. Each document was examined, fingered and quadruple-checked, every case examined in minute detail, every piece of equipment queried and inspected.

There was no logical reason for their paranoia. The islands have no secret laboratories, secret weapons or nuclear facilities. There's no valuable industry, unless you count ageing canning factories as harbingers of the Asia-Pacific's next economic tiger. The islands no longer have any strategic benefit and Japan's pacifist constitution means they're under no conceivable military threat. There's nothing to spy on. Absolutely nothing happens there. But still the Border Service plays out the role of Soviet nasties, like villainous extras in a *Rambo* film.

Oddly enough, there was a Russian television crew on the ferry that received only a cursory check, even though one of them looked uncannily like Rambo. He didn't actually resemble Sylvester Stallone, but he was wearing military camouflage with a black headband and a hunting knife strapped to his leg.

'That's our correspondent,' the Russian cameraman told me. 'He calls himself Rambo. It's his gimmick for Sakhalin television. A businessman here wants to be on television so he's paid us to come and do a story on him.'

We loaded our gear into a perestroika-era Niva van and headed off to the hotel we had booked, only to find it wasn't there. In its place was a Soviet gulag full of half-starved, filthy inmates crowded into decaying brick animal pens. At least that's what it looked like.

'Yes, this is the hotel,' the receptionist said. 'We have one room for three people.'

I lectured the crew about the lack of good accommodation in provincial Russia and the need to rough it for the sake of the story. Then I dragged five of our bags into the prison room and saw a man using our toilet.

'It's not your toilet!' the receptionist shouted when I complained. 'You have no toilet! Everyone shares that toilet.'

'Is there another hotel in town?'

She scowled and rang a number on an old bakelite phone. 'They're full,' she snarled triumphantly.

In desperation, we decided to chance our luck and loaded the gear back into the Niva to drive to the other hotel. This part of town lacked a single visible redeeming feature. Every building was a decaying five-storey Khrushchyovka, the 1960s generic Soviet building built to last all of 15 years. Bouncing down potholed streets past endless wrecked cars, cracked walls and rotting window frames, we eventually found the hotel, which appeared surprisingly fit for human habitation. But Rambo and his crew were checking into the last three rooms. One fat bribe later, the receptionist miraculously found us another ... with a bathroom!

Often as a correspondent, the discomfort is forgotten as you explore the wonders of the destination. This time nobody wanted to leave the room. A pall of bad weather had descended on the town: rain falling through fog onto mud, concrete and rust. But we were here to work, not to enjoy the delights of scratchy sheets with cigarette burns. So, reluctantly, we gathered our gear and went outside.

We plodded through the empty, muddy streets for what seemed like hours in search of someone to interview. The rain appeared to have driven everyone indoors. The drabness of the town made it hard to navigate but we fixed on a dead cat in the middle of an intersection as our marker. The grimy, dirt road right of the cat led to the town's only restaurant, and the left back to the putrid harbour where half-submerged ships lay deteriorating, abandoned after breaking down or just left to rot when there was no more use for them.

Straight ahead of the cat we saw our first human.

He swayed unsteadily. The man was clearly drunk, but he was the only living creature on the streets (apart from a slightly lost-looking cow) who was not employed by the ABC. So he seemed worth talking to.

'*Zdrastvuti!*' I said. Hello. 'I'm from Australia. May I do a short interview?'

His eyes focused slowly as he raised his head and attempted to stand straight.

'*Shto khochesh?*' What do you want?

'I'd like to talk to you about the Kurils.'

He scanned us blearily then smiled, revealing rotting teeth.

Geoff and Nathan moved in quickly with camera and microphone, adjusted settings, then nodded. The day wasn't going to be a waste of time after all.

'*Tak, kak zhizn?*' I asked. So, how's life?

He opened his mouth to answer and coughed up a gob of mucus. Then, for no apparent reason, he pulled out a knife. Before we could react he fell back in a perfect vertical decline and thudded unconscious into the mud.

Fortunately we had an appointment the next day with a man who was both sober and spoke English – Kunashir's mayor, Pavel Gomilevsky. He was young, educated and well travelled, part of the new generation of post-communist bureaucrats. A large portrait of President Putin hung behind his desk. As mayor, he was responsible for meeting Japanese delegations, but he saw no need for diplomacy.

'The Japanese, they are zombies!' he said when we started recording. 'How to explain such people? They are not normal like you and I. These idiots once call me and say I must meet them at the Japanese Friendship House. Like they own the islands! I say fuck you, you can come to my office!'

He was adamant Putin would never give up an inch of the Kurils.

'If Russian government give away islands is not true Russian government,' he continued. 'This territory is where I was born, my wife, my son. For me Russia is these islands. Russia forever.'

'What do you think of Japan's claim to these islands?' I asked.

'History says these claims are not honest. They do no honour to Japanese politicians, because these islands is Russian. In 1945 Soviet Union liberated all the Kuril Islands as a revenge for what the Japanese did. If they don't want to live in friendship well, it's up to them.'

A few years before, many islanders and even officials might have said something very different. When the enfeebled Boris Yeltsin was president, Russians felt emboldened to criticise their leaders. And the people here had much to criticise.

Like all remote Soviet border regions, the islands had been propped up artificially for strategic reasons. The few industries that were set up didn't trade with nearby Japan, but sold everything through central planners in Moscow. A huge military presence, a guaranteed market and state subsidies ensured the inhabitants had a passable standard of living. They were poor, but no worse off than anyone else in the USSR, and could be assured of jobs for life, free health care and education for their children.

The cold winds of economic reform blew hardest on outposts like the Kurils. When Soviet subsidies disappeared in the late 80s, everything that made life bearable went with them. Continuing paranoia over Japan meant they couldn't even take advantage of being on the doorstep of a rich neighbour. Instead, they were abandoned and trapped in a far-flung corner of a decaying state. In 1992, to make a point of their desperation to Moscow, the islanders held a mock poll in which they voted to secede to Japan.

Putin's more authoritarian rule put an end to such whining dissent. Nowadays, anyone suggesting they'd rather live under Japan's umbrella was branded a traitor.

'The traitors dreaming of only one thing, that these islands will be Japanese,' Mayor Gomilevsky said in disgust. 'Most of these people are nobody. Don't have good jobs. Don't have good kids. Kids are just as stupid as them.'

Roaming the streets of Kurilsk, it was hard to find anyone who wanted to talk at all. When I'd lived in Moscow as a correspondent in the 1990s, it was never a problem to gauge opinions. Every second person on the street could give an eloquent and passionate speech about life, politics or history. Now, at the very edge of Russia, nobody wanted to talk openly to a foreigner. A few people conceded off-camera how hard life was, but as soon as the camera was on they went straight to the official line of how much better life was under Putin and how proud they were to be Russian.

Japan had made one minor inroad into Kunashiri in the Yeltsin years, which it still maintained at huge expense. The Japanese Friendship House gives free language and culture lessons to the islanders and assistance to go on occasional charter boat trips to Japan, when the Russian authorities allow it.

It's a large, impressive building in traditional Japanese design with four full-time Japanese staff. Nearby is a Japanese-owned hotel catering solely to Japanese visitors. It's all supposed to be apolitical but the size and investment suggest the Japanese government sees it as a diplomatic foothold.

The islanders see it as the only place to get something for nothing. We watched about 20 residents ranging from schoolchildren to pensioners arrive for an afternoon lesson, removing their shoes and entering the classroom with a bow and the ritual greeting *Konbanwa*.

An elderly pensioner, Lubov Korsonova, told us it was the highlight of her week. 'It's very interesting for me to learn another language. Last year I was able to take the ferry to Nemuro and stay with a Japanese family.'

'Wasn't it expensive for you?'

'No, very cheap. Japan paid for the trip and I took a big box of tomatoes, cucumbers and potatoes.'

She invited us back to her house, which was 1950s Soviet meets *Teahouse of the August Moon*. It was decorated with Japanese calendars, tour brochures, dolls, lanterns, kimonos, fans and paintings of Mount Fuji, all courtesy of the Friendship House.

A shopkeeper had confided to us that Lubov was keen for Japan to take over. But, on camera, she would have none of it. 'I can say that the Kurils are a part of Russia,' she said. 'And in my opinion they should remain a part of Russia, under the jurisdiction of Russia, because we are Russian people and we are used to the Russian way of life.'

It was interesting to imagine how the islands would look if they had remained Japanese. The streets would probably be paved, the buildings modern. There'd be traffic lights, smartly dressed policemen, an efficient port, karaoke bars, clean well-equipped schools and hospitals, sushi restaurants, golf courses, five-star hotels, multi-storey car parks, perhaps even a giant bridge or underwater tunnel to the mainland.

Geoff, a former rugby league player who never minced words and who had spent years living in Japan, had no doubts. 'Mate, the Japanese would go apeshit over this,' he said. 'They'd develop the whole island just to make a point. They'd stick a dome over Kurilsk and keep it as a theme park so Japanese tourists could see the sort of shit the Russians did with it.'

On the other hand, the Japanese could have destroyed something priceless. Beyond the polluted harbours, decrepit towns and ramshackle military bases, the Kurils have something that might never have survived Japan's post-war development frenzy: a vast, unsullied wilderness.

It's complete coincidence of course. The Soviets had as much regard for the environment as a lungfish has for classical music. But it was so far away from Moscow they never got around to developing it.

We hitched a ride with some park rangers up to what is now the Kunashir *zapovednik*, or nature reserve. It's not easy to reach. The road only runs part of the way round the island, so we drove in a high-bodied truck that could bounce over the rocky coastline and, when necessary, just pull off into the water to continue the journey 'off-road'. It was a stunning contrast to Yuzhno-Kurilsk.

The forest was utterly pristine, a lush mix of fir trees, oak, maple, heath and meadows. We passed active volcanoes, hot springs and untouched beaches. The park covered most of the island and most of it had never even been explored.

'There are many places, in fact most of the area where a human has never set foot,' a young park ranger named Tikhon told us. 'Places where man has never ever been, only flown overhead in a helicopter or plane.'

Tikhon was only in his twenties but he was the chief park ranger. As a boy on the mainland he had read stories about the vast forests on the Kurils and dreamed of one day coming to work there. It was everything he'd imagined, with bears roaming the forests, whales passing the shoreline, and streams so full of salmon you could barely cross them. Inadvertently, the Kurils had become a refuge for plants and wildlife that once covered northern Japan but were being wiped out by overdevelopment.

'The nature of Hokkaido and Kunashir is similar but here it's much better,' he said proudly. 'In the last hundred years we haven't lost a single species. Nothing has disappeared. Sea lions from Japan escape here to live in peace, we have killer whales, lots of other endangered species, they're all doing well.'

He worried what would become of it all if Japan ever took over. 'We have a thriving colony of sea lions in the south. But the Japanese see them the way Iranians see wolves. They try to kill them because they disturb the fishing industry.'

The empty land and virgin forest were a developer's dream. But thanks to the isolation, the only development was a small collection of huts on one of the beaches. Not even the townsfolk came here except for some hobby fishermen who spent a few weeks a year in the *zapovednik* without their wives for peace and undisturbed drinking.

Some scientists had come once to study the environment and built a makeshift *banya*, a peculiarly Russian sauna of simple timber where sweat and buckets of cold water took the place of bathing. We joined Tikhon and his mates, one of whom could speak basic English, and spent the evening in a steam and vodka haze. Then we joined them in a hut for the best fish stew I have ever eaten.

'Japan would make this a five-star resort and put a barbed-wire fence around it to keep the bears out,' Geoff mused.

It was a shame to have to leave the *zapovednik*. Geoff was talking seriously about coming back for three months and shooting a doco on bears. As we drove back to town, I couldn't help wondering if another crew would come here in another 40 years on the centenary of the end of the war to do exactly the same story. The stubbornness on both sides seemed eternal.

With the first sight of Yuzhno-Kurilsk, we were glad to be going. The fog had rolled into town again and the rain had turned the streets into rivers of mud. Zombie-like drunks stumbled through the puddles.

The dead cat was still in the middle of the road. The unhappy Russians weren't going anywhere.

3. Zanzibar Blues

Zanzibar, January 2007

> I had intended to have gone into Africa incognito. But
> the fact that a white man, even an American, was about
> to enter Africa was soon known all over Zanzibar.
>
> Henry Morton Stanley, 1872, in his book *How I Found Livingstone*

The woman moved like a black shroud, appearing to float rather than walk along the beachfront. Only her eyes were visible under her dark chador. She averted them modestly as she passed Mercury's Bar, named after the island's most famous gay export.

I stepped inside to see giant photographs of Freddie Mercury in rock star mode pouting and parading on stage. A group of tourists were also gawking, marvelling that 'this is where that guy from Queen came from'. Freddie, real name Farrokh Bulsara, had indeed grown up in Zanzibar, in a traditional family of Persian–Indian descent, before moving to Britain. And Zanzibar's loss had been glam rock's gain. He became a gay icon belting out hits like 'Bohemian Rhapsody' and 'Fat Bottomed Girl' before dying of AIDS in 1991 at the age of 45.

The bar is popular with tour groups, who sip cocktails and watch boys playing beach football in front of golden sunsets. But few Zanzibaris dare come here. Their Islamist clerics have a problem with self-declared homosexuals, especially one of their own. The bar has twice been bombed, though in the murky world of Zanzibar's infighting few know if jihadists or rival bar owners were responsible.

Zanzibar has long been marketed as a tropical paradise 'where Africa meets Arabia'. The very name has become a byword for exotica (see the 1995 novel *The Wreck of the Zanzibar* set on the Isles of Scilly). It's been a successful formula in attracting up-market European tourists and down-market backpackers. But it doesn't take long to see why young Farrokh might have found life more agreeable in London.

The Zanzibar archipelago, formerly known as the Spice Islands for their cloves, cinnamon and pepper, has long been in the cross-fire of three competing cultures: Swahili African, slave-trading Arabic, and European colonialist. The culture with the biggest guns has always won.

The Portuguese had first crack after Vasco da Gama ran into it in 1498, but things came to a sticky end for them in 1631 when the Sultan of Mombassa massacred every white person. In 1698 the Sultanate of Oman took over, running a highly efficient trade in human cargo until Britain put the squeeze on slavery in the 19th century. In 1890 Britain established a protectorate over the archipelago, allowing the sultans to rule in its stead, until independence finally came in December 1963. The Africans wasted no time in seeking revenge for centuries of foreign domination, massacring up to 20,000 Arabs and Indians and driving out thousands more, among them a 17-year-old schoolboy with a penchant for pop music named Farrokh.

Thus, according to Zanzibar's schoolbooks, began golden days of peace and prosperity under the revolution's wise pan-African leader, Abeid Karume. He negotiated a union with the neighbouring mainland state of Tanganyika to form the new east African nation, Tanzania. But the union was very much on Karume's terms. He became Tanzania's vice-president while retaining the presidency and near total control of Zanzibar, establishing what was effectively a military dictatorship on the island. Ungrateful assassins killed him in 1972 but his despotic legacy continued. In 2000 his son Amani Abeid Karume took over as president and leader of the ruling party, Chama Cha Mapinduzi (CCM), the Party of Revolution.

None of this concerned tourists, of course, who jetted in from the Tanzanian commercial capital, Dar es Salaam, or took a three-hour ferry trip. We took the latter. It was cheaper.

It's rare as a foreign correspondent to go to a place where nice people take holidays. That's for travel reporters. So Vivien Altman, the producer, and cameraman, Dave Martin, were as excited as I was by the trip. It felt downright naughty. There would be good hotels, good food, even a chance to go swimming. The downside of course was that we'd be focusing on all the bad things that tourists can ignore.

The ferry disgorged us in searing heat on the main island of Unguja, where port officials collected our entry permits. We hauled our gear along the jetty, looking around for people watching us, feeling the paranoia that always comes when you bring a television camera to a police state.

Vivien had arranged for us to be met by the local journalist she'd hired as our fixer. In authoritarian states fixers are the unsung heroes of foreign reporting, not just guiding ring-ins around the complexities of the country but taking risks to help us get what the authorities don't want to give.

Adia (not her real name as even henchmen occasionally read) greeted us and suggested we move quickly. She had written articles for mainland newspapers that were highly critical of the Karume regime, making her a frequent target of police surveillance. As we drove into the city she gave us her take on the local politics.

'It is no longer Africans against Arabs,' she said. 'Everybody hates Karume. His people steal from everyone.'

It was hard to reconcile her negativity with the sheer beauty of the place. It was like a David Lean film set. Arab dhows sailed along a cerulean sea past blindingly white coral sand and swaying palm trees. We drove down cobblestoned alleyways into the old capital, Stone Town, passing spice markets, bazaars and 18th century Arab houses with giant hand-carved doors and windows.

'This is where all the young people buy drugs,' Adia said as we neared the hotel. 'There is no work for them. They have no hope. They just get stoned.'

'It doesn't look like a drug town,' I said, pointing to women shrouded in chadors on the street corner.

She looked at me as if I were an idiot. 'They're prostitutes,' she said. 'Can't you tell?'

We allowed ourselves an afternoon to settle in, enjoying the surface impressions of Zanzibar before starting the messy business of peeling back the layers. I wandered through Stone Town to the waterfront, marvelling at the strange hybrid of cultures. The barbarity of the slave trade had created a jewel of Arab civilisation off the African coast. Minarets and palaces sat alongside African shantytowns. Men in Arab dress mingled with African labourers in singlets. Most of the population is now black, but many light-skinned islanders of Arab descent could walk through the souks of Muscat without attracting a glance. Traces of British colonialism pop up unexpectedly – an Anglican cathedral in the middle of Stone Town, the decaying waterfront residence of David Livingstone before he started his final expedition in 1866. Adding to the confusing mix is up-market Western tourism, with bikini-clad Germans strolling out of beach resorts past fundamentalist mosques.

It was an extraordinary place to visit, but as Adia explained when we met her at her pokey office the next morning, it was less appealing to live there.

The 1964 uprising was supposed to liberate the blacks, but in the time-honoured tradition of revolution, one group of despots had simply replaced another. The Tanzanian government had obliged the CCM to hold multi-party elections since 1995, but they'd used cheating and violence to ensure nobody but their own could win.

Adia turned on her computer and displayed dozens of photos she had taken of victims of past elections. They were gruesome images of men, boys and women lying dead, beaten, burned or tortured. She explained it wasn't usually police who targeted opposition activists, but a shadowy youth militia that had earned the nickname janjaweed ('devils on horseback') after the roaming death squads of Sudan.

'They have training camps across the island. Many of them are next to police stations. I can try to take you to one but it is very dangerous.'

Adia was a useful source of information, but her obviously close links to the opposition made us nervous. As we drove back to Stone Town, we began to get the uncomfortable sense of being followed, only heightened when, for no apparent reason, a police car pulled us over.

'Where you from?' a smiling policeman asked.

'Australia,' I said.

'What you do here?'

'We're journalists.'

He stuck his head in the front passenger window and checked us out.

'You must give me money.'

'What for?' I asked.

He shrugged his shoulders. 'Give money.'

It was the first time a policeman had ever demanded a bribe from me without giving at least a made-up reason. It was clear we weren't going anywhere until we paid, so I handed him $10. He smiled and wished us a happy stay in Zanzibar.

The vaguely reassuring experience of standard beat police corruption temporarily eased my paranoia of being followed by secret police. But within minutes Vivien's mobile phone rang. It was the Foreign Ministry demanding to know where we were staying so they could look at our tapes.

'Why do you need to see our tapes?' Vivien asked. 'I can't remember the name of the hotel … The driver doesn't know its name either … We're about to change hotels anyway … No really … I'm not making it up … Of course. As soon as I know, I'll call you … Thanks, bye … Bye … Yeah, bye … Bye … Oh, shit!'

Vivien explained to us that the Foreign Ministry had rung on behalf of the Interior Ministry to inform us we would not be allowed to leave until they had reviewed all our tapes. Whatever sense we had of a holiday-style shoot vanished in an instant. If the police got hold of our tapes, we would certainly lose them. From now on, we would have to dub and secrete every tape, make sure we weren't followed and somehow stall on telling the authorities where we were staying. At the end of it, we would have to work out a way of getting out of Zanzibar in secret.

The first steps were the easiest. The foreign couple who owned our hotel agreed not to pass on our passport details to the police. And Vivien switched her sim card so the authorities couldn't call again. But getting away with filming dissidents for the rest of the week was going to be more problematic. Our only hope was that the government's security was as hopeless as the rest of its administration.

We caught a glimpse of the government's lack of governance the next day, when we left town to meet one its more prominent opponents on the other side of the island.

Naila Jiddawi was a feisty, middle-aged woman of Arab descent who ran a small beachfront hotel. She welcomed us in its empty dirt car park and invited us in for lunch. The hotel was run-down and there were no other guests. A few years before, she'd registered to run as an opposition candidate in the election. A crowd of janjaweed had promptly arrived at the hotel and burned her house down.

'They torched this house. They closed the hotel. The leaders were government people leading this group of witch doctors coming across there with their regalia and their drums forcing their way in here. When the time came to torch this place, they were singing – these are leaders of the ruling party – "We will get rid of all the Arabs, all the opposition parties. We will torch them." They were singing from place to place.'

After lunch, Naila took us to the neighbouring beachfront village to show how the discontent had moved far beyond the island's Arab community. Groups of black African women greeted her and began chronicling their own problems, as Naila interpreted.

'She says, you know the government does not have a social service to help people like her. She says you know when you go to town you want to bring rice, you want to bring flour and sugar, you can't manage it because you don't have money.'

The village had no amenities except a clinic with no staff and no medicine except Aspirin. The nearby school was just as badly off. The classrooms had no doors or windows and the children had to share the school's few textbooks. Naila had tried to open a free primary school in the village but the government shut it down after she refused to start each day with CCM propaganda.

'I won't conform to what they will want to sing,' she told us. 'There won't be those party songs here. It will be education.'

In earlier times, the United States had constantly criticised Zanzibar's dictatorship, even after it dropped its Marxist overtones and ethnic cleansing for more generic bastardry. As late as 2005, the US State Department condemned its electoral rigging and refused to send a representative to President Karume's inauguration.

Just months afterwards, the criticism softened. The US ambassador to Tanzania made a fence-mending visit to the islands, describing the rigged election as 'reflecting the will of the people'. It was bound to happen. Zanzibar might have marketed itself to Western tour groups as a peaceful paradise, but it was selling itself to the US as a front line in the War on Terror.

Ninety-nine per cent of the population is Muslim. It has traditionally been a moderate Islamic community, but Zanzibaris have not been immune to the call of jihad. At least two islanders were involved in the simultaneous bombings of the US embassies in Tanzania and Kenya in 1998 that killed 224 people. Radical Islamists from Saudi Arabia and Yemen were suspected of secretly training recruits. And the CCM repeatedly painted the opposition as closet Islamists, accusing it of sending militants to fight in Iraq and Afghanistan.

All of which deeply offended the opposition leader, Ibrahim Lipumba, who professed to be a pro-Western wishy-washy liberal. A large, dignified African in his fifties, he lived on the

Tanzanian mainland and only visited with a large contingent of bodyguards. We joined his convoy as it travelled to a supporters' rally in one of the many slums around Stone Town. The bodyguards stood in the back of open vans at the front and rear of the convoy, nervously scanning for militias.

A few hundred people had gathered to hear him, and his spin doctor warmed up the crowd, repeatedly mentioning that a foreign camera crew was filming. He motioned them to clap as Lipumba came to the front, but his appearance sent the crowd into genuine excitement.

'The young people of Zanzibar are tired,' he shouted. 'They don't have employment. They don't have good education. There are no health services. You are going to die in Zanzibar!'

I would have thought it was a gloomy message but the crowd cheered and clapped ecstatically. It was a rare treat to hear criticism like this in public.

'And if the Zanzibaris and people who believe in democracy are sidelined, it is possible for the hardliners, for religious extremists, to take over,' he warned. 'Supporters of Osama bin Laden can have a fertile ground in Zanzibar if we do not allow the democratisation process to continue!'

The last comment appeared aimed more at the camera than the crowd. The spin doctor jumped to his feet to lead the crowd in enthusiastic applause.

Ibrahim Lipumba expanded on his theme back at Civic United Front headquarters in the middle of Stone Town. While the government accused his party of backing terrorism, he claimed it was the government that was fostering terrorism by denying people the right to elect a moderate alternative.

'If the Civic United Front, which is a liberal party, is eliminated as a political alternative, the only other alternative ... and people are talking about it ... is to organise as Muslims. Just look at Somalia where you have the imams of mosques organising the government.'

Lipumba pointed out that his party was a member of Liberal International, a worldwide alliance of centrist parties. He proudly showed me a photo of him with David Steel, the former leader of Britain's Liberal Party, when Steel visited Zanzibar as an observer during the 2005 elections. Lord Steel had experienced a frightfully more interesting time than the usual Liberal Party junket, popping into CUF headquarters just as the government laid siege to it.

'This place was tear-gassed,' Lipumba told us. 'We collected 400 canisters of tear gas just around this particular area and people were beaten up.'

He gave me a DVD copy of the regime's greatest hits, all of them involving batons. Opposition activists had sat on rooftops during the voting to record police actions. There was nearly an hour's footage of people voting and being beaten, thrown into trucks and being beaten, thrown on the ground and being beaten, and in one case, a man being beaten unconscious, and then while unconscious, being beaten again. Police seemed to favour heads for the initial beatings, then bodies if the person failed to cooperate by crumpling immediately. Once on the ground the multi-skilled police would concentrate on beating their feet.

'If democracy fails in Zanzibar, certainly democracy cannot be able to prosper in the Arab states,' he said. 'So it is a very critical area. It is in the interest of people who want democracy to succeed in the Muslim world for democracy to first succeed in Zanzibar.'

The CUF wasn't looking like an alternative that a gambler would put money on. Lipumba admitted some of its younger members were becoming much more radical and difficult to control. Soaring unemployment appeared to be attracting Zanzibaris to extreme Islamist solutions. One fishing boat on the waterfront even had an Osama bin Laden face printed on its flag.

So how was I going to find the dangerous Islamic radicals? Fortunately, they were in the phone book.

The Islamic Propagation Organisation was banned from running as a political party, so it operated as a social welfare group and had an office in Stone Town. It was a small street-front stall with a phone and a handful of earnest-looking apparatchiks dressed in the conservative ankle-length Arabic robes called *dishdasha*.

Their leader was a young scholar named Sheik Azan Khalid. His family was descended from Omani Arabs and had clearly never married out. He was purely Arab in appearance and puritanical in outlook. The shopfront was too small and noisy for an interview, so he agreed to come to our hotel with two aides. They froze at the steps when they heard the hotel dog barking.

'We cannot enter a building with an unclean animal,' one of his aides announced.

I explained the problem to the owners, who agreed to lock their pet out the back, watching nervously as we began setting up to film.

Sheik Khalid was not one for small talk, giving monosyllabic answers as I tried to chat during the awkward minutes of rearranging furniture, putting up lights and attaching microphones before we could begin.

'So I understand you studied in Saudi Arabia.'

'Hmm.'

'And this was with Wahhabis?'

'Mm.'

Once the interview began, he seemed at first to fit the stereotype of a radical Islamist, telling me only sharia law should be allowed on the resort island and that tourists should be forced to dress modestly.

'The values of Zanzibaris have been degraded from the European influence, especially with the increase of bars.'

But as we talked, something strange happened. He began to sound more like a liberal democrat than a mad Islamist. He was clearly incensed by the government's crushing of dissent.

'The government does not respect the people or listen to their cries.'

And like Lipumba, he warned that the government was pushing people towards violence, saying people were nearing breaking point.

'Time will tell – humans are humans. They make their own decisions and there's a limit to how far they can be pushed. And we don't know what they'll decide to do.'

I wasn't sure what to make of him or his followers. He agreed to let us film him at the mosque the next day. But within minutes of our arrival, one of the mosque officials demanded to know if I was a Muslim, then ordered me to leave. Only the cameraman was allowed to stay. It was the first time anywhere in the world that I had been ordered out of a mosque for being an infidel. Tolerance was clearly not one of the movement's strong points.

Yet as I stood outside listening to the sheik's address, I was surprised by his remarks. He didn't rail against Western evils, but instead welcomed the Australian television crew and hoped we could show the world how Zanzibaris were suffering from the undemocratic government.

I was keen to talk to him some more, but Vivien appeared at the mosque with disturbing news. The Foreign Ministry had somehow managed to find her new mobile number and rung to demand we give up our tapes. They had told her they knew we had bought tickets to leave on the next day's ferry.

'Guys, we're going to have to get out of here now,' she said. 'There's a charter flight leaving in 90 minutes.'

We raced back to the hotel, loaded our gear and sped to the airport, watching nervously for anyone following. Nobody was. We checked in, dreading our names were on a watch list. They weren't. Minutes later we were on the small private plane, taxiing along the runway.

The intercom crackled with an unexpected Australian accent. 'G'day everyone, my name's Abdul, I'm your captain. Sit back and relax. We should have you in Dar es Salaam in 30 minutes.'

Zanzibar hadn't quite been the indulgent treat we were expecting. I felt tense and exhausted. Even the triumph of getting away was tempered by the obvious fact the secret police were as incompetent as they were brutal. Journalism has a habit of sucking the joy out of life. Looking down at Zanzibar's sweeping, pristine beaches, I had just one thought. I need a holiday.

4. No Man's Land

Spitsbergen, April 1999

> Svalbard, like other polar regions, has first and
> foremost been a man's world. Even today, the
> masculinity in some will greatly increase the moment
> they set foot on the tundra, as if the polar air itself
> affects certain glands.
>
> Svarthvitt Briger Amundsen, 2001

It was orientation day at the University of Svalbard and the
students were heavily armed, not with your average contraband
assault guns favoured in US campus killing sprees, but something
far more effective: Ruger Mini-14 big game rifles.

You can't expect to kill it with just one shot,' the safety
instructor, Fred Hansen, warned them, strolling along the line
of science students at the university's open-air shooting range.
'You need at least three or four rounds to kill it.'

Anyone attending the world's most northerly university,
deep inside the Arctic Circle, risks being in a real-life horror
film storyline – spunky sorority girls and geeky freshmen

go camping, know-it-all friend disappears, desperate female finds mutilated body, nightmare chase ensues. The island of Spitsbergen, in the centre of the Svalbard Archipelago, has only about 1800 human inhabitants. But there are an estimated 3000 polar bears.

'Four years ago there was a girl actually killed up in that mountain there from a polar bear, straight next to town,' Hansen continued. 'See the polar bear as one big target and aim straight for it.'

The students picked up their rifles and began blasting the outlines of polar bears in life-sized paper targets moving towards them on cables, struggling to brace their weedy shoulders against the powerful kickback. It was -20°C and they squinted against the blinding reflection of spring sun on ice. Nimilan, on his first day at uni, was doing his best to fire straight but was obviously having a disorienting day. It wasn't just the first time he'd picked up a rifle. It was the first time he'd seen snow.

'I am the only person from Sri Lanka here at the moment,' he told me between shots. 'So it's just a totally different place compared to Sri Lanka. The lifestyle is new, climate is new, snow is new.'

Nimilan had flown from the tropical subcontinent to study astrophysics at an Arctic outpost that was the exact opposite of his homeland. Spitsbergen, in the Svalbard Archipelago, is a 450-kilometre-long ice-covered island filled with black coal. The sun never rises for nearly five months of the year, then after a brief changeover period, never sets for the rest of the year. The North Pole is 1300 kilometres to the north. The Norwegian mainland is 1000 kilometres to the south. It's as close as you can get to the middle of nowhere and still order a cappuccino.

Norway takes great pride in administering this extreme outpost and goes out of its way to make it like the mainland. As well as a university, there's a modern town called Longyearbyen, claimed to be the world's most northerly. There are daily Boeing 737 flights bringing tourists and supplies including daily floral deliveries. The town boasts designer stores, gourmet restaurants and five-star guest lodges. There is also a filthy, impoverished Russian mining town complete with a statue of Lenin on Norwegian soil. The island has had a complicated history.

It began in 1596 when a Dutch mariner named Willem Barentsz arrived to check out reports of bountiful whales, found an island with jagged peaks and gave it the imaginative name Spitsbergen, meaning 'Jagged Peaks'. Eager cetological slaughter followed and by the 19th century the whalers were joined by Norwegian fur trappers, Swedish seal hunters, American coalminers and crazy brave explorers who felt it was a handy starting point to reach the North Pole. No country owned it or any of the other islands in the Svalbard Archipelago until World War One was over and the victors put their minds to re-drawing long-forgotten maps. The Versailles Treaty led to the Svalbard Treaty under which Norway formally took possession of the islands in 1925.

But there was a catch. The many countries with commercial interests in Spitsbergen insisted they be allowed to continue them with visa-free travel for workers. The newly formed Soviet Union quickly realised this was a way to get a foothold in the capitalist 'West'. It snapped up a Dutch coalmine called Barentsburg (after the Dutch explorer) and a Swedish mine called Pyramiden which it quickly transformed into model Soviet communities, shipping in tonnes of Ukrainian soil to establish Soviet-style public squares and gardens. During the Cold War they became a bizarre anomaly – Soviet towns full of communist iconography in a NATO country.

By 1999, when I was working as a correspondent in Moscow, Russian miners were still flying in and out of Spitsbergen to dig coal and occasionally making the news for all the wrong reasons (for example, a 1996 plane crash that killed 141 people). I was intrigued by why they would want to go somewhere that appeared to be even colder and more dangerous than Russia.

I had managed to persuade the then executive producer of *Foreign Correspondent*, Wayne Harley, that there was an important story here. But thanks to the difficulties of calling from Moscow, my cameraman, Dave Martin, and I weren't yet sure what the story was. We had an invitation to visit the Russians in Barentsburg and assumed we'd find something of interest in the Norwegian town. But it wasn't until the first night munching on a whale meat pizza in a Longyearbyen tavern (as mentioned in Chapter 1, this was where my descent into whale eating began) that I stumbled upon our 'talent', the TV term for the story's main character.

'You are from Australia?' a fellow beer drinker at the bar asked. 'Then you better call Jason.'

It was 10 pm but he assured me it wasn't too late to call. Arriving in late April we were already in the period of endless daylight, the sun travelling in a horizontal arc above the horizon.

(It would be late August before it set again.) One side effect is that people don't tend to sleep much, waiting for the dark months to start the human equivalent of hibernation.

I rang and a startled but distinctly Aussie voice answered: 'Heia!' It seemed some people did go to bed before 10 pm in spring, but after a short discussion he agreed to come straight up to the pub.

As a foreign correspondent I tend to avoid using Australians in stories unless there's a good reason. It's a hangover of once working in tabloid media when any report of a foreign disaster would begin with the equivalent of a brave Aussie being airlifted with an ankle injury from a landslide that killed 100,000 anonymous brown people. But Jason Roberts turned out to be a story in himself.

He had grown up on a farm in Victoria, become a stockbroker in Melbourne and London, then somehow ended up in Spitsbergen helping out a mate doing some diving under the ice for a research project. A visiting camera crew needed some shots of seals and asked him to take down a camera. He took some pictures and soon found himself being hired as a cameraman for Arctic shoots. Discovering a talent he had been unaware he possessed for spending weeks in an ice hide waiting for polar bears to give birth, he had become the go-to man for extreme documentaries and a favourite for filmmakers like David Attenborough. Longyearbyen, situated as far as it's possible to get from his old home, had become his new home.

'It's very hard to put into words what this place means to me,' he told me. 'Very pristine and not many people, which is very nice. There are not many places left on Earth that are as unpopulated as here. Some of the recent polar bear films we've done I've spent two years in the field. It's a bit of an adventure all the time. I like to say "another day in the office".'

Even better, he offered to show us around his office. He was planning to cross to the far side of the island in a few days to repair a field hut that had been damaged by a polar bear. 'Come along,' he said. 'You won't forget it.'

Apart from a souvenir store selling polar bear skins, the town centre seemed more village chic than wild frontier. There was even a newly built primary school. We filmed a class the next day and it could have been any school in downtown Oslo. The schoolteacher, Renate Tiefenthal, told us it was a complete change from when she moved here with her miner husband 38 years earlier. Back then, coalmining was the only industry and miners couldn't bring their kids to live in the town. During the dark winter months, when temperatures drop to -30°C, the community was completely cut off.

'I'm longing for some of the old conditions we had here, when all were friends, knew each other and were insulated the whole winter. Last boat left in November, first came in May. And we were friends and everybody knew everybody. But of course there are changes now to the better, especially for the workers. They weren't allowed to have families here, it was of course quite impossible.'

Until 1992 there wasn't even a food store, let alone a hotel. She had to order a month ahead. Then, with the coalmines starting to run down, Norway's government decided to develop

Longyearbyen as a modern town and tourist attraction. The investment paid off, with around 10,000 Norwegian tourists flying in each year, and the town boasted a supermarket with fresh food delivered daily.

'Now we have everything. Whatever you want – frozen bread, pears, meat, fish, everything.'

But 55 kilometres away, another side of island life remained consistently grim.

We hired snowmobiles and a guide to take us to the Russian mining settlement of Barentsburg. It was a long, slow slog along the coastline, the sea still frozen solid from the long winter. Despite the advent of tourism, the Norwegian authorities were careful to leave a gentle footprint on the environment. There were no roads between the settlements as cars and trucks would scar the permafrost. In summer, when the ice melted, the only way to travel round was by sea. The landscape was utterly pristine with no sign of rubbish. Then suddenly we came across rusting pipes and abandoned machinery lying in the snow. 'Welcome to Barentsburg,' the guide said.

In contrast to the modern Norwegian town, the Russian coalmining town could have been transplanted from Siberia. Everywhere was cracked concrete, rusting metal cladding, smokestacks pumping out filth, and gloomy five-storey apartment blocks. A marble bust of Lenin glowered across the main square.

For post-Soviet Russia, distracted by the turmoil under Boris Yeltsin, Barentsburg was no longer maintained as a strategic foothold. It was purely about money. There was still something of a market in northern Russia for the high-grade coal so there still seemed to be some point in keeping it going, and unlike most mines in Russia the workers were actually getting regular salaries.

One miner, Yuri Gabarev, said he didn't have to spend a single ruble except on vodka. 'Life is very hard on the mainland but here they send 30 per cent of my salary home for my family to live on and the rest of the money goes into my account. The meals are free so by the end of my time here I have all my money.'

But the rich seams were running out. The other Russian mine, Pyramiden, had been abandoned the year before. The future of Barentsburg was uncertain. Without a guarantee of higher wages, there was no reason for any Russian to want to live in Norway's high Arctic.

Jason, however, wouldn't live anywhere else. He met us at the snowmobile hire store the next morning to take us across the island. He assured us we'd be able to cover plenty of ground before night. (Not that there was any actual night happening for the next four months.)

'I say for locals who drive quite hard and fast, 10 minutes driving is about a day's walking. So you can work that out after a day's travelling how long it would take you to walk over.'

We rode up to his house on the edge of town to pack supplies for the expedition. The plan was to head south to fix his hut then over to the coast and, fuel permitting, ride across the frozen Arctic Ocean. Jason attached a small trailer behind his snowmobile to carry food for a hot meal and enough fuel for the return journey. I couldn't help noticing he had a .44 Magnum. 'Can't be too careful with polar bears,' he said.

For Jason, riding with a gun was normal. What he wanted to show off was the latest new accessory for Spitsbergen – a mobile phone. 'The first people have started to use phones,' he said, 'which is quite strange when you have an emergency situation, people on the edge of dying can maybe call home before they die, which has been happening lately.'

'So it's getting civilised?'

'It's getting very civilised and comfortable,' he said, almost regretfully.

As he strapped down six fuel canisters for the long ride he explained it was the life outside town that kept him here.

'It's mostly the adventure, I guess. You never seem to run out of things to keep yourself amused with, as long as you're not crazy about the opera, which we have a pretty bad chance of doing here. Outdoor activities are quite amazing. From the edge of town, you're in the wilderness. You're gone, just five minutes out.'

He sped off up the town's last road and I squeezed the throttle to follow. We were soon in a white wilderness, racing over snow and ice and dodging herds of reindeer.

'Arctic cows,' Jason yelled dismissively.

The temperature was well below freezing but the snowmobile suits were so wind-resistant there was no sense of cold. The hand warmers on the handles were so fierce I soon started to get hot and turned them off. As we reached flat ground Jason let rip and his snowmobile charged off into the distance. I followed as best I could, trying not to be fazed by the constant bouncing. As always, it was even harder on the cameraman. Dave Martin had slung the camera over his shoulder and had to endure it slapping against him with every bump. But he couldn't stop grinning.

We rode for almost two hours before the first stop. It was like riding a horse but many times faster with no need to rest. There was no vegetation but the landscape was stunning, from endless fields of snow to towering walls of blue ice and the jagged peaks that gave the island its prosaic name.

Jason pulled up in a sheltered valley for lunch, quickly setting up a gas burner and heating a warm stew while David filmed. As we ate, Jason told us more about the island's strange history.

'There has always been some type of spying on each side,' he said. 'Up until quite recently the Russian community had eight helicopters and the Norwegian government didn't have any helicopter support. So you could wonder what they were doing with eight helicopters and a base. I'm sure there's been a lot of submarines in the Cold War around these fjords and oceans.'

These days the only real enemy was polar bears. After lunch, we took a long detour to the hut to check out the bear damage that hunters had told him about.

We arrived in the late afternoon to see gaping holes in the hut walls. Jason had brought some building materials to seal the gaps. Judging by the mess inside, it seemed the animal had forced its way in and eaten half the mattress.

'Lovely animals, these polar bears,' Jason said as he hammered in a strip of cladding. 'They get carried away.'

Five kilometres away we found tracks of the animal that might have been responsible.

'It's definitely a young bear,' Jason said inspecting the paw prints. 'When a bear's young, you can tell from the track what type of a bear it is here. The male bears get a lot of fur at the bottom so they have more of a bend in the walk. You can see in the next track further on there's a slight bend, here the fur's coming through but it's such a little amount it's very difficult to tell if it's a female or male but it's definitely a young bear, quite a small track.'

'So it's just scooted off over the ridge?' I asked.

'It's just gone over the ridge here, and very recently.'

That put the bear close enough for Jason to load two guns: a signal gun to scare it off and the 44. Magnum in case it came straight for us.

Jason didn't need to ask if we wanted to follow the bear. He told Dave to spread the tripod on the trailer so he'd be ready to shoot when we found it.

Within seconds we crested a ridge and saw it standing on the horizon.

It was a young bear but clearly big enough to be dangerous. Jason kept us at a distance, more out of respect for the bear's safety than ours.

'You normally place yourself in front of it,' Jason whispered, 'and if it's inquisitive to come and have a look at you, you let it come and have a look at you. If not, you let it continue on its own business.'

Dave stifled curses as he tried to attach the camera to the tripod's frozen base plate, finally ramming it into place and buttoning on.

The bear heard or perhaps smelt us and decided to move on. I held my breath as Dave filmed the animal padding off into the distance. Definitely a good day at the office.

'Quite often they'll come to within 20 metres and just sniff and have a look and wander off, just wondering what you are,' said Jason. 'You're probably an alien in their world so they don't get to experience many people.'

'Do you ever get tired of seeing bears or is it still a thrill?' I asked.

'It's still a thrill. It's been quite a few now. I have no idea how many. But it's still a thrill. Different experiences and new things happen, you see a mother and cub come out of the den for the first time, it's quite an amazing thing. More people have been to the top of the Himalayas than have seen a polar bear mother and cub come out of a den.'

For Dave and me, filming a polar bear in the wild felt like a once-in-a-lifetime experience that would never be topped. Then Jason suggested we head out to an iceberg.

It was easy to know when we were on the ocean. It looked and felt like it had been snap-frozen, the wind having pushed the sea ice into sharp peaks that now resembled whitecaps. It was hard riding and I almost came off twice at high speed. Ten kilometres out to sea we found the iceberg jutting up from the frozen ocean. We rode up to the edge and dismounted. Jason and I climbed up it.

He broke off a piece of ice and sucked on it, inviting me to do the same. I was surprised to taste fresh water.

'It's a lovely iceberg,' he said. 'Glacial ice, it's frozen in the autumn with the sea ice. The water you just drank is probably hundreds of years old.'

Suddenly we felt a slight movement.

'The ocean's 300 metres deep below us,' Jason said. 'The sea ice is about a metre and a half thick. There's movement in the sea ice as the tide and the oceans come under here, so around the iceberg can be quite dangerous. This is quite small so it's not too bad.'

We stood for a while in silence. I had trouble taking in all we had seen that day and the sheer strangeness of sitting on an iceberg in the middle of the ocean. The cold was starting to seep through my bones but I didn't want to leave. Jason gestured it was time to move.

'Right now we're 140 kilometres from home, to put it nicely,' he said. 'It's now almost midnight.'

'Almost time to go back?'

'Almost time to go back.'

Reluctantly I walked back to the snowmobile and hit the ignition. The midnight sun still hovered above the horizon as we began the long ride home.

*

Seventeen years later Dave and I were back in Svalbard and things had changed. Jason was still there, running what was now a big production company for Arctic wildlife films. But the ice wasn't.

'This winter was impossible to do what we did 17 years ago,' he told me. 'The ocean was nearly not frozen anywhere on the west coast of Svalbard. The water was completely open up to the beach line, which we'd never experienced before. We experienced low sea ice years, but this was a no sea ice year.'

This time it wasn't the oddity of Spitsbergen Island that had brought us here, but an issue we had barely thought about in the 90s: climate change. And in Svalbard, even the Australian government would have trouble denying it.

'Since your visit last time, the climate has changed drastically,' Jason said. 'What we've seen in the recent years, no sea ice, or very little sea ice in the inner fjords in the winter, that's due to climate change.'

The warming waters meant icebergs and the icepack were fragmenting and drifting south. The effects had even been noticed in Britain, more than 3000 kilometres to the south. In May, scientists had been stunned to see an ice-breaking bowhead whale from Spitsbergen off the coast of the Scilly Isles.

Norway was responding to the crisis much faster than Britain. Its parliament had just voted to aim for carbon neutrality by 2030, a seemingly titanic ask for a country that relied on oil and gas exports for its prosperity. The pro-oil right-wing minority government was munching on parliament's carbon neutral sandwich and saying it was yummy. But it had also just granted 13 companies licences to explore for new oil fields in the Arctic. Some commentators were calling it 'the Norwegian Paradox'; fighting climate change at home while exporting the fuels that cause it. Some environmentalists were calling it 'the Norwegian hypocrisy'.

It gave a reason for Dave and me to extend a shoot on the mainland and fly up to Longyearbyen. The mining town had turned positively greenie. The big coalmine on the hill behind it was on its last legs, barely producing enough for the nearby power station. Scientists at the university were working on a carbon capture facility to remove all the CO_2 from the plant before it reached the atmosphere.

Eco-tourism was booming with the once remote outpost branding itself 'the accessible Arctic', even attracting cruise ships with more passengers than the entire population of Svalbard. Barentsburg was still operating, but Jason told us even the Russian town was reinventing itself as an eco-tourism experience with a big new hotel.

I had hoped Jason would take us round the island again but these days his 'day in the office' meant actually being in an office. Wilderness filming had become big business here and Jason had built up one of Norway's biggest production companies, providing logistics and locations for wildlife films. The downside was that he'd had to trade a snowmobile for a desk and computer and delegate much of the fun to employees. His company was even handling logistics for big-budget Hollywood movies needing icy locations. A large poster for the James Bond film *Die Another Day* hung on his office wall.

'That was a really shit film,' I offered.

'Can't comment,' Jason agreed.

He organised one of his guides, Tom Foreman, to take us out in the fjord to see climate change in action at a fast-receding glacier called Nordenskiöld. Tom had arrived in the high Arctic 18 months earlier with a Masters in Environmental Sustainability from Durham University and a desire to put it to use in a more interesting place than Stockton-on-Tees.

'If the weather stays like this we should be there in less than two hours,' he told us as he loaded up a small speedboat in the millpond-still harbour.

It didn't. As we hit the fjord the wind picked up and we were suddenly being drenched by high waves.

'What's the survival time in the water?' I shouted over the waves.

'Five minutes,' Tom shouted back.

We had survival suits that would automatically inflate in water but they weren't even remotely waterproof. I tried to hang on to the seat to cushion the constant bouncing as Tom struggled to manoeuvre the open boat through the heavy swell. There was no possibility of filming. Dave clung onto the waterproof bag containing his small camera as I imagined the iPhone in my pocket drowning and dying in salt water.

It took nearly three hours to work our way across the fjord and down a slightly sheltered bay to our first glimpse of Nordenskiöld towering in the distance. It was an awesome sight: a giant wall of blue and white ice spreading across the shoreline with three small mountains behind it framed by low cloud. I almost forgot for a moment that I was soaking wet and freezing. Tom told us it wasn't nearly as big as it used to be.

'It's gone back about five kilometres since the 50s or 60s,' he said. 'The glacier's back on its grounding line so it's all standing on rock rather than floating on the open ocean.'

There was even a large island sticking out of it that had only become visible after 2000 as the glacier retreated. It had been named Retreat Island.

'So 17 years ago where we are now would have been inside the glacier?' I asked.

'Yeah, it was about two kilometres further out.'

Suddenly the far end of the glacier began to fall apart. Giant walls of ice calved off the face and crashed into the water, sending surges of ice-filled waves under the boat. For several minutes we watched chunks of ice falling, each time making the sound of a rumbling explosion, till finally it quieted.

'This is a small face compared to some,' Tom said. 'When you see blocks the size of skyscrapers coming down, it's awe-inspiring. It's hard to believe we're having such an impact on things this big. They're such immense fields of ice. If you go over there there's actually a melt tunnel coming out, that's why the water's so brown.'

Our boat felt even tinier here than it had out in the fjord as we bobbed up and down over the ice scraping under us at the foot of the glacier. Tom, who had done logistics for Greenpeace voyages, was outraged by Norway's plan to keep drilling in the Arctic. Partly it was because of the inherent danger of oil spilling in remote, cold areas that were dark for months of the year. But it was also because of the speed of climate change he was seeing around him.

'Glaciers thin, glaciers grow, they get longer, they get shorter,' he said. 'I mean the ocean has been hotter in the past than it is at the moment, there's been times that in the past there's been no ice at all, but the time scales that this stuff changed over was geological time scales. Species and animals had time to actually evolve and catch up or die off in a natural way. The changes that are happening now on this planet are a mass extinction time scale, really fast, too fast for species to keep up.'

He steered the boat to a rocky outcrop on the side of the glacier for Dave to set up his drone camera to fly over the ice. I took the opportunity to strip off my soaking wet survival suit and clothes and put on a change of clothes that I'd packed in a watertight bag. I was naked and even more freezing before I found seawater had somehow got into the bag and those clothes were soaked too.

There was an old hunter's hut by the glacier and the original idea was for us to spend the night there. But a Norwegian man came out and warned Tom a polar bear was roaming the area. Tom curtailed the droning and got us back in the boat.

'There's an old Soviet mine on the other side of the bay,' he told us. 'It's abandoned but they've reopened the hotel.'

It took another half-hour to power through the waves to the old town of Pyramiden, one of the mining operations the Soviet Union purchased in the 1920s. The cloud had lifted and glorious late-afternoon sunlight illuminated the cracked and crumbling remains of a place that looked like a Siberian ghost town.

A giant rusting crane stood next to a rubbish dump of twisted metal and a decrepit disused power station. A cracked wooden walkway led past an empty preschool, workshops and storage buildings to a town square full of weeds, Soviet propaganda signs and a bust of Lenin. A man with a long beard and a polar bear rifle came out to greet us: the hotel manager, Sasha Romanovskiy.

After exchanging pleasantries with Tom he asked: 'Do you want renovated rooms or Soviet-style?'

The hotel was exactly the sort I remembered from my travels in Russia in the 90s: five storeys of cracked tiles, musty rooms and bad wall panelling. But it was in the midst of a major *remont*, the Russian word for rebuilding and redecoration.

A group of Russian tourists filled half the bar alongside some young American adventure travellers watching old Soviet propaganda films. It was one of those frequent moments as a foreign correspondent when you feel you're on hallucinogenic drugs.

The films showed Pyramiden in its heyday as a model Soviet community in Norway. There were schools, a hospital, sports club, town hall, hairdresser and bakery. Flower gardens ringed the main boulevard with the typically snappy communist moniker 'The 60th Anniversary of the Great October Socialist Revolution'. At its peak there was a thriving Soviet community of 1300 people.

Sasha explained it all went to crap in 1991 when the USSR dissolved as the Russian economy fell apart. Arktikugol, the state mining company that owned both Russian towns on Spitsbergen Island, decided it could only afford to keep Barentsburg operating.

'First they took the children. In 1993 the school closed down. Then the adults started to go home because of the financial situation. The last people left Pyramiden in 2000.'

The buildings decayed fast. The water pipes froze, ruining the power station. Wooden frames cracked in the fierce winters. Roofs were blown off. In the sunny months, rich Arctic tourists helped themselves to anything of value they could carry off.

'Unfortunately there was plenty of vandalism here, so tourists were coming on snowmobiles or private sailboats and breaking in, hunting for souvenirs. For example, we had two grand pianos. Now we only have one because one was stolen.'

Eventually a new management decided to cash in on the booming eco-tourism and reopen the old town hotel. Rather than aping the designer chic of Longyearbyen, they wisely decided to play on Soviet retro, advertising the hotel as a 'Soviet time machine'.

That it was. The food was as chock full of mayonnaise as anything I'd eaten in Siberia; the bar had 15 different types of vodka, and while the renovated room I stayed in was clean and comfortable, none of the taps worked. I loved it.

The main problem the hotel had was climate change.

'During the winter season people come here by snowmobiles. The fjord is frozen. But this winter the fjord did not get frozen and we had a pretty low season.'

I managed to dry my clothes overnight but as we headed back into the fjord the wind rose again, sending up a 2.5 metre swell that not only drenched us but threatened to sink us. Tom Foreman did his best to skirt the fjord but eventually gave up and sheltered in a small bay next to an abandoned nickel mine. A passing cruise ship agreed to rescue Dave and me while Tom waited manfully on his own for the wind to drop. I quietly mumbled an insincere offer to stay with him.

It was remarkable how quickly Spitsbergen had gone from uninhabited wilderness to a lawless wild north to multinational mining community to rich eco-tourist resort. Now the rapidly changing climate was threatening to transform everything again. I was glad to have seen two of its incarnations. I could only share the unease for the coming one.

5. Unnatural Selection

The Galápagos Islands, November 2004

Extreme tameness ... is common to all the terrestrial species ... A gun is here superfluous; for with the muzzle I pushed a hawk off the branch of a tree.

Charles Darwin, *The Voyage of the Beagle*

For a place that inspired the dog-eat-dog theory of evolution, Galápagos was once a pretty chilled-out place.

Charles Darwin visited in 1835 and was taken aback to see the animals in this isolated archipelago had absolutely no fear of Man. To his great amusement, he could simply bash birds to death, writing in his journal that they could be 'killed with a switch, and sometimes, as I myself tried, with a cap or hat'. What ho!

The young English naturalist was even more surprised by the sheer diversity of the islands. Close together but separated by deep ocean water and opposing currents, each was like a different world. 'One is astonished at the amount of creative force, if such an expression may be used,' he wrote between bird bashing, 'displayed on these small, barren, and rocky islands; and still more so, at its diverse yet analogous action on points so near each other.'

The islands played a big part in Darwin's revolutionary thesis of natural selection, in which he contended that God didn't actually design species. Instead, they evolved through a brutal and endless struggle for survival of the fittest.

If Darwin came back today, he could see another struggle for supremacy, involving a much stranger species than the marine iguanas or giant tortoises that he marvelled at on his first voyage: humans.

The tourist websites never mention this battle. It could be bad for business. Nature documentaries never document it. Humans aren't as exotic as the islands' other animals. But if you're staying on Galápagos and notice a plume of smoke rising above the national park headquarters or the sickly smell of gas, here's what it probably is: Ecuadorian riot police firing tear gas canisters to stop local residents assaulting park rangers.

In 2004 the riot squad were regular visitors from the mainland and the battles had a set-piece quality: on one side, park rangers cowered in their headquarters; on the other, angry and militant fishermen hurled rocks and sticks as they tried to force their way in.

This battle for supremacy was threatening the whole environment. The park rangers were in charge of protecting the land and marine life that made Galápagos famous. The fishermen were in charge of catching and killing marine life. And it seemed the rangers were losing.

'Morale? There's not such a thing I would say,' a ranger named Fernando Ortiz told me. 'From those of us who are seriously committed to conservation, for those of us who have been part of this place for a long time, right now it's like we're just touching the bottom. You know, I don't think things have been any worse ever in the national park.'

*

Galápagos has always sounded like a place somebody made up. There are penguins on the equator, giant tortoises that live for centuries, iguanas that swim in the sea, iguanas that climb up volcanoes, and fur seals, sea turtles, birds and plants found nowhere else on Earth. Each island is a different world from the other, with its own climate and landscape and a myriad of strange and matchless creatures.

I was planning a shoot in Ecuador and needed a second story to make it cost-effective, so naturally I started researching the Galápagos Islands, which are administered by Ecuador even though they're 1000 kilometres from South America. I knew about the amazing flora and fauna, but until I looked closer I had no idea of the other feature that made the archipelago unique – the most diverse ecosystem in the world had the most dysfunctional conservation agency on the planet.

Until relatively recently, Galápagos didn't have any human inhabitants to muck things up. The first only arrived in the 18th century: whalers and fur sealers who nearly hunted their prey to extinction. Pirates also used the islands as a base, introducing goats they could come back to slaughter for food. In 1832 the islands were claimed by Ecuador, which had just won independence from Spain, so it could set up an escape-proof prison colony. Three years later Charles Darwin dropped in while sailing around the world on the *Beagle* and made the islands famous for his controversial thesis on evolution. But it wasn't until the 20th century that people began to come in significant numbers.

Less than 2000 people lived there in 1959, when almost 98 per cent of the archipelago was declared a national park. As late as the 1970s it was still seen as a remote and nearly inaccessible destination, fit for only the hardiest adventurer or richest natural history film unit. But in the 1980s the economics changed. Mass tourism arrived as jaded travellers started looking for more exotic destinations. More importantly, in the 1990s Ecuador decided the world's second largest marine reserve would be a great place for commercial fishing.

The wildlife doesn't know it, but it won the booby prize when Ecuador wound up in charge of its protection. It's the country that gave the world the term 'Banana Republic', characterised not only for its economic dependence on bananas but also for the kleptocratic cliques who fought for the spoils of power. Ecuador has had a history of corrupt and unstable government, passing between quasi-democratic periods and military dictatorship, with some spectacularly disappointing rulers. When the islands were all but uninhabited, conservationists had no trouble in persuading the government to declare the land and surrounding sea a protected reserve. But during the 1990s, when there was huge demand in Asia for sea cucumbers, the government saw nothing wrong with allowing thousands of people to migrate to the islands to catch them.

Sea cucumbers are a sausage-like bottom-feeding creature common around the islands. They taste disgusting but are prized in parts of Asia as a supposed aphrodisiac. High world prices from 1992 led to a kind of gold rush mentality and intense overfishing. By the time the government tried to cap migration to Galápagos in 1998, the same time the bottom fell out of the world sea cucumber market (coinciding, perhaps not coincidentally, with the advent of Viagra), the population had swollen to 15,000. By 2004 it was close to 20,000. Half the community was involved in commercial fishing for a resource that was losing value and running out. The other half was devoted to eco-tourism or conservation. It was an explosive mixture.

In the months leading up to our visit, there had been a series of violent and largely unreported clashes between the national park and fishing cooperatives over the park's attempt to curtail the sea cucumber quota. To the rangers' horror, the government had buckled to the fishermen's demands and overturned the quota.

We flew in on one of the three daily flights from the Ecuadorian coastal city of Guayaquil and queued behind hundreds of tourists for processing. The once isolated community was now one of the most popular destinations for visitors to South America, with about 145,000 arrivals every year. (*International Traveller* magazine rated Galápagos number four on its countdown of '100 Ultimate Travel Experiences of a

Lifetime'. I only mention this because in 2014 the Isles of Scilly scraped in at number 100.)

Thankfully most tourists head straight to low-impact charter yachts to cruise around the archipelago. We headed into the town of Puerto Ayora on the island of Santa Cruz. The former outpost had become a typical South American tourist trap with hotels, resorts, restaurants and internet cafes crowded around the waterfront. Surrounding it were large new suburbs for fishermen and their families.

By chance, we had arrived in the middle of the latest crisis at the national park.

Our main contact at the park was ranger Fernando Ortiz, the director of the marine reserve and one of the most outspoken critics of the fishermen. He had been enthusiastic about our visit but when we met him at one of the town's main tourist cafes, specialising in soy lattes and banana pancakes, he was despondent.

'There is some really weird stuff happening at the park right now,' he said. 'The director is very weak. He won't go against the fishermen. I don't know how much longer I'm going to have a job.'

Fernando was a young Galápagan who had spent his entire working life in the park, first as a naturalist guide then as a park ranger and bureaucrat. Four months earlier he had rallied the other rangers to stand firm when fishermen tried to force their way into the park headquarters in protest at a ruling to stop the annual sea cucumber harvest. He tried to face down a mob confronting them with sticks.

As his fellow rangers videoed the scene for evidence, he shouted: 'We're not going to change our minds. We've been here a few days standing up for this principle and we're not going to change now. We won't budge. I've got nothing more to say on behalf of my fellow workers here.'

The fishermen had come to enforce what they saw as a coup against the conservationists. A former park ranger, Fausto Cepeda, who was now employed as an adviser to the fishing cooperative, had just been appointed as the new director. The rangers saw him as a traitor and were refusing to allow him to take up his position. The fishermen had come to try to force their way in so he could take over.

In the end the riot police had to beat the fishermen back while rangers took cover in the main building. But a group of fishermen managed to break through the barricades and storm in. The ferocity of the attack stunned the rangers, some of whom were beaten and bloodied. It also brought unwelcome international attention to Ecuador's mismanagement of Galápagos. Embarrassed by the ensuing headlines, the government revoked Cepeda's appointment. But a few weeks later it caved into the fishermen's main demand and overturned the park's ban on sea cucumber harvesting.

'The sea cucumber is now just about extinct,' Fernando told us. 'But there's nothing we can do about it. The fishermen have too much power.'

Their power came from a quirk in Ecuador's strange political system. Galápagos was classified as a province, giving it the right to elect two congressmen. That meant its tiny population had vastly disproportionate political representation. One of its congressmen was the head of the fishing cooperative. As the government had a knife-edge majority, it was terrified of losing his support.

'He's the Godfather,' Fernando said. 'The fishermen only account for a fifth of what Galápagos Islands produce, but they have more power than anyone else. You can say they're the most protected species here.'

Wandering round the waterfront the next morning, it was hard not to step on some of the other protected species. The wildlife of Galápagos is still surprisingly unafraid of humans, perhaps a genetic reflection of the millions of years there were no humans to disturb them. Huge iguanas lazed in the sun, not even blinking as we stepped around them.

We walked up to the national park service headquarters, a short walk from the town, to interview Fernando. He was cleaning out his desk. The park director had just sacked him as head of the marine reserve.

'Sorry guys, I can't talk to you here. Come to my house.'

A short time later he was breaking the news to his distraught wife as his young daughter played on her computer.

'I just got this memo today signed by the director. I was just removed from the marine resources area and I'm going to be stuck in natural resources. Basically what they, they have done is froze me. So, I don't know, what do we do? Do we fight it? Then I can be out of a job altogether.'

The news spread quickly around the small community. A family friend, Godfrey Merlen, came to commiserate. They both saw it as the beginning of the end for the park.

'Hopefully the person who is appointed for the marine reserve right now is going to follow up,' Fernando said. 'But they're not going to keep somebody there unless this person does whatever they ask him to do.'

Godfrey was one of the islands' more celebrated characters, an elderly but handsome English boat captain with a striking resemblance to a bearded Kirk Douglas. He had an aristocratic and bohemian bearing, like a 19th century lord who had decamped to more exotic climes to immerse himself in nature.

While Fernando worked out his next move, Godfrey took us to one of his favourite beaches to talk about Galápagos. He moved to Santa Cruz in 1973, when it was still a tiny settlement in an otherwise untouched wilderness.

'It was almost an unknown place, even in Ecuador, as it was a backwater with very little economy,' he said nostalgically. 'There were a few cows, which were sent to the mainland. There was a bit of salted fish exported but it was very, very low-key. It was very small boats doing bottom fishing and very few people.'

The changes in the past 15 years had troubled him deeply, Fernando's demise another worrying sign of the rot.

'People have seen dreams in Galápagos,' he said. 'On the mainland of Ecuador they've seen a way out of their poverty and their problems there and you can understand. They are people who never had anything.'

Before the advent of commercial fishermen, people like Godfrey had come only to enjoy nature.

There are 19 islands covering 8000 square kilometres and only four are inhabited. By a quirk of evolution, they are like a hothouse laboratory of evolution.

Volcanic activity threw up the islands in the middle of the Pacific Ocean at the precise confluence of three currents, two of them warm and one of them cool – the Humboldt Current. This not only made them a melting pot of different species, but the nature of the islands meant they all developed separately. The different terrain and height means the ecosystems range from sun-baked desert to cool rainy forests. This has not only given rise to an extraordinary range of flora and fauna, but the distance between the islands means they developed in isolation over millions of years. Out of some 5000 animal species and plant varieties, 40 per cent are found nowhere else on Earth.

We spent two days exploring some of the islands by boat. Everywhere we went was like a different world. There were iguanas, giant tortoises, flightless cormorants, boobies, tropical penguins, albatrosses and mockingbirds. We splashed over the waves past green sea turtles and walked on beaches covered with sea lions. Once, as we waded into shore, we even saw what is now one of the rarest creatures – a sea cucumber.

'People started seeing this place as a gold field and I think to this day Galápagos is seen as paved with gold and a place to solve all your problems,' Godfrey told us. 'But it isn't.'

The sea cucumber has never been one of the natural wonders of Galápagos, but it is crucial to the ecosystem of the entire marine reserve, an area of 133,000 square kilometres only second in size to the marine park of the Great Barrier Reef.

Apart from being a food source for fish and crustaceans, sea cucumbers vacuum up dead and decaying matter and oxygenate the water. As Godfrey explained, a marine reserve without sea cucumbers was like a garden without earthworms.

More importantly, the conflict was paralysing the park's management. In seven years it had had eleven different directors. Every few months a director was appointed or dismissed in the seesawing of influence between conservationists and fishermen.

We went back to the park headquarters as the latest director was holding a crisis meeting with staff. The Environment Minister had just arrived from the mainland to lay down the latest philosophy for the park. Fabian Valdiviezo was not a politician but an urbane former diplomat who had just been appointed to the plum job.

'It's essential to change what's being done here in Galápagos,' he told the rangers. 'Until now conservation has received a lot of attention, but the people's standard of living has been neglected.' Fernando sat unhappily at the other end of the table.

After the meeting, I asked the Environment Minister why the park director had been replaced so many times. He explained that it was hard to appoint anyone who was independent of the warring parties. The law setting up the national park reserved the director's post to native Galápagans.

'Galápagos has a small population so the available jobs are limited, and so in one way or another, the few technical people in the Galápagos are aligned in one way or another to those who make use of the marine reserve,' he said. In other words, they were either pro-conservation, pro-tourism or pro-fishermen.

Fernando saw the main villain in the piece as Rogelio Gyuacha, the local congressman and head of the fishing cooperative, on whom the Ecuadorian government depended for survival.

'He is a businessman of fishing. He has not been out on a fishing boat for years. He doesn't know any more what it means to be out fishing.'

We caught up with the congressman at the waterfront. He had invited us to meet him on his large fishing boat, where he was making a point of cleaning the engine. But he looked more like a prosperous businessman than a working fisherman. He denied that he was merely pushing commercial fishing interests.

'I think differently,' he said. 'I don't advocate for just one group of people but my interest as an MP is for all of us here in Galápagos to have a good standard of living and respect the laws of the province.

'The situation for the fishermen is very difficult right now in spite of the fact that they have always been very patriotic and fought for sovereignty here in Galápagos. They've passed laws to cause the fishing sector to disappear in Galápagos, so the fishing sector has had no choice but to take action.'

He had recently wrested control of the fishing cooperative from a poor fisherman named Tity Torres, who had a reputation for being less militant. In the small community of Galápagos, he was also close to many of the rangers. Strangest of all, Fernando Ortiz was his best friend and godfather to his children.

'Can you imagine, the head of the marine park and the head of the fishermen being best buddies,' Tity's wife, Ivonne, laughed when we met her at the family home. 'It's fascinating to listen to them argue with each other over dinner.'

Tity and Ivonne invited us out with them for a day on the water to show the fishing community's side of the story. Typical of most fishermen, they had only a small tinnie and used hand-held lines. A small compressor on the boat was used to go underwater in search of more valuable catch like lobsters. For all their political clout, most fishermen struggled to make a living. There were simply too many licensed fishermen for all but the largest operators to make a decent living.

We moved around the reserve for three hours, stopping at various points where Tity hoped there would be fish. After a full morning's work, the entire catch consisted of one medium-sized fish.

'This is worth a dollar a pound,' Ivonne said.

'So it's not much for a morning's work is it?' I asked.

'Not for three people especially. It doesn't even cover the cost of fuel.'

Fernando and Tity had become friends through Ivonne, who had worked with Fernando as a naturalist guide before meeting her future husband. Despite their friendship with Fernando, the couple had joined the protest where the fishermen tried to storm into park headquarters.

'As the wife of a fisherman I will tell you we depend on the sea cucumbers. Whatever my husband makes during the sea cucumber season, thank God we can save and use it for the rest of the year,' she said.

She believed there would be more violence if the park tried to stop the next harvesting season. 'If they don't get the sea cucumber, there's going to be a social problem. They won't have enough for a living and I don't know what's going to happen in my family, or other families of fishermen.'

While they disagreed strongly with Fernando's views, they shared his belief that a sensible solution could be found to the problem if the government only had the will. For years it had been promising to build a processing plant to make fishing more profitable and find alternative jobs for fishermen who wanted to leave the industry. But the promises had come to nothing. Fishermen had been frozen out of the only other significant industry, tourism, which was monopolised by big mainland operators, many with close links to the government.

'All most people get from tourism is high prices,' Ivonne said.

We motored back to shore to find the government had at last taken drastic action to resolve the crisis. But it wasn't what Tity and Ivonne were expecting. Fernando told us he had just been informed his contract with the park would not be renewed. Another 123 rangers, nearly a third of the park's staff, had also been dismissed.

'They don't want to have anybody there who they cannot control, anybody who's going to be doing things legally or anybody who, who's going to really you know assume a position that can be read as conservation,' Fernando said angrily. 'You know they just want some puppet to do whatever they want them to do and that's it. That's not me, that's for sure.'

Within days the announcement had paralysed the park management. With no marine director and a drastic shortage of rangers, sea patrols were suspended, leaving a free run for poachers. Fernando doubted the park would again have the ability or the will to protect the environment.

'The national park service has built up a reputation because of what it has done in this marvellous environment,' he said in disgust. 'All of that is going to go into the sewers because again of a political circumstance.'

And down it went. Despite the best efforts of remaining rangers, the park never really got on top of the environmental problems. In 2007 UNESCO put Galápagos on its World Heritage in Danger List. Conservationists were appalled when it was taken off the danger list three years later, warning it was still in peril.

Evolution normally takes millions of years. In Galápagos, the supremacy of Fisher Man took less than a generation.

6. Finding Reinado

East Timor, March 2007

> **The nation is divided, half patriots and half traitors,**
> **and no man can tell which from which.**
>
> Mark Twain

My stomach troubles were hitting peak awkwardness as we scrambled down to the bloody riot outside Dili's Government House. The UN office where we'd been filming had just dispatched a rapid response team and we followed them, me calculating how many minutes I could hold out before retreating to the hotel bathroom. We arrived to see the government headquarters on fire and police grappling with rebels as smoke filled the waterfront. My cameraman, Dave Martin, shouted at the driver to turn the car around so we could make a quick escape if things turned nasty. I thought I heard the pop of small-arms fire over the growling of my stomach.

'Quick piece to camera, Dave!' I moaned, wondering why I'd eaten the hotel salad.

We ran towards the melee and set up for a shot. 'Make it fast!' Dave shouted.

I tried to think of something profound to say but all my effort was going into holding in my breakfast. 'This is the worst conflict since East Timor's independence five years ago,' I began. 'The next few days will show if oh shit bloody hell we've gotta go.'

Dave glared at me and I kept talking, finally straining out a sign-off. Dave snapped off shots of the fighting until we spotted a group of angry men with large knives heading our way. He scooped up the camera and tripod and raced back towards the car. I followed as fast as I could with clenched buttocks. The car was still facing the riot, the driver standing nonchalantly beside it puffing on a cigarette.

'Turn the bloody car around!' Dave shouted. One five-point turn later we roared down the potholed road towards the safety of the hotel and its porcelain toilet.

We had spent four days watching protests by disgruntled former soldiers build slowly towards this confrontation. It started peacefully enough, with about 500 ex-soldiers and supporters marching through the city centre. They had gone on strike complaining of bad conditions. The government declared it a mutiny and sacked them, reducing the national army by a third. The mood was ugly but nobody was expecting any bloodshed. We'd interviewed the Foreign Minister, José Ramos-Horta, and he'd dismissed the protests as a legitimate grievance being played up by gangsters and street gangs.

But the main thing he'd been interested in talking about was how he was organising a Tour de Timor bike race to boost tourism.

These were supposed to be golden days for Australia's nearest neighbour, a new nation rising from the ashes with bountiful foreign aid and caravans of foreign experts and earnest NGOs. Suddenly it was all falling apart.

Over the next month East Timor came close to civil war.

Townships went up in flames as unemployed youths and opposition followers joined the ex-soldiers' revolt. Even some police took sides with them and gun battles erupted between loyalists and rebels. The government called for outside military help. An Australian-led International Stabilisation Force was quickly assembled to quash the violence. Eventually the fighting stopped and many of the uprising's leaders were jailed. But resentment continued to simmer across the country.

At the heart of the conflict was a regional divide that had seemingly grown out of nowhere after the Indonesians left.

For centuries the island had been divided into east and west. Portugal colonised Timor in the 16th century but in 1620 the Dutch seized the western half. After the Netherlands lost its colonial empire in 1949, West Timor became part of the new nation of Indonesia. East Timor remained under Portuguese rule until the Marxist-leaning Fretilin (Revolutionary Front for an Independent East Timor) declared independence in 1975.

Days later Indonesia invaded with the tacit approval of the US and Australian governments amid fears East Timor would turn communist. Fierce resistance continued in the countryside until Indonesia finally withdrew in 1999, leaving the corpses of tens of thousands who had died of disease, starvation and bullets during the long occupation.

But over the past few years another east-west divide had grown within East Timor. The new national army was dominated by former resistance fighters from the western part of the country, including the capital Dili. Soldiers from the eastern half claimed they were being lorded over and bullied by western officers.

It was hard to know how much substance there was to the complaints. There were bound to be tensions when scattered resistance forces were brought under a unified command led by Dili. But in the economic and social hardship of East Timor, the perception took on a life of its own.

For all the aid money pouring in, most of East Timor was desperately poor. Everybody wanted someone to blame, and the idea of regional discrimination became a powerful rallying call for many from the east who'd grown frustrated with the lack of spoils from independence and blamed the Fretilin-led government in Dili. Some easterners even accused westerners of having colluded with the Indonesians. In marketplaces in Dili fights would break out between traders from the east and west.

Political instability added to the problems. Fretilin dominated the government and parliament and many of its senior figures were Portuguese-speaking exiles who had only returned to East Timor after the Indonesians were driven out. The Prime Minister, Mari Alkatiri, had spent the occupation in Mozambique. The government's harsh treatment of the eastern soldiers confirmed to many that Fretilin was out of touch with the people's suffering. The sacked soldiers had declared their loyalty was not to the government, but to East Timor's ceremonial President, Xanana Gusmão, a legendary guerrilla fighter who had led the resistance in the bush. He and his close ally José Ramos-Horta, who had represented the resistance at the UN, had repeatedly clashed with Fretilin politicians, accusing the party of authoritarianism.

But perhaps the main problem was that it was a small young nation with a large number of guns. Egos and gunpowder were an explosive mix in a country still struggling to build up basic institutions, especially when many of the main players had until recently been guerrilla fighters.

In hindsight, the big mystery was why nobody had seen it coming. After the horrors of Indonesian occupation, which ended with Indonesian-backed militias trying to raze Dili to the ground, there had been romantic hopes that East Timor could somehow avoid the dysfunction that almost always accompanies the birth of war-torn nations. Few imagined that independence fighters would turn on each other so viciously. Even after what I'd seen at Government House, I wouldn't have thought that 10 months later the bloodshed would be continuing and that I'd be scrambling through the hills of East Timor trying to avoid being shot by Australian soldiers.

*

I've been to many conflict zones, usually with Dave filming, and we've run the gauntlet of foreign armies from Chechnya to

Colombia. But this time we were trying to meet up with a rebel leader, Alfredo Reinado, who had recently escaped from prison and was being hunted by the Australian SAS. A few weeks earlier, he and his men had been in a gun battle with Australian soldiers that had seen five of his fighters killed. Reinado and most of his followers had slipped through the Australian encirclement and disappeared into the bush. With Australian combat helicopters scouring the hills trying to hunt him down, we'd set ourselves the optimistic goal of finding him first.

We had two big advantages that I hoped would help us succeed, apart from the fact I was no longer suffering chronic diarrhoea. First, we had a guide who knew the area intimately, a Timorese woman and childhood friend of Reinado called Ina Bradridge. Secondly, Reinado had told her he wanted us to find him. There was just the small matter of him and his men marching up to 40 kilometres a day across the mountains to avoid the helicopters combing the countryside for him, which meant our following him on foot, let alone catching up with him, might be impossible.

Before leaving Australia, I'd sought advice from my reporter colleague Mark Corcoran, who'd once served in the Australian navy and had done a stint with the military's spy agency, the Defence Signals Directorate (DSD). He warned me that if we used mobile phones to communicate with Reinado, the SAS would be onto us. But when I arrived in Dili to start the wild rebel chase, Ina assured us they'd be speaking in dialect and code to confuse any DSD technicians who might be monitoring mobile phone calls from Darwin.

The irony was that Alfredo Reinado had been trained by the Australian Defence Force that was now trying to capture him.

He'd been just seven years old when Indonesia invaded, and he was subsequently forced to work as a porter for the Indonesian army. He later fled to Australia with a boatload of refugees and was interned in the Curtin Detention Centre. After he was granted asylum he learned the trade of tugboat captain in Western Australia. After independence he returned to East Timor and joined the new navy, rising quickly through the ranks to major and even being sent back to Australia for intensive training with the ADF. Eventually he was made commander of East Timor's military police. But a headstrong temperament and outspoken manner led to a rocky relationship with his superiors. When the violence flared in 2006, he was one of the most effective rebel fighters, accusing Fretilin of plotting a dictatorship. His followers led an unsuccessful assault on Dili, and Reinado was soon arrested and imprisoned on charges of murder.

In February 2007, when the government thought the revolt was over, he busted out of prison with more than 50 inmates and took to the hills, taking a large cache of guns from a border post. Reinado claimed the border police gave him the weapons, as Fretilin was illegally arming its supporters ahead of the upcoming election.

East Timor turned again to Australia for help and SAS soldiers were dispatched from the International Stabilisation Force to catch him. After the earlier battle with Australians, I doubted it would end peacefully. And with the SAS likely tracking us, there was a small but worrying chance we could find ourselves in the wrong place at a very bad time.

Ina had grown up with resistance fighters in the bush and was close to the former commander turned President Xanana Gusmao. She arranged for us to interview him in Dili and to her disappointment he was highly critical of Reinado and wanted him to surrender.

'He crossed a limit that a state can permit,' he told me.

Reinado claimed to be supporting Gusmao against his Fretilin opponents in parliament. But Gusmao said he could not tolerate Reinado seizing weapons.

'How can a soldier, a military man, living outside the institution, go to a police post and borrow weapons? If he went there to borrow some food from them, to borrow a pencil to write his plea or something, but borrow the weapons? What for? This is something that we cannot accept.'

Afterwards, Ina told me she couldn't understand the President's position. She saw Reinado as a hero fighting for justice. 'He love nature, he love his people, he's a very nice man. He's different compared to Timorese men. He's very different. He love his people too much. Xanana is always fair in any decision he made but this time, I don't know why he makes a decision like this. This is really a surprise for the people. I mean people are quite shocked.'

There was no doubt Reinado still had popular support. Ina drove Dave and me to the town of Same, Reinado's old stronghold, where he had fought the Australian soldiers. Pro-Reinado slogans were daubed on several buildings. A dozen of his followers met us secretly to say they could take us into the mountains to find him.

As they made preparations, Dave and I waited in a small restaurant trying to look like tourists. We soon weren't alone. Two muscular white men with military haircuts entered the restaurant and sat down at an adjoining table. One of them wore a Hawaiian shirt. He picked up a menu and pretended to read it as he scanned the room in our direction. He didn't make direct eye contact and I noticed he was holding the menu upside down. They couldn't look more like SAS if they were wearing T-shirts labelled *Undercover*.

Ina suggested we leave and I stood up as a cramp suddenly hit my stomach. For the second time it seemed I'd eaten something inadvisable. 'Give me a minute,' I muttered as I headed to the bathroom.

Five minutes later I staggered out past the plainclothes commandos as we pretended not to look at each other. Ina drove us around town several times to make sure nobody was following then headed down a dirt road to a bamboo field. We got out, grabbed our gear and followed her through the bush to a clearing where our guides were waiting. Without a word they moved out and we scrambled to follow.

On Ina's advice we were carrying only a small camera kit concealed in a backpack and a dozen large bottles of drinking water. She assured us villagers would feed us on the way. But even with a relatively light load it was hard to keep up with the Timorese. They moved quickly through the hills while Dave and I struggled to push through the thick undergrowth, grabbing branches and bamboo shoots for balance and continually slipping in the dirt. After an hour we seemed to be walking around in circles. Ina and four of the men talked constantly into mobile phones to Reinado and his men, getting updates on where they were heading. None of them seemed concerned at being monitored by the Australian military. Ina told us helicopters were hovering near Reinado and they had to keep changing direction. Occasionally I had to stop and head off behind a tree to relieve myself, vowing next time I'd bring canned food to East Timor.

It was stiflingly hot and humid, and as much as we tried to ration our water Dave and I were soon guzzling it down. We were close to collapsing as we finally stopped at a bush hut on sunset. Ina told us we would rest there for the night. Some women from a nearby village appeared with food for us: boiled chicken and a kind of stew.

Our guides wanted to talk about the gun battle Reinado's men had fought with the Australians a few weeks earlier. They asked why Australia was covering up Reinado's victory. 'They shot 12 Australians,' one man said. 'Why is nobody talking about that.'

They wouldn't believe me when I told them no Australians had been killed, just five of Reinado's men. I explained that if Australian soldiers had died, it wouldn't be covered up. 'The relatives would know, the media would know. The army would have to announce it.'

But they were not convinced.

There was only a small wooden platform to sleep on and I huddled on it next to Dave and Ina. The others disappeared down to the village or slept on the dirt floor. As I began to drift off to sleep it started pouring with rain, the water dripping through the grass roof onto us. After the fierce heat of the day I was soon shivering with cold. I lay awake until just before dawn.

The scratching of chickens in the brush beside us woke me a short time later. Soon the women were back preparing our breakfast. Half an hour later a man in a makeshift military uniform arrived at the camp and said he'd like to be interviewed. Ina told us he was a member of parliament who had left Dili to support Reinado's struggle. She translated as he told us Fretilin had betrayed the resistance and abandoned the people. It felt good to have an interview with a rebel in the can and I thanked him for his time. We shook hands as he started to move out. Then for the first time I noticed his cap, which I had somehow not registered in my fatigue. It had *Shit as Fuck* written on it.

'Dave, did you notice the cap?'

'What about it?' he asked.

'Check the frame.'

'Oh fuck! It's unusable. Get him back.'

We tried to call out to him but he had already disappeared into the bush and Ina was keen to keep moving.

'Why the fuck did he have a cap with *Shit as Fuck* on it?' Dave lamented.

Now we really had to find Reinado.

Within an hour the early morning cool had turned again into searing heat. We hiked down a mountain, stopping once and hiding under thick tree cover when we heard a helicopter overhead. At the base of the mountain was a fast-flowing river.

The guides held on to Dave and me as we crossed, fighting not to slip in the water with our camera gear. Then we started climbing.

For the next four hours we traipsed up steep hills, our small loads feeling like millstones. None of the Timorese showed any sign of fatigue and seemed annoyed at our slow pace. Dave and I were soon parched and drinking water at every rest stop. I could feel dehydration setting in and our water was almost all gone.

At lunchtime we reached a village called Sasema where the SAS had come two days earlier searching for Reinado. Two of the huts had been blown down. The villagers stood in a crowd demanding angrily that we hear what had happened. A man told us the army had landed two helicopters in the village at 10 pm, the wind from the rotors knocking down the huts. Soldiers had stormed out of the choppers and rounded up all the men.

'The worst thing is what the Australians did to the houses and the farms, and hitting the young people, and tying them up,' he said. 'They tied them up and pushed their faces into the ground. They broke furniture and they told people to put their hands up on their heads. Women and men.'

Two young men showed us plastic cords the soldiers had used to bind their hands before interrogating them.

'They're 10 times worse than Indonesia,' the man said, nearly spitting in disgust. 'The Australian military is very bad.'

We continued climbing hills trying to catch up to Reinado. Dave and I were now completely exhausted and our water was all gone, and still we seemed no closer to reaching him.

Three times we struggled to the top of steep hills only to turn round and stagger back down as word came that Reinado's men were changing direction to avoid the helicopters. I marvelled at how fast they must be moving. It was now clear we were not going to be able to catch up with them on foot. Reluctantly, Ina told us we would have to head back to Same. Close to sunset we arrived where we had started nearly 30 exhausting hours earlier, at the clearing where Ina had parked the car.

'We'll try to meet him on the road,' she said.

We left our guides and, after buying water, drove for hours down dark dirt roads, Ina continually calling as she tried to arrange a rendezvous. She had grown tired of us asking how close we were and told us to be quiet and wait. I had given up hope when she suddenly stopped the car and ran in front of it. I turned on the headlights and saw her embracing a bearded man in the darkness. Dozens of armed men in military fatigues stood around them, tense and silent.

I walked up to the man she was hugging. He was wearing an Australian army uniform.

'Major Reinado, I presume,' I said. He nodded. 'You're a very hard man to find.'

He shrugged. 'I don't know,' he said. 'This is the nature of this. But somehow, yeah, we can meet here.'

'The Australian Army hasn't found you yet,' I said.

'I don't know. You're not one of them?'

'No, not me, definitely not the Australian Army. Have they been pretty close the last few days?'

'They're always close.'

I couldn't help but admire his chutzpah in wearing an Australian uniform, the ultimate two fingers up to his Australian pursuers. But months in prison and weeks on the run seemed to have robbed him of some of his bravado. He looked tired and stressed and painfully thin. Ina had tears in her eyes and said she was worried by how sick he looked.

I didn't know how much time we'd have so I kept asking him questions.

Would he consider surrendering?

'I don't never have a word of surrendering. I'll surrender to justice, not to any command, any force.'

Why had he taken weapons from the border post?

'We're just a few guys, we go there and ask and they gave me more than we wanted. The question here, is it more right for me to have this weapon to defend the people rather than to give it to the political party?'

Would he fight Australian soldiers again if they surrounded him?

'I never want to shoot any Australian.'

'You did fire at them the other night.'

'I defend myself because they are firing at us first. They're surrounding us with helicopters going everywhere so they land in our area and fire on our men so we have to protect ourselves, we have to defend ourselves.'

Did he have any regrets that he could have shot Australians in the battle?

'That was a fair fight. They also men, we also men, we are soldiers, we are trained to fight. The question here is what are the interests they are fighting for? I'm here fighting for our dignity, the sovereignty of our country.'

Why was he fighting Fretilin?

'You're there to serve the people, not to conquer the people. They have been giving their weapons to civilians, radical Fretilin supporters, to create something exactly like Mozambique and Angola. I know they have a plan in 2007 to kill all opposition leaders and influential people and also people like us standing against them. I don't want that to happen in this country. Communism doesn't belong in this country.'

He grew angrier as he talked. It seemed he had reached a stage where there would be no compromise, no prospect of trust, and the only end would be bloody.

'As a military man, I have to take sides,' he continued. 'I have to get out there and stop them because this institution belongs to the people, to stand up to defend the people, not to kill the people. So as a military man I stand up to stop my institution to take more action to kill more people. You say I'm wrong?'

Suddenly we heard the unmistakeable sound of helicopters approaching. Reinado hugged Ina and without a word disappeared into the darkness with his men.

Ina was sobbing as we drove off. 'He looks so sick. He's lost so much weight. It's not fair. He's just trying to defend the people.'

She took us to a small guesthouse in the hills to spend the night. The next morning we began the long drive back to Dili. It was the day before the program's weekly broadcast so we needed to script and edit the story overnight. But first we had to talk to the Australian military.

We arrived in Dili in the early afternoon and I saw a unit of Australian soldiers patrolling the streets. I asked them where the Australian headquarters were.

'Dunno,' a young soldier said. 'Somewhere.'

One of the strangest things about working as an international journalist is how much easier it is to work with foreign military forces than my own country's. I've managed to film with more than a dozen armies without trouble, even the Russian and Chinese military. I've travelled with the Indian Army, gained regular intelligence from the US Army, relaxed with French and Latvian soldiers and enjoyed espresso with Italians from the back of their armoured personnel carrier in Kosovo. But no matter what war Australia has fought, the army has always known its real enemy is Australian journalists.

In Vietnam the great Australian war correspondent Neil Davis spent most of his time with US and South Vietnamese troops because he found his countrymen so hostile. I've known Australian correspondents in Iraq who were turned away from the safety of an Australian army base to chance their lives in insurgent territory. The ADF spent years refusing to embed journalists in Iraq, unlike ever other coalition power, with rare exceptions like the radio comedians Hamish and Andy. In Afghanistan I had to ask the US and British military what Australians were doing because Canberra refused to give out any information. So when we finally found the Australian base in Dili I thought it prudent not to mention we'd just interviewed Reinado and that I had the tape in my pocket.

We were met by the Australian commander Mal Rerden, a gruff brigadier who seemed to take an instant dislike to me. As head of the International Stabilisation Force he was obliged to handle foreign interviews, meaning I didn't have to apply for permission from the black hole of Defence PR in Canberra.

'We have to obviously locate Reinado and we're working very hard to do that and you know the nature of the terrain is very rugged, but we have got very well-trained, very well-equipped and very well-led soldiers involved in the operations and I've got great confidence in them.'

Despite the earlier gunfight, he said his men were doing their best to avoid bloodshed. 'The people that were involved in the operation and in particular the five that were subsequently killed were armed and they were carrying out actions that threatened the lives of my soldiers.'

He accused Reinado of 'terrorising' civilians and did not believe the complaints of ill treatment we had heard in the village of Sasema. 'Our soldiers are highly trained, they've been conducting their operations in a very professional manner, and they have a great deal of understanding of the need for sensitivity and respect for civilians when they're conducting their operations.'

We now had all the material we needed for a story, just little time to put it together. A cameraman who'd been shooting for ABC News, Craig Berkman, had waited an extra few days in Dili for us in case we got lucky with Reinado. So at least we'd have another body to do the editing. But it was an all-nighter of scripting and cutting.

We finished just in time to take the tape to the local TV station in the morning to send the story to Sydney on a satellite feed we'd booked only to find the one technician who knew how to feed had decided, without warning, to take the day off. I demanded his phone number and rang him but he refused to come in for the booking, saying he had to go back to his village to fix his radio. After the hell we'd gone through to find Reinado, it seemed we'd miss the broadcast because of one stubborn technician. Dave and Craig broke the story down into segments and spent the day desperately combing internet cafes to try to email the vision on painfully slow feeds to Sydney, where the segments were edited together, colour graded and sound mixed with just 30 minutes to spare before the *Foreign Correspondent* broadcast.

We watched the story going to air that night on the ABC's international channel, Australia Network. We celebrated quietly in the hotel. We didn't want to be seen round Dili by anyone from the Australian military.

The Defence department in Australia went ballistic. One officer in Defence PR called on us to be prosecuted, apparently unaware East Timor wasn't part of Australia. The army never found Reinado. Instead, he emerged from the bush months later and did something so horrendous it was almost beyond belief.

In February 2008 he led an ambush on José Ramos-Horta, one of the only people in government who'd tried to respond to the soldiers' grievances and who had succeeded the Fretilin leader Alkatiri as prime minister. Ramos-Horta was shot in the stomach. Reinado was shot dead by police who intervened.

The wound suggested he'd been fired on at close range, leading many to believe he'd been executed.

It was impossible to know what had happened to Reinado's mind in those months on the run to make him do something so appalling. I tried to contact Ina but she didn't respond. I could only imagine the mental anguish she must have suffered at seeing what her hero had done.

Ramos-Horta survived the shooting. East Timor continues to struggle on from the legacy of the rebellion and the bitterness of lost hope on that troubled island.

7. Go Global Warming!

Greenland, July 2007

Journalist: 'How do you find America?'
Ringo Starr: 'Turn left at Greenland.'
Media conference with the Beatles, 1964 US tour

The icebergs were closing in and Kenneth Hoegh was getting worried. It wasn't out of fear the boat could be damaged; it was built for navigating the ice-filled fjords, and the constant scraping of ice on the hull that reminded me of the *Titanic* was just part of a normal commute. But today the icebergs were so plentiful Kenneth feared we wouldn't be able to reach the farm where he had a pressing appointment.

He began an animated conversation with the Inuit captain in Greenlandic, a language that sounded to me like they were swallowing marbles.

'He thinks there's a small channel we can get still through,' Kenneth said.

'We can't drive there?' I asked.

He laughed at my naivety. 'All the settlements are like small islands. Even though they're connected by land there are no roads between them.'

Around us was a fjord of astonishing beauty. Thousands of small bergs that had calved off the glacier bobbed and collided in the intensely blue water. It was July and the sun shone bright and hot but the cool of the ice produced a strange feeling of outside air-conditioning.

Kenneth went back to the captain as another berg smashed against the side.

It was our fourth day in Greenland and the ice and emptiness and near 24-hour sunlight were still messing with my slightly jet-lagged mind after the 4-hour flight from Denmark.

We had landed in Narsarsuaq, where a porter helped Dave, me and our producer Marianne Leitch carry our cases of gear to a hotel opposite the runway. I asked what there was to see in town only to find there wasn't one. The US military built the airstrip in World War Two as a refuelling stop for combat raids on Europe and a small hotel was eventually built to cater for tourists fresh off the plane. But the nearest town was a 20-minute boat ride away along the fjord. Greenland's settlements all hugged the narrow coast around the giant ice cap that covered more than 80 per cent of the island. The only connection between them was by air or sea.

The icebergs were more plentiful this summer thanks to rising temperatures speeding up the ice cap's annual melt. Glaciologists were warning the accelerating melt could raise sea levels around the world. But many of Greenland's 58,000 residents couldn't be happier, and none more so than Kenneth Hoegh.

'I hope that this greenhouse effect won't run out of control totally,' he told me as he returned to the stern of the boat. 'But just a little bit of extra warmth, ah, that would be good for us.'

Kenneth was a government agricultural consultant on an island that until recently had very little agriculture. The few farmers had raised tough sheep that could handle the harsh winters, and had grown small quantities of hardy, quick-growing vegetables like potatoes. Most food was imported from its old colonial master Denmark, which still controlled Greenland's defence and foreign policy. But since the mid-90s the average annual temperature had risen nearly two degrees. Now, in 2007, this inappropriately named land of ice was suddenly turning greener.

'Now they are willing to grow turnips and potatoes commercially,' Kenneth said. 'It used to be only for the farm and now they are willing to invest a lot of money into growing them commercially on a larger scale. Instead of 10 tonnes per hectare of potatoes, you might be able to harvest 15 tonnes now. It's very nice for us now that we are getting more and more sure that this tendency that we have seen in the last 10 to 12 years seems to be lasting.'

Kenneth was a native Greenlander, meaning he had both Danish and Inuit heritage, but like many on the island he looked like a Dane, with blue eyes, red hair and a red beard. Suddenly he was the man of the moment, advising farmers how they could capitalise on global warming.

The boat finally scraped into an icepack on shore and we hopped the last five metres to shore to meet today's client, an Inuit farmer named Ferdinand Egede.

Egede, a squat taciturn man with a farmer's weathered face, proudly showed us around his new vegetable plots of potatoes, turnips and cabbage. They were all growing well, but Egede said he was worried about the lack of water.

'The mountain has very quickly become free of snow,' he said. 'Usually there is some snow that feeds the creek, but now there's very little.'

'On the way out here I was thinking that you should have a permanent irrigation system,' Kenneth told him.

Despite the years of unusually high temperatures and unusually scarce water, Egede said he didn't believe in all this talk of global warming.

'I really don't believe that pollution is to blame for Greenland getting warmer,' he said. 'The eighties were very cold, while the nineties were a bit better, and now it's also good. That's the way it is.'

Greenland seemed fertile ground for a new branch of our National Party.

Popular myth has it that the Viking Eric the Red, who arrived by longship in the late 10th century, named the island 'Greenland' as a marketing ploy to attract settlers to its icy shores. For the same reason, Viking settlers of a much greener island to the southeast called their more fertile home 'Iceland' to scare others away. Both stories are probably apocryphal but there was no doubt that Greenland, at least on its narrow south coast, was starting to live up to its name.

'Greenland was actually much greener when the Vikings were here,' Kenneth said. 'The Middle Ages were much warmer. They were even growing cattle. Then the climate changed.'

We headed back through the ice to clearer water and Kenneth took us to some old Viking ruins a few kilometres down the fjord. Just near the shore were the crumbling foundations of what had once been a turf-covered communal house.

'It would have been completely sealed up for warmth with just a small entrance and a chimney,' Kenneth said. 'Can you imagine the smell?'

He sat in a pile of stones that still bore the signs of a chair. 'This is where a man would sit in winter telling lies about killing polar bears!'

At its height, the Viking settlements were thought to have 3000 inhabitants, trading polar bear skins, walrus ivory and narwhal tusks with Norway. When the once-mighty Norwegian kingdom declined in the fourteenth century and trade ships stopped coming, the isolated Vikings had to survive on hunting seals and farming.

I followed Kenneth as he pointed out the remains of abandoned farms. 'That's probably an old storage house for storing foodstuff for the winter,' he said, pointing at a large mound of rocks. 'It was probably used from year 1000 until around year 1500.'

The only substantial building was an old church that still had most of its five-metre high walls, if no roof. Kenneth explained that the last record of Viking settlement was a letter found in Iceland describing a wedding in the church in 1408.

'Then nothing. Nothing more was heard of them. They just disappeared.'

It wasn't until 1721 that Denmark, which had taken over the Norwegian empire, sent a party of missionaries to Greenland to see if any Christians were still alive. All they found were Inuit, who they proceeded to baptise regardless. At first it was thought the colonists had been killed by the Inuit, who started moving across from North America in the 13th century. Another theory was that the colonists had just intermarried with the Inuit and lost their Viking ways. The latest theory was that they were victims of climate change.

Greenland endured a long cold spell from the 14th to late 15th century called the Little Ice Age. It would have devastated the crops and cattle farms. Struggling to adapt, the people could have faced a relentless battle to sustain themselves, the communities shrinking and weakening until they abandoned Greenland on rare trading ships stopping off on the way to Iceland or Norway, or simply died out.

Denmark sent new settlers to colonise the territory and they fared better, but there are still fewer than 60,000 people living on the world's largest island. (Nerd alert: Australia is more than three times larger but it's classified as a continent rather than an island because it sits on its own tectonic plate. Greenland is part of the North American tectonic plate.)

The ice cap is uninhabitable and only small Inuit communities have managed to endure in the Arctic north. Most

Greenlanders live on the grassy, fjord-indented coastal strip in the relatively temperate south and southwest. While it had been self-governing since 1979, Denmark still provided about A$800 million a year, equal to A$13,000 per person.

But now the temperatures were rising, with earlier springs and much longer growing seasons, things were looking up for Greenlanders. Our next stop was the first cattle farm in 600 years.

Sofus Frederiksen, a lanky, dour man of the land, had few words and even fewer cattle. But he was proud of each and every one of them. All 16.

'I really like my cattle,' he told us at his farmhouse. 'They're very gentle and good-tempered.'

We walked up a steep hill behind his farmhouse where the entire herd was grazing. He knew each animal by sight, though he insisted he hadn't given them names. He had a uniquely personal way of studying them. Without a word he dropped to his knees and crawled into the herd, whispering softly to a cow. We watched as he crept around to each of his 16 cattle for a chat. I had been to cattle stations in Australia with more than 100,000 head and never seen a grazier talk to any of them.

Sofus knew this was a miniscule herd but saw it as a prototype. He wanted to study intimately how each animal coped over the year so he could experiment with different breeding stock to build up the herd. After six centuries without bulls and cows, there wasn't any past experience in Greenland to go on. But he was confident he was onto something big.

'I hope so. Warming temperatures can't be bad when you're working with agriculture.'

We went back to the Narsarsuaq hotel to try to get some sleep in the bright late-night sunshine. My room was hot and stuffy from the constant glare so I opened the windows to let in the outside air-conditioning. I turned on the room TV and found the local Greenlandic station had shut down for the night. But the TV was picking up a Canadian channel and suddenly Al Gore was on the screen warning about the perils of climate change.

It was Live Earth, a global broadcast featuring 150 bands with numerous politicians, activists and indigenous peoples in traditional dress, all demanding action to combat global warming. It felt strange to be in one of the only places on Earth (outside oil company executive bathrooms and News Corporation newsrooms) that was actually looking forward to it.

Scientists were taking a bleaker view. The Intergovernmental Panel on Climate Change, which reviews global data, had predicted the previous year that the melt could raise sea levels by 20 centimetres over 50 years. But a glaciologist I had spoken to in Copenhagen, Professor Dorte Dahl-Jensen, told me those estimates were already out of date.

'You might even double it so you're up 40 or 50 centimetres of sea level change during the next 50 years and that's quite serious. This will affect a lot of people that are living close to the ocean.'

'So the speed of the melt is actually increasing?'

'Yes that's right, and we would never have believed that just 10 years ago.'

It was highly unlikely the changes were a natural variation, like the medieval warm period or the Little Ice Age. Scientists like Professor Dahl-Jensen were collecting ice cores from the Greenland ice cap that showed carbon levels over the past 100,000 years. Today's carbon measurements were off the scale. Cores from other glacial areas like Antarctica looked back even further, showing carbon levels were now the highest in 400,000 years.

Of course that's just what smarty-pants scientists with their fancy satellites, monitoring stations and ice drilling were saying. Sceptics could cite the authority of Farmer Egede.

The next day we were back on the water dodging icebergs to meet Kenneth in his home in Narsaq, the nearest town along the fjord. It was a typical ordered, picture-postcard Greenlandic town with brightly coloured houses looking over an ice-filled bay. On the edge of town was a rough suburb of largely welfare-dependent Inuit plagued by alcoholism and violence. But Kenneth and his family were from Greenland's comfortable middle class and a striking demonstration of the island's mixed heritage. His wife and sons looked Inuit while his seven-year-old daughter looked like a Danish princess.

The town had actual roads, and after lunch Kenneth drove us to an experimental station testing just how far Greenland's green revolution could go. A series of open plots and greenhouses were growing vegetables that were once unthinkable so far north.

'We are testing new things that we probably would have hesitated a little bit to test in the past – like broccoli, like different types of cabbage. They're growing fine.'

It meant Greenlanders could at last have access to fresh milk and vegetables. Kenneth said they might even be able to export meat to Denmark, marketing it as totally organic produce.

'Bit of an irony there, isn't there, if you've got an export market for organic meat that's a result of global warming?' I asked.

'Yeah, you could say so, but there's always something good that comes out of something bad. We are right on the limit of agricultural production. We are next to the Arctic desert, to the cold desert, and the cold desert is retreating and that's good for us.'

One entrepreneur in Narsaq was already capitalising on the melting ice, turning it into export beer.

Early the next morning Dave and I joined a fishing boat catching ice. The captain, Kurt Hansen, had been fishing the bay for 23 years, always seeing the ice that calved off the glacier as a nuisance. Now he and his crew were collecting it.

'We look for the shiny ones, the ones without any sand,' he explained.

Every time he spotted one he pulled the boat alongside and his men used a grappling hook to drag it onto the boat. Soon the deck was full.

'This is quite new and I really don't know how it will go,' he said, still puzzled by his new occupation.

Back at the dock we were met by a young Inuit businessman named Salik Hard. He carefully selected the cleanest specimens to be taken back to his microbrewery.

'This ice is very old,' he said, 'between 2000 and 180,000 years old. It's the purest water in the world.'

As he drove us to the brewery he explained that water was the core ingredient of beer and the brewer's biggest challenge was removing all the impurities from it.

'Melted ice has no minerals whatsoever and is absolutely pure, and brewers all over the world spend a lot of money taking all the minerals out of the water but we don't because it's so pure. So that's every brew master's dream to have such pure water.'

Salik had brought a brew master named Rasmussen Broge over from Denmark to perfect the beer. We watched him go through the painstaking process of adding the malt and hops, boiling it and leaving it to ferment.

We sampled some of the completed product, then a bit more to be sure and another couple of cans just to make certain it was good.

'Thish ish not too bad,' I said, giving the highest Australian compliment.

'The water is actually perfect for brewing with,' Rasmussen said. 'I could make the same water if I had a filter. In normal tap water I take out whatever kind of stuff is in there, but I don't have to adjust anything here. It's perfect to brew on right away, which is perfect.'

'Itsh very tashty,' Dave confirmed.

Salik said he was already taking orders internationally, marketing it as being made from 100,000-year-old ice.

'But the best thing was a couple of weeks ago when we sold the first beer in Greenland. It was much more important for me personally and deep inside my soul it was the best feeling I have ever felt.'

But even in Greenland there was a downside to the melting ice cap.

The last farm we visited with Kenneth was a five-hour boat ride down the fjord. It was to be an overnight trip. 'It's a long way but you're going to enjoy it,' Kenneth promised.

We arrived to find a military transport vehicle with tank tracks waiting on the dock. Beside it stood a tall fair-haired man named Stefan Magnusson.

'Welcome to Isortoq,' he shouted.

'Thank you. I love your ride!'

'Yes, it's an old Norwegian army vehicle. Constructed in Sweden. You can go anywhere in the wintertime, summertime, it's an all-round land vehicle. It can even swim! You need that around here.'

Stefan lived on this isolated farm with his young Inuit wife who was a qualified butcher. Which was handy for Stefan as he was farming reindeer.

He drove us up a hill to the slaughterhouse he had constructed next to his house. It was built entirely from stainless steel.

'It meets all EU standards,' he boasted as he pulled down a handle making the door slam shut with a violent clang. Marianne squealed in shock and Stefan roared with laughter.

'Come to the house. We're having a reindeer barbecue!'

We lugged our gear to the cosy wooden house where Stefan's wife was chopping up imported vegetables for salad. Stefan slapped fresh reindeer steaks on the grill.

'This one's name was Johnny,' he said.

'So you get really sentimental about your reindeer, do you?'

'Oh yeah, I cry every time.'

Stefan talked animatedly about his life's adventures over the sizzle of the steaks. A native Icelander, he had travelled all over the world, spoke six languages fluently and decided to move to this remote farm to make his fortune in reindeer. He now had 2000 head roaming over 140,000 hectares but the changing climate was threatening to make him seek his fortune somewhere else. It was becoming impossible to round up the herds for slaughter.

'The temperature is significantly warmer than it used to be 10, 12 years ago. We used to have three stable months of snowmobile conditions but now we can barely get three weeks.'

'So what are you going to do?'

'I don't know. Maybe lay down and put my four feet in the air,' he said, laughing. 'Tomorrow I'll take you to the glacier and you'll see what I'm talking about.'

We gorged on venison and settled in for stories and vodka as the boat captain played a piano accordion, the sun finally dipping down to the horizon for what passed as night.

'I'm going to put you in the loft to sleep,' he said. 'It's very comfortable. We once had a tourist stay there, a Bosnian general.'

I paused.

'What was his name.'

'Ratko.'

'Not Ratko Mladić!'

'That's the one.'

'The war criminal?'

'Well he didn't talk much about what he did. He just came here to hunt reindeer. At first he said he was a Croat. I asked him about the war and he said it was a beautiful country and suddenly one day everyone started fighting each other.'

I slept uncomfortably in the mass murderer's bed. Next morning we set off towards the ice cap, three kilometres from Stefan's farm. As we descended the hill a squadron of mosquitoes attacked.

'You might want to put these on,' Stefan said, handing us mosquito masks.

We flung them onto our heads as mosquitoes swarmed into our eyes and ears. A small combat unit flew into my mouth. Stefan didn't bother to protect himself, striding off seemingly unfazed by the aerial attacks.

Dave dissolved in expletives. 'They're inside the bloody lens. I've got mosquitoes in every friggin' shot!'

We continued walking, slapping our faces and arms to try to kill the flying beasts, hundreds descending to take each swatted mosquito's place.

'Yes, it comes with the territory,' Stefan said. 'You get used to them. Not far to go now. Just over yonder.'

Half an hour later we finally escaped the insects and stood on a ridge looking at the awesome majesty of the ice cap. It towered over us, a wall of solid white.

Stefan told us it was retreating fast.

'That's where the glacier was 10 years ago,' he said, pointing to a spot 100 metres in front of it.

'That was all ice?' I asked.

'Yes, all ice.'

A river now flowed where the ice had been.

'Three years ago we saw a new river coming from underneath the ice. And the melting is going through the crevasses and I think there is a huge lake underneath the ice cap just over there yonder. From here to there it's close to 100 metres. And down there it's even more, close to 200 metres that has been melted away.'

We had decided to blow the rest of our budget on hiring a helicopter from Narsarsuq Airport to see the melt from above. Stefan rang the Swedish pilot and guided him to land in a field next to us. Stefan was excited to come up with us as he was considering using helicopters or ultralights to round up his reindeer from the air next season now the snow was becoming too sparse for snowmobiles.

We took off over a stunningly panoramic vista of ice, lakes and mountains, Stefan guiding the pilot in fluent Swedish towards his herds.

'Their natural habit when we have warm weather like this is to go up to the glacier to cool off, to get away from the mosquitoes and all the bugs, and they stay there mostly during the day and then in the evening they will go down back onto the green land for the pasture.'

We soon found hundreds of reindeers up on high ground and Stefan practised rounding them up.

'Can we keep them together?' he said to the pilot. 'Right, right, right. Yes, that's good. Those ones in the lake, we'll get them at the beach. Don't go any further that way, go to the right and then we can make them swim across.'

The helicopter mustering was working a treat, if you didn't count the hire cost of A$1000 an hour.

'I live in a great place, yes?' Stefan said turning back to me. 'I think I live in one of the greatest places on the planet.'

The sheer size of the ice cap was staggering, even the small part we could see from the helicopter. It towered three kilometres into the air. Deep crevasses split through the top of it with giant spouts of water pouring from its face as icebergs calved into the fjord.

Stefan opened up a map to follow where we were. He frowned. The map bore little relation to what we were seeing.

'On older charts this lake here did not exist in 1952. It's unbelievable. Nothing that is on the old map, that is based on aerial photographs taken in 1953, nothing on the map makes sense where the edge of the ice is. There are new lakes that have formed and the ice has retreated several hundred metres in some areas.'

Everywhere we flew was the same. Where the map showed ice cap was now a lake or open land.

'All this land that you are seeing here used to be covered up with ice 10 years ago. The global warming and the climate change is a fact, you have the physical fact right here in front of your eyes!'

We flew in silence for a while, awed by both the beauty of the land and how quickly it was changing. Scientific graphs and projections are one thing. Actually seeing the change was visceral.

Like all Greenlanders, Stefan was trying to look on the bright side. After all, global warming was going to be good for many of his farmer neighbours. 'We will just have to observe it and how far it is going to go and try to live with it. I have to adapt. Yeah I'm a fan for it because the next generation is going to benefit from it. I'm not going to benefit from it but the next generation is going to benefit, at least the generation living around the Arctic Circle. So you gotta try to see the positive in the negatives.'

We dropped him at his house and continued on to Narsarsuaq to catch our flight back to Denmark. It seemed Greenland's 58,000 islanders really did have reason to be hopeful. Shame about the other seven and a half billion humans on planet Earth.

8. Aryan Nation

Sri Lanka, January 2010

> I strongly believe that Sri Lanka belongs to the
> Sinhalese, but there are minority communities and
> we treat them like our people. They can live in this
> country with us. But they must not try to, under the
> pretext of being a minority, demand undue things.
>
> Sarath Fonseka, ex-army chief and self-appointed hope of minorities

It was a squeeze to fit all the asylum seekers on the bus but
at least the chains on everyone's wrists meant they wouldn't
be fighting for elbow room. The short trip from the town jail
to the courthouse was the last step in their unsuccessful bid
to reach Australia. They'd paid a Tamil businessman up to
A$20,000 each to be taken to Australian territory and were
ferried offshore in fishing boats to wait in vain for a promised
ship, slowly realising they might have been duped. After 10 days
bobbing in the ocean, a Sri Lankan navy ship found them and
took them by force to the mainland naval base at Matara near
the tourist town of Galle.

A two-month stay in prison followed where they were abused and beaten by prisoners from the majority ethnic group, the Sinhalese. Now they were about to face justice for attempting to leave Sri Lanka 'illegally'.

The bus disgorged about 150 men who were led to a courtyard to await their fate. Happily for me their guards appeared too dim-witted to spot anything unusual in a white reporter walking in and filming them removing the prisoners' chains. I smiled and waved at the guards and zoomed in on the chains rattling into the dirt.

The men looked despondent but their fate was arguably better than if they'd managed to board a ship. Three months earlier the Australian Labor government had managed to persuade Indonesia to intercept a boat carrying 254 Sri Lankans before they could reach Australia. The opposition Coalition was drawing up plans to bring back indefinite offshore detention. Politicians were competing to sound toughest on 'queue jumpers'. The obvious question these Tamil farmers and labourers had to be asked was: 'Why didn't you read *Hansard*?'

The answer perhaps – apart from the lack of good internet connections in rural Sri Lanka and the fact that they could barely read English – was that this was a rather unpleasant time to be a minority Tamil in Sri Lanka. In July the military had finally wiped out the rebel army of the Tamil Tigers along with thousands of civilians who had the misfortune to be in the way of the government's mortars and shells. The Sinhalese were still celebrating the triumph, and not in a conciliatory group-hug kind of way.

Inside the courtroom, a judge gave the would-be refugees a stern lecture in Sinhalese, a language many of the Tamils had trouble following. Bail was denied for more than 30 men the prosecutor asserted could be rebel fighters. The others would only be released when their relatives paid a hefty bond. Then they were put back in chains and led outside where their families cried out their names as they were loaded onto the bus and returned to prison.

More than 100 people had come to hear the verdict and they milled around the street in the blazing sun trying to work out what the fine was and how they could raise the money. Everything they had was in the hands of the people smugglers.

I began interviewing them and a cacophony of voices answered.

'Sir, not safe in Sri Lanka, not safe in Sri Lanka!'

'No money, no jobs, no food!'

'The Tamil people cannot stay here,' one man shouted. 'You have to pay money, then go to Australia to save your life.'

'But Australia says if people come by boat they will be sent back to Sri Lanka,' I said.

'But there is no government help to go by the flight,' a woman answered. 'That's why they go by boat.'

A distraught mother called Namadeva Pathmanathan told me she hoped her son would try to reach Australia again if she could get him released.

'There is no money here,' she said. 'We have no land, no food, no house, nothing. Just want [to go to] Australia.'

The lethargic police finally stirred from their midday stupor and noticed the commotion, shooing us away.

I had come here with a Sydney producer, Ian Altschwager, and the ABC's Bangkok cameraman, Dave Leland, to find out what had happened in those last tumultuous days of a 26-year-long civil war. Sri Lanka had barred any media, aid groups or even the UN from going near the Tamil Tigers' last stand, a narrow enclave about the size of Central Park on the island's northeast coast.

More than 300,000 civilians had been trapped in the area and the psychopathic Tigers had prevented them from leaving, believing their presence would stall the Sri Lankan military's offensive. It didn't. An indiscriminate rain of heavy artillery killed rebels and civilians alike before the army stormed in and executed the senior Tigers. Video evidence smuggled out to human rights groups suggested the army had also executed the Tigers' families.

Even now the area was still closed off to outsiders, and most of the civilians who survived were being held in isolated camps while the authorities decided whether they were fighters or non-combatants. The Tigers hadn't hesitated to use child soldiers so the government saw even small children as suspect.

The brutal military offensive, thought to have killed tens of thousands of civilians and which Amnesty International and Human Rights Watch condemned as a war crime, was later described by Australia's former prime minister Tony Abbott as 'probably unavoidable'.

About two million Tamils live in Sri Lanka; close to 13 per cent of the population. Their presence on the island goes back more than 2000 years, though many were brought over from southern India by the British in the 19th century to work in tea plantations.

Attempts to campaign for equal rights were violently suppressed in the 1970s leading to armed revolt by a group called the Liberation Tigers of Tamil Eelam (LTTE) in 1983. It soon morphed into the Tamil Tigers, one of the most ruthless and bizarre insurgencies of the 20th century.

The Tigers (an animal that doesn't exist in Sri Lanka) were led by a megalomaniac named Velupillai Prabhakaran. Think L Ron Hubbard with an army, or Hannibal Lecter with a business plan. He was a fan of Clint Eastwood films and pioneered the use of suicide vests and female suicide bombers. He turned the movement into a cult where he was feted as a demi-god by his adoring followers, including legions of fierce young female warriors. Prabhakaran demanded total obedience and insisted every aspect of the struggle be recorded for posterity. There was even a Tiger film unit comprised of teenage girl soldiers who would shoot both bullets and video in battle.

By 2002 the Tigers/LTTE controlled 15,000 square kilometres of territory including a large 'homeland' in the north called Eelam with a fleet of warships and an air force. They carried out regular assassinations and bombings in the rest of the country.

Sinhalese civilians watched on helplessly as successive governments seemed unable to protect them. Tamil civilians were caught between an insurgency that expected them to fight for it and Sri Lankan security forces that assumed they did.

When people disappeared off the streets it was hard to know which side had done the snatching.

Both sides signed a meaningless ceasefire in 2002, but the tide only really started turning in 2005 after the Asian tsunami wiped out the Tigers' navy and most of their coastal bases. It might have been an opportunity for genuine peace talks if either side had had a genuine interest. Instead, the government resumed a full-scale military offensive in 2006 escalating to the final bloodbath in May 2009. Prabhakaran was one of the last to die, along with his 12-year-old son.

If there was any sign the government's victory had led to a policy of reconciliation with Tamils rather than triumphalist payback, it hadn't registered on the young men trying to flee to Australia.

That night we waited outside the prison as the families who had raised the bond money or found guarantors came to buy their relatives' release.

Namadeva embraced her son Krisanth as he emerged dirty and dishevelled with a long beard from two months inside. He told me he was already thinking about trying to reach Australia again.

'Yes, I like to again, maybe.'

'On a boat?'

'I cannot say anything, that's it.'

I wanted to ask him more but he and his mother just wanted to go home. He invited us to come to his distant village later in our journey, promising to explain to us why he had tried so hard to leave.

Back in the capital Colombo, Sinhalese were still celebrating the victory, none more so than the man who claimed full responsibility for it, President Mahinda Rajapaksa. The heavy-set, mustachioed Rajapaksa was hoping the defeat of the Tigers would bring him a crushing victory at the election to be held in a week's time. He had called the poll a year early to 'seek a fresh mandate'.

The presidency had been as outstanding a success for his family fortunes as it had been for the military leadership. Rajapaksa had installed two of his brothers as ministers: kid brother Gotabhaya as Defence Secretary and older brother Chamal as Ports and Aviation Minister. Rumours of massive corruption swirled around Colombo but they were drowned out by state media's adulation of the President. He was spawning his own cult of personality, with television advertisements not only singing his praises but declaring he should be crowned king.

We waited in a sports stadium on the city's edge for his latest rally. The stand was filled with enthusiastic supporters watching schoolchildren marching in formation and performing gymnastic displays on the field. The roar of a helicopter announced the President's arrival. It circled the cheering crowd and landed beside the stadium. Moments later, to martial music, the President entered the arena clothed in a pure white robe with a long scarlet scarf. The rally could have been choreographed by Leni Riefenstahl.

Rajapaksa gave a rousing speech to the crowd, peppered with references to the military triumph, before settling down to watch more athletic displays by Sri Lankan children.

The government had ignored or rebuffed every request we'd made to interview officials about what had happened in the offensive. So I slipped past the President's security detail and stepped up to the stage where Rajapaksa was standing.

'Sir, we're from Australian television,' I shouted as security guards rushed up to grab me.

Rajapaksa turned towards me and his guards stopped, uncertain of whether they could hit me in front of him.

'There is much concern about Tamils coming to Australia in boats,' I continued. 'Will that problem be solved?'

'Yes, don't worry, I think it is solved,' he said with a politician's oily smile under his thick moustache. 'Most of the problems. Because it was organised by the LTTE because that was their way, you know. They were drug dealers and traffickers. Drugs, arms and smuggling humans.'

He turned away and his guards pulled me back, scowling with rage. I thanked them and walked back to the crowd.

Rajapaksa was now chatting with some Buddhist monks seated next to him on the stage. Most people in the West think of Buddhism as an innately peaceful religion, the perception coloured by images of the Dalai Lama, vegan restaurants and chanting Hollywood celebrities. In Sri Lanka it's more war-like.

Buddhist fanatics had long been at the vanguard of championing Sinhalese superiority over the mainly Hindu Tamils. In 1959 a monk assassinated the President after he allowed the Tamil language to be used in schools. In the 1970s and 80s monks took part in and sometimes led vicious pogroms against Tamil civilians that left thousands dead. Their fundamental belief was that Sri Lanka was not a land of many ethnic groups with equal rights, but a Buddhist Aryan nation.

While the Nazis appropriated the term Aryan to denote German racial purity, the term actually refers to descendants of a prehistoric people who settled what is now Iran and northern India and spoke an Indo-European language. (The Nazis also appropriated the Sanskrit symbol for good fortune, the swastika, giving it a whole new meaning.) Under Sri Lanka's extremist Buddhists, the term Aryan had again come to denote racial superiority.

In Sinhalese mythology, Sri Lanka was conquered by a light-skinned prince who was driven out of northern India 2500 years ago. Prince Vijaya and his followers defeated a race of demons on the island and, on the direct instructions of Lord Buddha himself, founded a Buddhist kingdom.

Anthropologists and ethnographers class modern-day Sinhalese and their language as Indo-Aryan. The language has almost nothing in common with the Dravidian Tamil dialects of southern India. While Sinhalese are overwhelmingly Buddhist, a religion emanating from northern India, Tamils have retained the Hinduism of the south. (Strangely enough, many of the LTTE leaders were Christians, having no apparent trouble reconciling their faith with suicide bombings, child soldiers, mass terrorism and using Tamil civilians as human shields.)

For Sinhalese extremists, Aryanism plays to the idea of being a separate race to the darker-skinned Tamils and a perception that Tamils were not real Sri Lankans but the foreign descendants of invaders and interlopers.

Hardline monks weren't just backing Rajapaksa. They were conferring an ethnic and religious legitimacy for wiping out his opponents. But Rajapaksa's quest for victory had encountered an unexpected hurdle thanks to the one man who had as much blood on his hands as Rajapaksa did.

Field Marshal Sarath Fonseka, who had directed the offensive, was also contesting the presidency, hoping to capitalise on the mantle of national saviour. Rajapaksa had sidelined him after the victory to the backroom post of Chief of Defence Staff. In November he had resigned to announce he was running for the top job. It seemed a brave, even foolhardy, move to take on the authoritarian Rajapaksa, who was rapidly bringing the state's institutions under his personal control. But the old warhorse, who had once been gravely wounded when an LTTE suicide bomber attacked his motorcade, was not a man to be scared easily.

I door-stopped him after a rally in Colombo and he seemed stiff and unfriendly, more a military man than a politician. He didn't have much to say but handed me a copy of his talking points listing dozens of allegations of high-level corruption by Rajapaksa and his cronies, claiming they had trousered tens of millions of dollars from government projects. For example, it accused the Defence Minister, Gotabhaya Rajapaksa, of a 600 million rupee fraud (about A$5.5 million) in upgrading MIG aircraft. It also alleged the Rajapaksas were behind the murder of 14 journalists.

'Little time does the Secretary of Defence waste in eliminating his "adversaries" which dares to threaten his "livelihood",' the pamphlet stated. 'My condolences are with the kith and kin of the other "eliminated" journalists as well.'

The nation's Tamils had thrown their full weight behind Fonseka's campaign. It seemed odd that Tamil leaders were enthusiastically backing a man whose forces had killed thousands of Tamil civilians, but they saw him as the lesser of two great evils. They were not only cheering him at rallies but organising Tamil villages to vote for him.

Many Sinhalese were also tiring of Rajapaksa. Sinhalese journalists found themselves facing a difficult decision: join the chorus of adulation for the President or risk disappearing. One of the last independent newspapers was the *Sunday Leader*. We arrived to meet its editor Frederica Jansz and found an armed guard standing outside the entrance. Inside was a large photo of the paper's previous editor, Lasantha Wickrematunge, who had been murdered the year before.

'I hold the current government, the Rajapaksa government, completely responsible,' she told me. 'Whether they initiated the attack I don't know. We have no proof. Whether they killed Lasantha I don't know. Again we have no proof. However, the fact that Lasantha's investigation has gone nowhere is proof I believe that his killers are close or are known to the highest authority in this land.'

Wickrematunge was only one of dozens of journalists to have been killed, beaten or abducted since Rajapaksa came to power. Not a single case had been solved.

'We have continued to be threatened and harassed. We have continued to receive death threats, both myself and my news editor and editor of investigation desk, all women. The reality is that there is very little press freedom in this country. Most of the press has been cowed into submission. They're too afraid to be free any more or to write without any kind of self-censorship.'

Later we drove to Namadeva and Krisanth's village in the northern town of Batticaloa. He and his family were living in a decrepit rented cottage, having sold their house and land to pay the people smugglers.

Squatting on the floor over a lunch of coarse rice and vegetable curry, the now clean-shaven Krisanth said none of his family had ever been involved with the Tigers. But he had taken the boat to avoid being killed as a traitor.

'I feared for my life and wanted to go somewhere I could live happily. No one in my family could get work. I wanted to go so I could look after the family.'

He explained that his father had been abducted and murdered in 1992 as the civil war raged around them. Four years ago his uncle disappeared. Last year while he was running a small shop in town – he had an old photocopier and charged to copy documents – anonymous phonecallers told him he would be next.

'When I was in that shop I received threats. I'd already lost my father. My uncle also disappeared. I didn't want this to happen to me as well.'

The shop provided barely enough income for the family to eat. As the only breadwinner, he felt a responsibility to try to find work in Australia. Despite the family's history of persecution, he saw no point in applying for a visa from the Australian High Commission.

'My elder brother applied but was rejected. He went to Colombo for an interview, and a lot of money was spent. Therefore we were a bit sceptical and did not reapply. He also applied to the Swiss Embassy but that was rejected too. After all this we gave up.'

I explained to him that under the UN convention you could not apply for asylum if you were still in the country you claimed was persecuting you. He would have to find a way to leave Sri Lanka legally to go somewhere like India or Indonesia. Only then could an Australian mission consider his application. He would probably have to wait there for years. It seemed to make him even more determined to get a boat, no matter how dangerous that might be.

'If there is an opportunity to leave Sri Lanka, to flee Sri Lanka by any means, I will not hesitate, even if it poses a risk to my life.'

'There have been a lot of changes to the immigration law in Australia and a lot of debate in our parliament about migration,' I said. 'Were you aware of any of this?'

'Yes. Not much, but to some extent. I'd heard other people talking about it.'

'Did that influence your decision to go to Australia?'

'Yes. It would make it easier because of the problems we have here. The only way to be granted the appropriate status for our problems was to reach Australia. We just wanted to reach Australia. We departed believing that our problems would be solved. We fully believed it.'

After lunch he invited us to come to a cricket match he was playing with some friends. It was a social match but they were serious players, often spending hours a day practising. Since the Tigers' defeat they had cut practice short.

'I'm 24 years old and I've never felt that we have rights,' Krisanth said. 'Now today if we go to a ground to play cricket we can't stay out after 5 or 5.30 pm. Even now it is scary.'

It was his turn to bat and he showed himself to be the best player, hitting the balls with long, powerful strokes that sent his opponents racing to the furthest edges of the field. It occurred to me he and his mates would make perfect migrants to Australia: sports mad, already speaking rudimentary English and desperate to work hard and build new lives. I doubted any of them would get the chance.

After the match Krisanth told me his dream was to become a professional player.

'So who would you rather play for, Australia or Sri Lanka?' I asked.

'Australia or South Africa,' he said.

'You don't support Sri Lanka?'

'I can't support Sri Lanka.'

We left him and drove north to Jaffna, the capital of the former Tiger homeland. The government claimed to have begun a rebuilding program and we had gone through the laborious process of obtaining all the necessary travel permits. But at a checkpoint outside Jaffna Sri Lankan soldiers refused to let us pass. They would not even look at our permits. We rang the officials in Colombo who had granted us permission and they refused to intervene.

We began the long drive back towards Colombo, spending the night in a filthy small hotel. It was a long time since it had seen any tourists. Most of the rooms were closed up and I had to share a bed with the producer, Ian Altschwager. As we were getting ready to sleep our Tamil fixer knocked on the door.

'I have some people for you to meet,' he said.

He took us downstairs where two Tamil men were waiting for us. They explained they were government doctors who had been working in a clinic in the Central Park-sized enclave when the final offensive began. I remembered hearing interviews with the doctors during the fighting. They had been in daily phone contact with foreign media talking about the shells falling around them and the civilians dying. They had been the only voices countering the government's claim that no heavy artillery was used in the attacks.

Afterwards, they disappeared until weeks later they were paraded to the media at a press conference in Colombo, retracting all their claims and saying the Tigers had forced them to invent stories.

'The press conference was a lie,' one of the doctors told me. 'They put us in jail and charged us with making unauthorised statements. They told us we would only be released if we said it was all untrue.'

They said Sri Lanka had systematically shelled hospitals on the front line. Every hospital had been hit with mortars or artillery. They showed me photos they had taken of the destruction and of dead or horrifically wounded civilians, many of them children. They said they were explaining this to us so we would know what had really happened but asked us not to use them in our story.

'In six months I hope to move to the UK with my family,' one doctor said. 'Only then will it be safe for me to talk.'

We stayed in Sri Lanka until election day, watching Tamils line up to vote for Fonseka. It was in vain. Rajapaksa won easily, 58 to 40 per cent. Fonseka's best results were in the northern Tamil areas where he had led attacks. If Fonseka had thought he could escape the ruthlessness he had helped Rajapaksa deal out to other opponents, he was soon set right. Within days he was arrested and charged with committing 'military offences'. He was later convicted of corrupt military supply deals and sentenced to three years in prison.

Back in Australia, I had one more interview to do to complete the story.

Gordon Weiss is an Australian journalist who had been the UN spokesperson in Sri Lanka, meaning he had been privy to information about the offensive that was totally at odds with the government's claim of doing everything possible to avoid civilian casualties. But under the UN's strict rules he had been forbidden to speak out. An Australian aid worker I knew said the enforced silence had taken a heavy toll on him.

'He's a broken man,' he said.

Weiss had just resigned from the UN and moved home to Australia with his young family. It meant for the first time he could say what had really happened when I met him at his home in Newcastle.

'About 300,000 civilians were within range of all the armaments that were being used, small and large, being used to smash the Tamil Tiger lines,' he told me. 'The end result was that many thousands lost their lives. I have heard anything between 10,000 and 40,000 people and that's from reliable sources who had a presence inside the zone.'

'So up to 40,000 civilians could have been killed in those last battles?' I asked.

'That's right.'

The government's estimate of civilian casualties was about 40,000 less.

'They repeated a number of things that were either intentionally misleading or were lies. One senior government civil servant remarked at the end of the war that the government insistence that the figures were very low was a ploy. It was a ploy to allow the government to get on with its business.'

He was just as critical of the Tamil Tigers. 'We have pretty good testimony that the Tamil Tigers were killing people consistently to stop them from getting out.'

But that didn't excuse the Sri Lankan military.

'If one looks at the numbers of civilians who died during this time, I think it speaks for itself that not enough care was shown in order to preserve the lives of the innocent.'

'Do you think senior government officials, even President Rajapaksa himself, should be investigated for war crimes?' I asked.

'Well I think as is the case with war crimes, it's a question of the chain of command and where the buck finally stopped.'

He was obviously relieved to have left Sri Lanka but was still haunted by what had happened. He did not believe Rajapaksa had any intention of dealing with Tamil grievances.

'The Rajapaksa administration is seen as being closely tied to Sinhalese nationalism and to Buddhism and I don't think that the administration feels inclined to deliver any serious reconciliation for the Tamil community in Sri Lanka, but we'll have to wait and see.'

When it was aired on *Foreign Correspondent*, our story caused a diplomatic explosion as Gordon Weiss's estimate of 40,000 dead was quoted in headlines around the world. The Sri Lankan government and much of the Sinhalese community in Australia began a furious attack on Gordon Weiss's credibility and our broadcast story. The ABC was flooded with more than 500 complaints, many sent from the same IP address. It triggered a formal internal inquiry. I had to draft a response to every single point of complaint. Weeks were spent writing justifications for every phrase in the story, including defending my description of Matara as a port rather than a seaside town. Some complaints asserted that I had not even been to Sri Lanka but faked the entire story from Australia. The Sri Lankan High Commission in Canberra lodged its own complaint, claiming falsely that we had not requested any interviews with Sri Lankan officials.

It was gratifying when the inquiry finally dismissed every complaint and upheld the story. But I sensed I might have greater trouble persuading the ABC to invest in a Sri Lankan story again, which was undoubtedly the purpose of the complaints.

By now the atrocities in Sri Lanka were beyond dispute. Video footage obtained by Channel 4 in Britain showed the targeted shelling of hospitals as well as Sri Lankan soldiers torturing and summarily executing prisoners. Perhaps the most shocking footage showed soldiers sexually defiling the naked bodies of female Tamil fighters who had died of gunshots to the head.

In 2011 a UN report ordered by Secretary-General Ban Ki-moon backed Gordon Weiss's claim of indiscriminate shelling and unlawful killing. It stated that the exact number of civilian deaths could not be determined but that his estimate of 40,000 was plausible.

By November 2013, as Britain was demanding an international inquiry into Sri Lanka's alleged war crimes, the new Australian government boldly sided with China in resisting any condemnation or calls for sanctions. Instead, it moved to forge closer ties with Rajapaksa to 'stop the boats'. In 2014 the Immigration Minister, Scott Morrison, commended the 'very close cooperation' as he met Rajapaksa to gift two patrol boats for the Sri Lankan navy to intercept asylum seeker boats. He denied Tamil asylum seekers now being returned to Sri Lanka by Australia would risk any persecution.

When Tony Abbott reflected in March 2016 on his brief term as prime minister, cut short by his own party room, he cited the decision to keep silent as others condemned Sri Lanka to be one of his greatest achievements.

'I'm sure that the Sri Lankan president was pleased that Australia didn't join the human rights lobby against the tough but probably unavoidable actions taken to end one of the world's most vicious civil wars,' Mr Abbott mused thoughtfully.

But by then Rajapaksa's own rule was over. In 2015 he suffered an election swing so severe that not even police torture, media suppression and electoral fraud could protect him.

The new President, Maithripala Sirisena, pardoned Field Marshal Fonseka. The new Prime Minister, Ranil Wickremesinghe, alleged Australia had made a deal with Rajapaksa to stay silent on human rights abuses in exchange for cooperation in cracking down on people smuggling. He called Australia's close relationship to Rajapaksa 'a mystery'.

Frederica Jansz eventually fled Sri Lanka after Gotabhaya Rajapaksa personally threatened her life. By her account, he rang her in 2012 saying: 'Yes, I threatened you. Your type of journalists are pigs who eat shit! I will put you in jail! People will kill you!'

As an educated, middle-class Sri Lankan of means she was able to fly to the United States and apply successfully for asylum.

When I last heard, Krisanth was still trying to find a way out.

9. Dire Strait

Taiwan and the South Pacific, June 2005

Even if one tree falls down, it wouldn't affect the entire forest.

Chen Shui-bian, Taiwanese President, 2004

We will smash the separatist schemes of the Taiwanese independence movement at all costs!

Zhang Mingqing, Chinese government spokesman, 2004

It was my first trip to Taiwan and the first time a man had ever hung a 2.5-kilogram weight from my penis.

We had two days to kill before flying out with the Taiwanese President to the South Pacific so I decided to use the time productively shooting a story on genital kung-fu.

Yin diao gong is an ancient martial art forgotten in mainland China, but like many Chinese traditions it's been kept alive in Taiwan. In essence, it involves tying a sash around your genitals and using a hook on the end to lift weights. Advocates say it releases huge amounts of qi, the life force at the heart of Taoist medicine.

My cameraman, Geoff Lye, and I watched slack-mouthed as the mainly geriatric practitioners lifted astonishingly heavy weights. One man invited me to sit in a chair with a hook on top, climbed some steps behind it, attached it to his own hook and, after much grunting and mental preparation, lifted me into the air. With his penis! He later told me eight of them were in training to pull a 747 jet.

I was amazed by their pluck and there was no way I could manfully refuse their invitation to try. An old man tied a sash into a slipknot and mimed how I should attach it to my loins. (You basically place your penis and scrotum through the knot and tighten it to taste.) Standing next to old men swinging 20 kilograms between their legs I was almost embarrassed when he handed me a mere 2.5-kilogram weight. But as soon as the weight dropped I winced in pain. More experienced practitioners had lifted up to 200 kilograms. My introductory weight was enough to make me limp back to the hotel and lie in the foetal position for 12 hours. This was not a martial art for wimps. But I digress.

The point is, Taiwan is an odd sort of country with a tradition of taking on impossible odds – even if they prove embarrassing or painful.

Officially, the country doesn't even exist, despite having 23 million people, the same population as Australia. Mainland China calls Taiwan a renegade province run by 'evil splittists'. The Chinese Communist Party (CCP) has repeatedly threatened to invade the island, just 180 kilometres across the Taiwan Strait, if it formally declares independence.

Yet Taiwan has long claimed it's actually the real China and the communists in Beijing are just usurpers. Until 1971 it even held China's seat on the UN Security Council while most countries refused to recognise the communist government on the mainland.

Once the UN bowed to political and demographic reality and gave the seat to Communist China, Taiwan fell into diplomatic and national limbo. Most of the international community now agrees Taiwan is not an independent country, even if some, like the US, warn it will defend Taiwan militarily should China attack.

But in 2005 Taiwan was fighting a valiant rearguard battle to win back international support. It was offering huge economic assistance to any small country or failing state that agreed to give it diplomatic recognition as a sovereign country. The man behind this was the diminutive native-born President, Chen Shui-bian. He was about to fly to the South Pacific to shore up alliances and we were coming along for the ride.

We had already spent a day travelling around Taiwan with him. Short, bespectacled and slightly nerdish, President Chen seemed an unlikely man to be challenging the world's most populous country. But what he lacked in raw charisma he made up in sheer determination. He had risen by force of will from the humblest of origins, growing up in a dirt-poor family of tenant farmers.

'When I was a child, we often didn't know where our next meal was coming from,' he told me in an interview. 'At that time my father didn't have a regular job, our family didn't own a piece of land to plough and my parents were illiterate.'

His mother still lived in the simple cottage of his childhood and he invited us to join him as he visited his birthplace. We flew down on his official plane with his wheelchair-bound wife, Wu Shu-chen.

Chen was obviously the hometown hero: 25,000 people lined the streets waiting for his arrival. I walked up the line of spectators doing vox pops, holding up a microphone and asking people their thoughts, and nobody had a bad word for him.

Random woman: 'He's very close to the people and he's the president of all the people so we give him our support.'

Random man: 'I like Chen because he's a native of Taiwan.'

Chen worked the friendly crowd giggling and handing out Taiwanese $10 coins in red envelopes to mark Chinese New Year. I formed the impression it wasn't just his humble, populist manner that endeared him to them. They also saw him as a Taiwanese patriot who wasn't afraid to stand up to China. Unlike any leader before him, Chen had come close to uttering the unutterable.

'We state that Taiwan is already an independent sovereign country,' he told me.

It was a carefully calibrated statement, stopping just short of a formal declaration of independence that could trigger an invasion. Even with US protection, the threat was real. China had more than 1000 missiles pointed at Taiwan and was working assiduously to assert its territorial claims. During a recent visit to Beijing, Australia's Foreign Minister, Alexander Downer, had said a Chinese invasion wouldn't necessarily invoke the ANZUS treaty and oblige Australia to fight alongside the US.

Downer's statement had left Chen fuming. 'I must say that I feel sorry for that,' he told me diplomatically.

The Chinese Communist Party has always insisted Taiwan must return to the fold of the Motherland. The irony is that the CCP has *never* ruled Taiwan, even for a single day. Even China's historical claim is tenuous – you can count on one hand the number of years Beijing has ruled Taiwan since the 19th century.

After passing between indigenous, Han Chinese, Dutch, Han Chinese, Spanish and Han Chinese rule, the island (then called Formosa) was seized by Japan in 1895 when China still had an emperor. Japanese occupation continued until the end of World War Two, when the Allies handed Taiwan to the Republic of China, led by the warlord Chiang Kai-shek and his Nationalist party. Four years later communist revolutionaries overthrew the Nationalist government and declared the *People's* Republic of China (PRC). But before the Reds reached Beijing, the Nationalists decamped en masse to Taiwan, declaring Taiwan to be the new base of the *Republic* of China (ROC) as they prepared to retake the mainland. For decades the big China and the little China engaged in a bizarre face-off, each threatening to invade the other.

Chen Shui-bian represented the third force in this long-running dispute: native-born Taiwanese who didn't want to pretend they could one day reconquer the mainland. They just wanted their own country.

Chen had spent his youth fighting the Nationalists' brutal dictatorship. (Chiang Kai-shek's atrocities included the 1947 massacre of as many as 30,000 Taiwanese civilians to suppress protests.) In 1985 Chen was jailed for libel for eight months over articles in a pro-democracy magazine he edited. 'We published this underground political weekly magazine and we appealed for fully-fledged freedom of speech,' he told me matter-of-factly. 'Unexpectedly I was imprisoned because of these activities.'

The easing of one-party rule allowed Chen to enter politics. Tragedy soon struck when his wife was run over by a truck and paralysed while they were campaigning.

'We should be able to walk hand in hand in the streets in Taipei but now it is me pushing my wife and her hands are always cold and I constantly ask why? And how come? And I did feel like giving up.'

But Chen continued to devote himself to the cause, helping found the main opposition group, the Democratic Progressive Party. As well as opposing the Nationalists, it also proposed giving up any claim to the mainland and becoming an independent island country.

By 1994 Chen had become mayor of Taipei. In 2000, to Beijing's horror, he was elected president on a pro-independence platform, ending 55 years of Nationalist rule. In 2004 he stood again but the day before the election he was shot in the stomach in an apparent assassination attempt. His Vice-President, Annette Lu, who was standing beside him was shot in the leg. His office released graphic photographs of his wounds, provoking an outpouring of sympathy. He survived the shooting and managed to scrape through to win a second term by the narrowest of margins: just 29,000 votes out of nearly 13 million.

He may have looked and sounded like a suburban solicitor, but he was one stubborn little 'evil splittist'.

'The world cannot sit by idly to see an undemocratic China deprive the freedom, democracy and rights of Taiwan's citizens,' he told me.

It wasn't just the mainland's communist leadership who woke up twitching and banging walls every time they thought of Chen Shui-bian. The anti-communist Nationalists he had ousted in Taiwan also thought he was a little *hùnzhàng* (son of a bitch).

Until Chen came along, relations between the former mortal enemies had been steadily improving. After the Tiananmen Square massacre, the communists and Nationalists found a common cross-strait language in authoritarian capitalism. There was booming trade, endless backslapping banquets and even tastier business deals for the Nationalist elite. Talk was turning to a future Hong-Kong-style reunification where the Nationalists would still run things with Beijing's blessing. Then that little *fèi rén* (loser), Chen Shui-bian, came along and ruined everything.

The Nationalists' point man on relations with mainland China, Sui Qi, agreed to meet me to discuss the President. With a sour expression that could see him cast as Dr Evil, Sui could barely conceal his contempt for Chen, saying his presidency was illegitimate. He point-blank accused him of organising a fake assassination attempt to win the recent election.

Above: Isolated Faroe Island villages are now linked by massive underwater freeways. *Eric Campbell*

Left: Our fixer Bjørt Samuelsen in traditional dress. *Eric Campbell*

Below: Turf roofs deaden the sound of the Atlantic storms and waterfalls. *Eric Campbell*

KURILS

Above left: The unspoilt wilderness of the national park was a pleasant contrast to the Russian settlement. Top right: Enjoying the hotel facilities in Yuzhno-Kurilsk. Above right: The unfortunate former cat became our navigational marker. Below: Nathan English and I take a break from filming to enjoy the fumes that give the islands their name 'Kuril', from the Russian 'kurit' (to smoke). *Geoffrey Lye*

Summer's day at Longyearbyen after an ice-free winter, just 1300 kilometres from the North Pole. *Eric Campbell*

Hotel manager Sasha Romanovskiy with a former resident of Pyramiden. *Eric Campbell*

Tom Foreman guides us around the glacier as he explains why we're all doomed. *Eric Campbell*

Dave Martin flying his drone camera. He had to be quick in case of polar bears. *Eric Campbell*

SPITSBERGEN

Abandoned coal mine in the high Arctic.
David Martin

At its peak, 3000 people lived in the Soviet mining town of Pyramiden in Norway.
David Martin

Soviet iconography. *David Martin*

GALAPAGOS

GREENLAND

Above: The seals seem happy to be in the shot with Brett Ramsay, Vivien Altman and the author.

Left: A summer cruise.
David Martin

Below: Stefan Magnusson pointing out glacial melt. *Eric Campbell*

GREENLAND

Ferdinand Egede's ice-bound farm. *Eric Campbell*

Viking ruins. *Eric Campbell*

Left: The Falkland Islands offer visitors penguins and ... um... *Brett Ramsay*

Below: Enjoying the balmy summer weather with Brett Ramsay and Vivien Altman.

Prisoners apparently love to dance. *Eric Campbell*

Above: Reykjavik, the country town that took on Wall Street and lost. *Brett Ramsay*

Right: A protest against British and Dutch government demands to cover Icesave losses. *Brett Ramsay*

Below: Author attempting a visual financial metaphor with the only two members of the Viking society with suits. *Brett Ramsay*

SPRATLYS

Top: The BRP *Sierra Madre* is home to a platoon of Filipino marines guarding an underwater reef from besieging Chinese coast guard ships. *Wayne McAllister*

Above: Marines paddle out to pick up blockade-busting supplies dropped from a navy plane. *Wayne McAllister*

Left: Making a satphone call from the deck of the *Sierra Madre*, taking care not to fall through the rusting deck. *Wayne McAllister*

ANTARCTICA

Top: With producer Brietta Hague, just after we landed on King George Island. *Dave Martin*

Above: A long way from home. Sign outside the Bellingshausen base pointing to Russian towns. *Brietta Hague*

Right: Dave Martin downloading the day's footage in his room at Bellingshausen. This is the gear he brings when he's travelling light. *Eric Campbell*

Top: The Russian science base, with its Chilean neighbour in the background. *Brietta Hague*

Left: Tinned sausage, pasta shells, salami and lashings of tomato sauce at the Russian mess. *Eric Campbell*

Below left: Dave and Brietta filming from the Trinity church in Antarctica. *Eric Campbell*

Below rigth: Father Sophrony Kirilov kisses the altar during a liturgy at Antarctica's Trinity church. *Eric Campbell*

Above: The author at Collins Glacier, which has retreated nearly two kilometres in 50 years. *Brietta Hague*

Right: And chilling at the Russian science base. *Brietta Hague*

Below: Producer Brietta Hague filming gentoo penguins. The red poo (guano) means they've been eating krill. *Eric Campbell*

CUBA

LA PALABRA ENSEÑA,
EL
EJEMPLO GUÍA

Above: Dave Martin and I expressing eternal socialist fraternity between the ABC and Cuba. *Brietta Hague*

Left: The Kaehler boys Cliff and Seth, who were once Castro's BFFs. *Brietta Hague*

Below: Our fixer Josue Lopez takes a nap. *Brietta Hague*

One of these men is not Cuban. *Josue Lopez*

The author smoking a cigar, just to be culturally sensitive.
Josue Lopez

Left: The Carriles family has to trek three kilometres through the bush to reach their farm. *Josue Lopez*

Above: The family inisisted I ride a horse to their farm while 79-year-old Abuelo walk. *Josue Lopez*

Below: Pretending to understand Spanish as Kenia explains organic rice farming. *Brietta Hague*

Brietta showing Kenia the fine points of filming. *Josue Lopez*

And farewelling her 'Cuban family'. *Josue Lopez*

'I think he lied and he staged the shooting incident,' Sui said. 'He had to cover up his lie one after another and it was just like Watergate. We simulated the shooting and based on all the evidence he provided, things just don't match. The whole thing was most likely faked.'

He also said Chen was risking war.

'If there's an accident or there's a miscalculation on the side of Beijing, then a disaster will take place,' he warned. 'As long as the Beijing leadership feels it is compelled to do so, feels that it has no other way to avoid a conflict, it feels that Taiwan independence is a certainty, I have no doubt that Beijing would resort to use of force.'

In contrast to old Nationalists like Sui Qi, young Taiwanese seemed completely relaxed about Chen. I fell in with some university students at a night market, a bustling throng of open-air food stalls cooking dubious animal parts in gas-heated woks. The students said they thought of themselves as Taiwanese and saw China as a foreign country.

'We don't really have any direct connection with mainland China,' a girl named Fongshwin Yeh told me. 'I have no idea of the name of any government minister there. I've never been to mainland China.'

The feeling of Taiwanese identity was even deeper in rural areas like Chen's village. After two generations of Japanese rule, many had seen the Chinese Nationalists as just another set of brutal invaders. But feelings were much more divided in the big cities where the bureaucracy, courts, military and big business were still dominated by Nationalists. Making things even more confusing was that Taiwan now felt more Chinese than mainland China.

Taipei doesn't exactly evoke the ancient wonders of the Middle Kingdom. It's full of concrete monstrosities on badly planned streets that have collectively been whacked with a giant ugly stick. But thanks to the 1949 exodus, there are people from every Chinese province: a kaleidoscope of regional dialects, customs and cuisines all crammed into one city on one island/'renegade province'. Chinese culture had been Westernised, as in Beijing, but not vandalised.

For all the Chinese Communist Party likes to boast of preserving China's 5000-year-old heritage, it spent years trying to obliterate it. During Mao's Cultural Revolution in the 1960s, Red Guards were sent out to smash ancient Chinese buildings and destroy their libraries and artworks. If the Nationalists hadn't carted most of Beijing's treasures to Taiwan in the late 1940s, the party fanatics would have surely destroyed them. (This is a point raised whenever Beijing demands Taipei's National Palace Museum returns 'stolen' artefacts from the Forbidden City.)

So Taiwanese, like Singaporeans, were proud of their Chinese heritage. But that didn't necessarily mean they saw themselves as part of China or wanted to be ruled by a dictatorship as oppressive as the one they'd shaken off.

Even so, Chen Shui-bian was facing formidable opposition from the Nationalists over his flirtation with independence. The last thing he could afford was to lose any more international support. Which was why he was about to fly to the South Pacific with his chequebook.

And so, nursing bruised pride and aching genitals from my run-in with a 2.5-kilogram weight, I limped down to the hotel foyer to catch a taxi to Taipei's military airport.

A US presidential tour could hardly have been larger. With so few diplomatic allies, chances for official travel are scarce and Taiwan makes the most of any visit, no matter how tiny or obscure the destination. Two large Air China passenger jets had been laid on to carry more than one hundred politicians, officials and media. All the President's senior ministers were joining him for the tour. Dozens of military officers and officials in dark suits formed a line through the terminal to wish him a successful journey, the President shaking hands with each one of them as he edged towards the plane.

Minutes after we took off, Taiwanese fighter jets appeared on the horizon and escorted our flying convoy until we left Chinese airspace. It was the biggest diplomatic delegation to ever visit Palau.

The Republic of Palau has a smaller population than the village Chen grew up in – just 21,000 people spread over 250 islands east of the Philippines. It's effectively a client state of its former territorial master the US, which still provides its defence and social services. It even uses the US dollar as its currency. But it has a vote at the UN so Taiwan was throwing everything possible at the government to keep its favour.

The coral archipelago came into view three hours after we left Taipei. The media plane landed first, giving us time to scramble out next to the runway and set up cameras and tripods to record the President's arrival. Scores of schoolchildren stood on the tarmac holding Taiwanese and Palauan flags. It seemed the entire government of Palau had turned up to greet him.

The Taiwanese returned the favour the next day, with the entire cabinet coming to a sports field to witness the inauguration of Palau's recently re-elected President, Tommy Remengesau Jnr. (The 'junior' is to distinguish him from his father who had also been president). It was a peculiar sight. Half the podium was filled with President Remengesau and his rather beefy Micronesian ministry. The other half was filled with the government of Taiwan, sweltering uncomfortably in the tropical sun in dark suits. President Chen sat next to President Remengesau. Other world leaders could only send their regrets.

Tommy Remengesau (Jnr) began proceedings by excitedly reading out a letter of apology from his US counterpart. 'First, from the United States: Laura and I regret being unable to attend. My thoughts will be with you on that historical day. Sincerely, George W Bush.'

The crowd cheered and screamed and the Taiwanese ministry clapped politely.

The ceremony was followed by an obligatory banquet, after which President Chen was taken on a scenic boat trip around the islands. Palau is one of the main tourist destinations for Taiwanese, direct flights from Taipei being part of the economic bounty flowing from diplomatic recognition. The Taiwanese media pack was frantically shooting every part of the trip, reporters doing running commentary on fish types, geographical formations, temperature and wind conditions.

Excitement was building ahead of a promised bonus sequence for the evening news. The President was going to dive!

The twist was that Chen Shui-bian couldn't swim. But he was not a man to be daunted by practicalities.

The boat stopped at a particularly scenic location of reefs and rainforest and Chen went below deck to change. Minutes later he emerged in a full wetsuit with mask, snorkel, flippers and a kickboard. For once, the media pack was quiet. The only sound was the *sloop-thunk-sloop-thunk* of the presidential flippers as he stepped determinedly towards the back of the boat. Flanked by four bodyguards in matching wetsuits, he descended gingerly into the water. Each diver held a presidential arm or leg to support him as he dipped his head below the surface. The entourage paddled him slowly over a reef. A dozen television cameras rolled. Officials on the boat held their collective breath. Two nervous minutes passed. Finally Chen raised his head, pulled away the snorkel and beamed. The delegation applauded in gratitude and relief.

The following day the caravan moved on to the next diplomatic giant – the Solomon Islands, population 470,000. This time a traditional ceremonial dance greeted Chen at the airport with dozens of men in grass skirts and masks pounding the tarmac in time with drums while three men waved spears at the visitors. Again the entire government had turned out to greet them. They all headed to the Solomons' best hotel for a formal banquet with the prime minister, Sir Allan Kemakeza, and more traditional dancing. The Taiwanese delegation applauded as Sir Allan declared Taiwan was an independent sovereign country. It wasn't much in diplomatic terms but … Actually it wasn't much.

Chen had come bearing gifts and the next day was spent unveiling new aid projects and inspecting Taiwanese-funded development projects from a hospital upgrade to a rice farm. It was impossible to know just how much Taiwan was spending on its allies as the President had access to a special slush fund out of which he could allocate money for friendly countries without public scrutiny.

But the cost of the game was ever rising, with mainland China just as determined to stop any country recognising Taiwan. The communist leadership made it clear that countries could choose either the People's Republic of China (PRC) or the Republic of China (ROC), meaning if any country recognised Taiwan it would lose all diplomatic relations (and therefore most of its trade) with the mainland.

The two Chinas were now in a furious bidding war over some of the world's least sought-after countries. The previous year Taiwan had managed to persuade the Solomons' nearest neighbour, Vanuatu, to switch diplomatic recognition from the PRC to the ROC. Just weeks later, mainland Chinese officials flew in with promises of even more money and Vanuatu promptly switched its recognition back to the PRC.

Even so, Chen Shui-bian's entourage took great exception to any suggestion they were involved in chequebook diplomacy, insisting any economic assistance was simply part of a deep and abiding friendship between nations.

The Solomons' Prime Minister Kemakeza took a more straightforward view.

Sir Allan agreed to meet me in the late afternoon at his home where he was having a short rest in the stifling heat. He was an agreeably laidback PM, opening the door in his singlet and taking some urging to put on a shirt and tie for the on-camera interview. He admitted the PRC was also offering money for diplomatic recognition.

'They approach me and my ministers, my officials at international conferences,' he said.

'So could there be a time when the Solomons switch recognition?' I asked.

'Maybe,' he shrugged. 'I cannot predict the future.'

Before flying out, Chen Shui-bian agreed to speak to me again. His frustration at being a diplomatic outcast was apparent.

'Why has Taiwan become an orphan of the international community? I would ask all the democratic countries in the world including the United States, Japan and Australia to put themselves in Taiwan's shoes and see how they would feel.'

And if only international diplomacy worked that way, he might be on to something.

We left the visit early to fly home, missing out on the final diplomatic titan, the island of Guam. I couldn't help but be impressed with Chen's stubborn if perhaps quixotic determination, and felt the journalist's natural sympathy for the underdog. I couldn't imagine I'd be back in Taiwan three years later to play a small role in his downfall.

*

By 2008 the 1000 ballistic and cruise missiles aimed at Taiwan were the least of Chen Shui-bian's problems. His Nationalist enemies had found a much more potent weapon to attack him. The heroic democrat, the poor farm boy who had climbed so high, the patriot who had stood up to the Chinese superpower, the ordinary but brave man who had sacrificed his life to a noble cause, had done a very silly thing. He was now accused of corruption.

The evidence was in a series of copied receipts my travelling companion had brought from Queensland.

Ligi Li was a middle-aged Taiwanese-Australian fashion designer based at Sanctuary Cove. If Chen looked an unlikely man to take on China, Ligi Li looked an even less likely woman to take on the President. She could barely walk thanks to a recent accident and was palpably nervous about contacting a television program to tell her story. She imagined she was in danger and had hired two female bodyguards to protect her.

'I feel very proud of myself,' she told me, sounding more uncertain than confident. 'I am strong enough, brave enough to say go down to the President Chen Shui-bian. He is a liar.'

President Chen may have endured dictatorship and the wrath of China, but his real problems began when Ligi Li went shopping.

During frequent business trips to Taipei staying in the Hyatt Hotel, she spent more than a quarter of a million dollars, on items ranging from accommodation to wedding banquets, diamond rings, iPods, underwear, even mosquito zappers for her Gold Coast villa. She may have spent with abandon, but as a careful businesswoman she made sure she kept receipts.

One day her cousin asked if she could have all the receipts to give to the First Lady, Chen's wheelchair-bound wife, Wu Shu-chen.

'My cousin, Li Pi-chun, told me the President's wife is collecting all the unwanted invoices for charity,' Ligi Li told me.

Anywhere else in the world it would have seemed a strange request. But not in Taiwan, where receipts are like lotto cards. To discourage black market trading, the government holds regular receipt lotteries with big cash prizes, publishing the winning numbers in newspaper advertisements. People don't just hang on to receipts. They often give them to charities. So Ligi Li saw no harm and potential benefit in giving her receipts to the First Lady.

The problem was, Wu Shu-chen wasn't actually collecting for charity. She was collecting receipts for herself and claiming reimbursement, saying they were items she had bought for diplomats. The heavy expenditure hadn't raised suspicion. It was all paid out of the President's special fund for secret diplomatic missions.

It was never clear what happened to raise Ligi Li's suspicions, but she said she soon feared she was involved in a scam. 'They love Hyatt Hotel invoices, it's exactly Presidents' specification, you know meet their dining, wining dignitaries standard,' she said. 'I started to doubt about, something is fishy so I questioned my cousin. You know she told me the President, he has absolute power and we have government machine. Why you have to worry about?'

Ligi Li said she did worry. She asked the Hyatt Hotel to print out all the receipts and sent samples to the prosecutor's office.

Sure enough, the receipt numbers matched the First Lady's claims.

The receipts caused a national sensation. Wu Shu-chen was arrested and charged with fraud. Three presidential aides were also charged, leading to speculation President Chen might have knowingly allowed his slush fund to make payments to his wife. He was immune from prosecution as president, but only until his term ended the following May. Chen looked certain to end his rule in ignominy. Ligi Li felt no qualms about what she'd done.

'He promised to take us to a bright future, a better future, and he himself is so corrupted. I cannot tolerate that.'

The previous months had seen massive protests against Chen, many of them led by his former supporters. He was under intense pressure to resign.

I had mixed feelings about covering the story. I genuinely admired Chen and it seemed such a stupid way for him to lose his legacy. When he first became president he cut his own salary, saying it was excessive. The amount his wife had taken in fraud was less than that salary cut. It seemed absurd he would risk everything to indulge his wife's greed, no matter how much guilt he must have felt over her disabilities.

To my surprise, Chen agreed to let me interview him in the presidential palace. I included the controversy in a list of areas I told his office I wanted to discuss but Chen seemed genuinely affronted when I raised it.

'How do you respond to these very strong attacks?' I asked him. 'Are you a corrupt president? Did your family steal from the state?'

He was silent for a few seconds, then denied any wrongdoing. 'If something hasn't happened, it hasn't happened,' he said. 'For political reasons it's easy for people to distort, to discredit and to mislead. As political figures we are quite helpless.'

The prosecutor disagreed, announcing Chen would be charged when he stepped down as president.

Adding to my sense of discomfort, a Nationalist-owned TV station bought my story on Ligi Li from the ABC and broadcast it across Taiwan. I was now a party to Chen's humiliation.

In March 2008 the Nationalists swept back into power under President Ma Ying-jeou. Chen stepped down in May and was arrested less than an hour after he left the presidential palace. Further investigations revealed more financial irregularities, including illegal overseas transfers of campaign funds.

In November he was taken to the prosecutor's office in handcuffs, and waving them above his head, he shouted, 'Political persecution! Long Live Taiwan!' He was later openly mocked at a conference of judges and prosecutors, with a prosecutor waving his arms in handcuffs and shouting, 'Political persecution!' to the laughing crowd.

The judicial reckoning was astonishingly harsh. In September 2009 Chen was sentenced to life in prison. After several appeals and an attempt at suicide, he was finally released on medical parole after six years in a cell, his political legacy in ruins, his body racked with suspected Parkinson's disease. He left prison in a wheelchair.

It was a tragic end to a crazy brave career. And China – the big one across the Taiwan Strait – couldn't have been happier.

10. Malvinitis

The Falkland Islands, June 2006

We have ceased to be a nation in retreat. We have instead a newfound confidence – born in the economic battles at home and tested and found true 8000 miles away.

Margaret Thatcher, victory speech to Conservative rally, 3 July 1982

Do you think this will jerk me off?

Margaret Thatcher sitting astride a field gun during a visit to the Falkland Islands, January 1983

We had just driven past the crashed Argentine helicopter when we ran smack-bang into a group of British soldiers getting ready to attack. The Scottish sergeant was screaming orders in an incomprehensible accent but his fellow Scot commandos knew exactly what to do. Soon the air was filled with deafening gunshots as the heavily camouflaged soldiers raced from their dugouts towards the enemy, peppering the air with bullets.

It would have been a terrifying scene except for the small detail that the enemy didn't actually exist. The soldiers were just doing one of their regular drills. The Falklands War ended in 1982 and there had been no hostilities since. Just don't tell that to the Brits.

To this day Britain maintains one its largest and most expensive military garrisons on a group of islands that nobody guided by logic or self-interest would want to invade. Soldiers drill by firing bullets at an imaginary enemy, which represents the supposed enemy, Argentina. That enemy is a Western-style democracy that in every other respect is one of Britain's closest allies. The two nations work together on international peacekeeping operations, and in Cyprus British troops had just served under an Argentine commander.

But after withdrawing from fighting real enemies in Afghanistan and Iraq, Britain has no intention of withdrawing forces from the Falklands, where its troops prepare for an invasion its impoverished ally Argentina couldn't possibly mount, even if it wanted to, which it doesn't. Some people might find that stupid. The British military believe it's eminently sensible.

'I suppose we're scared by what happened in the past,' Britain's naval chief, Sir Alan West, told me as we shivered on a freezing hilltop. 'I mean, they told us effectively they wouldn't be using force then and then they did it.'

I had come to the Falklands to look at the legacy of one of the strangest wars of modern times, when Britain and Argentina threw their full military might at each other over islands Argentina didn't need and Britain didn't particularly want. The Argentine writer Jorge Luis Borges described the conflict as 'a fight between two bald men over a comb'. Had he run British or Argentine foreign policy in 1982, nearly 1000 men might not have been killed nor hundreds more crippled, blinded and otherwise maimed.

Unhappily for them, Britain was headed by the terrifyingly coiffed Margaret Thatcher while Argentines suffered under the oily bouffant of General Leopoldo Galtieri. Both saw armed conflict as a beneficial move in what was, politically as well as personally, an extremely bad hair year.

On 2 April 1982, the much-despised Galtieri ordered his armed forces to retake a group of islands in the South Atlantic called Las Malvinas that the dastardly Brits had seized in 1833. Crowds of patriotic Argentines turned out to hail a leader they otherwise regarded as an utter swine.

Margaret Thatcher responded by ordering her armed forces to liberate the islands, which Britain called the Falklands, from the beastly Argies. Crowds of patriotic Brits turned out to praise a leader they otherwise regarded as an utter sow.

I was a hairy 22 year old at the time and it was my first exhilarating brush with war reporting, running a satirical article about the conflict in a student newspaper I was editing in Sydney to avoid finishing a law degree. It was the least significant contribution to the war's coverage on the planet. But having tasted the vicarious excitement of covering a conflict a mere 12,000 kilometres away, my destiny was set. So, too, was Maggie's and Leopoldo's.

Britain went on to win the war and a newly popular Margaret Thatcher won re-election. Galtieri's military dictatorship collapsed in disgrace and Argentina became a democracy with a constitution forbidding armed invasion. I went on to become a professional journalist, of sorts, and cover wars from war zones. And I vowed to one day visit the islands to see where my 'career' began.

The islands are a less than compelling tourist destination: 500 kilometres east of South America and not really on the way to anywhere except Antarctica, which is why most of its visitors are cruise ship passengers stretching their legs on the way to the Antarctic Peninsula.

Nobody lived there until the 18th century when European seafarers started claiming sovereignty. The history is complex, but in essence goes like this: a ship from one country would claim possession and put up a few huts. A short time later a ship from another country would come and burn down the huts so it could claim possession.

Britain first established a small settlement in 1765 on the main island, West Falkland, unaware that the French had just settled the other main island, East Falkland, the year before. Spain bought the colony from France and threw out the British, who returned in force a year later, only to abandon their garrison in 1774 due to the rebellion brewing in Britain's American colony. (They left a plaque on the island to reserve sovereignty.) In 1816 Argentina declared independence from Spain and claimed the islands for itself. After sporadic attempts to settle them, Argentina finally set up a military garrison in 1832. Three months later a British warship was able to force the Argentines to surrender (largely because the Argentine commander had just been murdered in a mutiny). Depending how you look at it, this was either the latest act of maritime gang warfare or a legitimate and permanent territorial claim under international law. Britain, of course, took the latter view. Argentina continues to claim it was an act of piracy.

I never lost my desire to visit the Falklands, but little news ever came out of there and I could never see an excuse to suggest a story – until a chance conversation with a gay Jewish nationalist in Buenos Aires in 2004.

I was filming a story about Latin America's first gay marriages. A young Argentine named Esteban Cichello-Hubner was getting hitched to his long-time love Leo under a new arrangement by the city council to recognise civil unions. This was a radical step in macho, Catholic South America and Esteban took pride in being a trailblazer. He had grown up in a Jewish family in Buenos Aires' worst slum and escaped through sheer determination and daunting intelligence. Short and unimposing but brilliant and determinedly charming, he had won a scholarship to Oxford University and later become an adviser to both Israeli Prime Minister Ariel Sharon and Argentine President Carlos Menem. Along the way he had become a close friend of the soccer idol Diego Maradona, which greatly impressed the gay football team Leo played in. We were filming their practice one night when Esteban confided that he was suffering from an incurable disease. He called it 'Malvinitis'.

'For we Arrr-gentineans the Malvinas is like Jerrr-usalem for the Jews,' he said wistfully, rolling his 'r's like a romantic lead in a *telenovela*. 'I have suffered greatly from it. You really must go there and tell our story.'

Next to gay rights and Leo, the Malvinas/Falklands were Esteban's greatest passion. He told me how as a teenager opposed to Galtieri's regime he had unquestioningly joined the crowds outside the presidential palace to cheer the invasion.

'I hated the Falklanders and I hated the British and I felt very, very angry about the situation. I was blind. Like many Argentinians.'

Esteban was no ordinary Malvinitis sufferer. For 17 years after the conflict, Britain barred Argentines from the islands, presumably out of fear 1000 undercover soldiers might try to sneak in on a package tour. But in October 1998 Esteban used an Israeli passport he had picked up while working in Jerusalem to slip in as a tourist on a flight from Chile. (Chile supported Britain's invasion of the Falklands thanks to bitter rivalry between Galtieri and the equally odious Chilean dictator, Augusto Pinochet. While both men butchered thousands of leftists, they never bonded over their mutual serial killing. However, Pinochet and Thatcher became BFF.)

Esteban's aim was to touch the soil of what he saw as the lost heart of the Motherland and return on the same flight a week later without anyone discovering he was the 'enemy'. But once again the battles of Great Powers intervened. A day after he arrived, Britain served a Spanish arrest warrant on Pinochet, who was in London for medical treatment. An outraged Chilean government banned all flights from British territory, leaving Esteban stranded in the Falklands for nearly three months.

Eventually Esteban fessed up to being Argentine, but the authorities had no choice but to let him stay. He used his time diligently, setting out to meet every resident on the islands to understand their villainy, even writing of his experiences in the local newspaper under the headline I AM AN ARGIE.

'I had enough time to discover this place and fell in love in certain ways with this place and to realise that this place was not what I as an Argentinian thought it is. I thought that this place was very British in many ways and I discovered that the islanders, they are not monsters. They are very nice people.'

Esteban had now directed his Malvinitis into a quest for solving the conflict. It was an ambitious goal. While Britain enjoyed close relations with Argentina, the friendship stopped at the shores of the Falklands. Argentina was still claiming sovereignty and doing everything it could to make life hard for the islanders by restricting flights and trade. Britain had put a permanent 1300 strong military garrison on the island out of fear its ally might reinvade.

'I will take you there,' Esteban promised. 'I will arrange everything. I will even try to bring Maradona.'

It was a year before I was able to take him up on his offer, flying back to Buenos Aires with Spanish-speaking producer, Vivien Altman, and Brisbane cameraman, Brett Ramsay, to meet up with Esteban. He hadn't managed to persuade Maradona to join us. (Despite sharing Estaban's Malvinitis, the fallen soccer star apparently had some pressing rehab commitments.) But Esteban had found someone equally intriguing to take with us: an Argentine war veteran.

'His name is Sergio Delgado. He is a wonderful man. Perrfect for your story!'

Sergio Delgado was one of thousands of teenage conscripts sent in with the invasion force and the experience had scarred him for life. He looked older than his 43 years, with a craggy face and sad eyes under his thinning long hair. Sergio had suffered years of post-traumatic stress disorder and drifted from job to job, haunted by the mental and physical injuries he endured during his 10 weeks on the islands.

'I had psychological problems,' he said when I first met him. 'I had to have treatment. I was unwell for a long time and needed a lot of care. I was in a bad way.'

In April 1982, at the age of 19, Sergio had just completed his compulsory military service and was returning home to Buenos Aires when news of the invasion came. He was ordered back to base and told his military service had been extended. A few days later he found himself on a ship to Las Malvinas. His unit was sent to guard an exposed mountaintop without shelter or provisions while their officers stayed in the capital, Port Stanley, hastily renamed Puerto Argentina. They dug trenches to sleep in and scrounged for food to stave off starvation, barely surviving the freezing wind and rain until the last day of fighting when Brits overran their position. His rifle jammed and he was nearly killed by a shell without having fired a shot in the entire war. The soldier who shared his dugout died in front of him. Sergio and his surviving comrades had never returned to the islands.

He had been drinking all night with his army mates before he arrived at the airport to meet us just before dawn. The men from his former unit insisted on coming to see him off, after staying up with him singing, laughing, weeping and swapping war stories. There were a dozen of them: chubby, middle-aged men who had once been skinny, frightened teenagers. The realisation that one of them was going back had affected them all deeply. Amid backslapping, cheek-kissing, tears and manly hugs, one of Sergio's fatter friends took off his T-shirt and gave it to him to bury on the battlefield. Sergio's family and friends had come to see him off too.

'I just want to say I'm really, really happy because the people who love me are here,' he said awkwardly, posing uncertainly for our camera. 'I'm delighted that my mother is here, my nieces and nephews. I would have loved it if my daughters had been here, but thanks to everyone. I'll be back soon.'

It was a huge event for a veteran to be returning. While hundreds of British veterans toured the Falklands each year, Esteban believed less than two dozen Argentines had gone back. Even after the ban on Argentine nationals was lifted, the Argentine government and official veterans' groups refused to organise tours as travelling on international passports would effectively acknowledge British sovereignty. Sergio was only travelling because Esteban had assured him he'd be safe and the ABC had agreed to cover his costs. There was no other way Sergio, or any other war pensioner, could afford the flights and accommodation on the islands. One plane a month from Chile was allowed to fly to the islands through Argentina, returning a week later. All the other passengers boarding in Buenos Aires were Falkland Island residents returning from holidays in 'enemy' territory.

In keeping with Argentina's insistence of sovereignty, the plane flew out of the domestic terminal without even a passport check, the boarding pass listing the destination as Malvinas. Sergio's tears started flowing at the first sight of the islands from the air, as Esteban whispered reassurances. But I knew we were in for a frosty welcome. Like all commercial flights, the plane landed on the military airstrip at the British base. Perhaps unwisely, I'd mentioned in an email to the Ministry of Defence that I would be travelling with two Argentines.

'Your decision to bring Argentine nationals has caused considerable controversy,' the PR officer wrote in reply. 'They will be required to leave the base without delay.' The officer gave me a cursory handshake when we arrived but declined to meet Sergio or Esteban. This wasn't just rude. It was surreal. I had once watched British officers in Kosovo exhorting gobsmacked Serbs to live in peace and harmony with Albanians, just days after NATO had been bombing the Serbs and as Albanian paramilitaries were burning their homes. Now a British officer, acting under official policy, was refusing to even shake hands with two Argentine civilians 24 years after the war had ended.

We left the base with strict instructions not to film it, as Brett and I looked around for vantage points we could film from later without being seen. Esteban and Sergio had not noticed the officer's snub and started chatting excitedly as we drove along the road towards Stanley, passing lonely hills and stony fields with nothing but the occasional flock of sheep and lines of landmine warnings.

Sergio's eyes welled up again.

'What do you remember?' Esteban whispered to him in Spanish.

'I remember my *compañeros* [companions], that was the first thing that crossed my mind. *Compañeros* who aren't here any more.'

The mountains looked the same, but Esteban and Sergio were stunned when we reached the outskirts of the capital, Stanley, which Sergio remembered as Puerto Argentina.

'Wow! Look, Stanley looks so different!' Esteban exclaimed.

'Stanley or Puerto Argentina?' Sergio asked.

'Argentina? Is this Argentina?' Esteban said, laughing 'Well, it isn't now!'

While Sergio had only seen Stanley full of Argentine soldiers, it had changed dramatically even since Esteban's visit in 1998. The town emanated wealth, with new roads, shops, restaurants and suburbs. Except for rows of brightly coloured Scandinavian kit homes, built to withstand occasional Antarctic weather, it looked like a prosperous growth centre in rural England.

Before the war, the Falklands had been a kind of feudal outpost of poor tenant farmers working for the London-listed Falkland Islands Company that owned all the land. Britain had refused to grant the islanders British citizenship, fearing it could set a precedent for its other overseas territories, most of the inhabitants of which, it might be noted in passing, were not white. But after fighting to defend the plucky islanders, everything had changed. Not only were they accepted as fully-fledged Brits but the land was redistributed to the tenants and the community was given economic rights over the rich fishing resources. There were even negotiations with oil companies to search for what were believed to be huge offshore reserves.

We dropped our gear at the hotel and set out to explore the town centre. It looked like an English theme park, with row houses, quaint cottages, bright new red phone boxes, charming teahouses and Union Jacks hanging from every official building. Even the rolling hills looked faintly British. (Interestingly, a 1927 British film called *The Battles of Coronel and Falkland Islands* was filmed on the Scilly Isles because of their perceived similarity to the Falklands. This is true.)

The sun was shining but a bitterly cold wind swept across the bay, whipping the water into whitecaps. The chill didn't seem to bother the islanders going about their business, and Esteban soon ran into a group of Falklanders who remembered him from his earlier visit. They welcomed him warmly, chatting away in a hybrid British accent that strayed from West Country to middle-class London. Sergio spoke no English and stood back shyly.

The most extraordinary thing about the community was how small it was. After 20 minutes walking we were seeing the same people two or three times. The official population of the islands was just 2900, about two people for every British soldier, sailor and airman. And only about half of them appeared to be British. Many of the passers-by were Chilean, and many more were black. Esteban explained that the Falklands gave work permits to Chileans to do menial jobs that had once been done by Argentines. They filled the rest of their workforce needs from St Helena, a tiny British territory in the middle of the South Atlantic. St Helenians would travel by ship to the island of Ascension, where military flights from the UK stopped to refuel. Then they'd catch the military flights to the Falklands in search of work.

'They are second-class citizens,' Esteban said. 'They cannot vote, they cannot stay permanently and they do all the worst jobs.'

He took me to dinner in a pub run by St Helenians. I started talking to the bar staff and was amazed to find they had slightly cockney accents. I'd never heard of St Helena but the barman reminded me it was where Napoleon had been exiled, which gave an indication of how isolated it was: 4000 kilometres from South America and nearly 2000 kilometres from Africa. He recommended I go there one day to do a story. 'It's a free day boat ride from the airport but it's wurf the trip,' the barman said. 'Great food, nice people, just no bloody jobs.'

So who were the Falklanders for whom Britain had waged war and now spent billions of dollars defending?

'In my opinion the Falkland Islands became a country club for the rich Falklanders that live around the world during the year and in summertime they come here,' Esteban said. 'In my opinion there are only 200 Falklanders, really Falklanders here. The rest are 500 Chileans, 400 St Helenians, and Australians and New Zealanders that in their own country were losers so they came here.'

The long-time Falklanders call themselves 'kelpers', after the abundant seaweed round the coastline, to distinguish them from more recent arrivals. Despite my best efforts, nobody on the island could confirm how many 'kelpers' actually lived there.

Sergio was desperate to go back to his old position on Mount Longdon, and we'd organised one of the 'real' Falklanders to help him do just that. Patrick Watts made a living as a tour guide taking visitors out to penguin colonies but his real passion was showing British war veterans around the battlefields. He had an encyclopaedic knowledge of the conflict, thanks to lapping up as much information from veterans as he dispensed. In all the years since the war he had never met an Argentine veteran and saw it as a chance to fill in the details from the other side. Patrick spoke schoolboy Spanish and, with Esteban simultaneously translating, he and Sergio were soon talking excitedly about the war like long-lost friends.

Patrick was tall and thin with a scraggly grey moustache. As well as being a military buff he was a ham radio enthusiast. At the time of the invasion he ran the Falkland Islands Radio Service and broadcast live as the Argentines stormed onto the beach, later forcing their way into the station and holding a gun to his back.

'But I told them in no uncertain terms they weren't allowed to smoke in the studio,' he said. 'I couldn't stop them taking over, but I said if you're going to smoke you can go outside.'

In his reserved British way, Patrick was as excited as Sergio about heading up to Mount Longdon, a bleak, grassy peak just visible from Stanley. We headed off in Patrick's Land Rover as he went into tour guide mode, rattling off what the islanders had suffered in the invasion, pointing out the house where three women were accidentally killed by a Royal Navy shell in the final battle. (They were the only Falklanders killed in the entire war. Britain lost 253 of its 28,000 military personnel, while Argentina lost 635. The Argentine government chose not to repatriate their remains as they were already considered to be on Argentine soil.)

As we left town we passed a staggering amount of war detritus, from wrecked attack helicopters to rusting artillery. Minefields were everywhere. The Argentines laid them all over the islands, often dropping them from the back of helicopters. The marshy ground made it prohibitively difficult to de-mine, so vast areas were simply fenced off to stop livestock wandering in and getting blown up.

We parked at the bottom of the mountain next to a mine warning sign and started the long climb to the top. There was almost no vegetation on the hill and the wind was picking up strongly, making it hard to keep a steady footing on the steep, marshy track. Oblivious to the weather, Sergio raced ahead with a boyish excitement and started shouting as he reached the summit, with Esteban giving a running translation for Patrick.

'My position! Patrick, my position!' he yelled, panting heavily. 'It was much deeper and it had stones above it. It was here – this was my location. I was here.' He ran over to a rock and lay on it. 'This is the place where I told you I saw a dead English guy!'

Patrick was fascinated to hear it was the Argentines shelling their own men. 'So the shells were coming from Stanley up here! Argentine shells were coming here to hit the British.'

'Sí, sí, sí!'

Sergio seemed half in the present and half in the past as a frightened teenage conscript. 'Cold! It was freezing. It was unbelievably cold. Unbearable. It was so uncomfortable –

that's what I remember most. When I was in there, I could hear the bombs falling around me. I could hear the sound of the shell fragments hitting the ground. The debris was flying everywhere.'

He pulled up a trouser leg to show the deep scars from a shell that hit him, then recalled how a British soldier had rushed over and bayoneted his friend, before noticing Sergio.

'He was saying, "Come on come on," and pointed a weapon at my head. And so I said, "Please … my legs" – maybe in poor English, but he understood. Without dropping the weapon he lifted me up by my pants and saw that I was wounded so he put his weapon away. It was an Argentine weapon! He must have said, "Wait here," then he went away and came back with a nurse who spoke some Spanish. He checked me over, gave me morphine and told me that my comrade was dead and that they were getting me out of there.'

Patrick was clearly fascinated to hear the details of what Sergio had seen and been through. The stories were horrific. While the Argentine officers had stockpiled food in Port Stanley, the conscripts were left to starve. The men would take turns to hike across the mountains to try to scrounge food from the islanders.

'Hunger came over us after the first week or 10 days, at first we dealt with it, there was a farmhouse over there, we went over there to get food, then found there were two sheep heads far away. I went to look for them with a friend of mine, it took us 10 hours to get back, we risked our lives to get them. We didn't care.'

Once, Sergio found a transport helicopter that had just crashed and stole a side of beef from it. It was soaked in gasoline but they ate it greedily, trading part of it with other units for cigarettes.

They had no idea why they were guarding the mountain or what they were supposed to do when the British came. All they could think of was trying to survive the cold and hunger while they waited for the bombs.

'Well it's just so interesting for me to hear him tell his side of the story,' Patrick said to me. 'How did they occupy themselves? You know, what was life like for them? We wanted them out of the place as fast as possible and by any means, you know. Now I'm glad this guy's alive. It's great to meet him.'

But while Patrick didn't feel any animosity to Argentines, he was as hostile as ever to Argentina. 'Here we are, 23, 24 years on and their position hasn't changed. They still claim the islands. They still don't recognise our right to self-determination. They don't recognise our government. So really nothing has changed in all those years to soften the feeling. Yes, we can forgive what happened in the war but we can't change the attitude of the present day Argentine government and that's the sad fact of this. All these men were killed and at the end of it all, governmentally between us, nothing's really changed at all.'

Argentina's democratic constitution, brought in after Galtieri's dictatorship collapsed, enshrined the principle of Argentine sovereignty over the Malvinas but outlawed the use of force to recover them. Instead, the government began a spectacularly unsuccessful policy of offering the islanders money to leave. Since the election of the more nationalist, left-leaning government of Néstor Kirchner in 2003, Argentina had been taking a harder line, restricting the use of its air and sea space around the islands. Injured islanders couldn't even be evacuated to Argentina. Emergency flights had to go hundreds of kilometres further north to Uruguay.

(Public feeling in Argentina remains deeply resentful of British 'occupation'. In October 2014 an angry mob tried to lynch *Top Gear* host Jeremy Clarkson while he was filming in Patagonia. The attack was blamed on the crowd mistaking his number plate H982 FKL for a gloating reference to the 1982 invasion, rather than him being one of the world's most obnoxious people.)

We left the mountaintop as the wind picked up to gale force, after half an hour trying to find Sergio who had wandered off on his own. He somehow managed to find his way back to town by nightfall. By the next day the weather had turned from vile to horrible. The wind was blowing horizontal sleet, sending the temperature towards zero. We had only brought summer clothes with us, it being the middle of summer and all, but venturing outside was like stepping into a giant freezer in a wind tunnel with someone hurling buckets of water on you. All flights around the islands were grounded and we were stuck in the hotel, which with every passing moment seemed to be morphing into Fawlty Towers.

I had forgotten how truly appalling British hotel food could be. The breakfast immediately brought back memories of backpacking in Britain in the 1980s, each day beginning with greasy fried egg, fried bacon, fried sausage and fried tomato on a plate of fat. Despite being a short flight from Argentina, there was no trace of South American culture. The cuisine combined the worst of 1950s England without the curry. Vivien already had food poisoning from the night before and, with the phone not working, sat miserably on the hotel computer, waiting five minutes between clicks at a pound a minute to try to rearrange our schedule by email.

As we waited for the storm to clear, Esteban explained to me his solution for the Falklands/Malvinas. 'Before I thought that the Falklands should be Argentinian and only Argentinian but now I realise that a solution needs to be found for the sake of everyone involved in the conflict,' he said. 'In this claim, I believe that a solution can be reached with imagination. Three flags here, one British, one Argentinian, one Falkland. You can call it the Autonomous British Argentinian Falkland Islands. And the Falklanders will be autonomous. Like a child that will have a father and a mother, but a grr-own up child making its decision. And I believe this agreement will save the Argentinean pride, and also the British pride, and the Falklanders will have what they want, and that's autonomy.'

I asked him why the Falklanders would trust Argentina.

'You are forr-getting our charr-isma!' Esteban said. 'We will charm them.'

The following morning the weather improved to merely filthy and Sergio went off with Patrick to poke around the battlefields, with Esteban interpreting. Vivien, Brett and I spent the time meeting other islanders to sound out Esteban's proposal.

Trudi McPhee was another of the 'kelpers'. We met her at a shearing shed where she was in charge of the clip, joking and ordering around the shearers over the buzz of blades and the static of BBC World Service radio. She was a cheerful, nuggety woman in her fifties, descended from one of the islands' oldest families. Her ancestors had migrated four generations earlier from a similarly harsh climate on a Scottish island.

'My dad, he always says, silly old blighters they went from one cold windswept island to another,' she laughed. 'He thought they could have went somewhere a bit warmer.'

Even so, she insisted she wouldn't live anywhere else. 'Not for the world. I think it's wild, it's sort of rough and it's just a way of life that we've always been used to. It's the freedom and it's a good place to live.'

The Argentine invasion robbed them of their freedom. 'You know, after just going along naturally, and next thing you hear on the radio saying there'd be an important announcement at eight o'clock. And we listened and the governor came on and he said, you know, there's an invasion. It should probably happen before dawn. And you know you think, oh God! And Patrick Watts at the radio station kept us up to date of what was happening. And we could hear when they first come in to Stanley and they were shooting. And when they overrun the radio station, it was really frightening.'

Many of her neighbours, including volunteers in the Falkland Islands Defence Force, were interned in a barn as security risks. She was allowed to keep farming but worked every day in the gun sights of soldiers guarding her.

'It was 74 days of you know, very uncertain. The trouble is you know, one Argentine might say it was okay, but the next one might just shoot you. It was a very scary time.'

When the British finally came, she escaped her farm and offered her services as a guide. At great risk, she led a group of marines in darkness towards an Argentine position, wearing white gloves so they could follow her in the moonlight. The position was Mount Longdon. They were likely the soldiers who attacked Sergio's position and killed his friend.

Trudi refused point-blank to meet Sergio. She was one of the few islanders who'd stubbornly insisted on avoiding Esteban during his enforced stay. 'I haven't spoken to any Argie since the war and I'm not going to now,' she said. It was a matter of principle. She'd been minding her own business in 1982 when the Argentine military invaded and made her a prisoner in her own home.

'I was furious,' she said. 'You know, how dare they come and invade our cabbage patch!' And she was just as critical of the new democratic government in Argentina. 'They're putting pressure on us every way you move. They interfere with the fisheries, they interfere with the flights. Anything you name, if they can make it awkward for us, you know they're just like a big bully sitting on your shoulder and whichever way you try and move, you know they're there.'

I started asking her: 'Could you ever see yourself living in a political settlement, whereby —'

She cut me off. 'No I definitely could not. That is definitely not on either. If Argies come here, Trudi's off.'

The British government was little more compromising than Trudi. While the islands enjoyed self-rule, the peak of political power was still Her Majesty's governor, who governed from Government House down the end of Thatcher Drive. It was a handsome workplace and residence resembling a 19th century Surrey estate transported to the South Atlantic beachfront. British marines had fought hard to defend its grassy approach from invading Argies but eventually withdrew to prevent it being destroyed. We walked in as staff were busily preparing for another invasion, a forthcoming visit by Foreign Office and Defence officials.

It was as though we had entered a high level embassy rather than an obscure administrative centre for a few thousand residents. Primly dressed staff bustled around the well-appointed rooms beneath portraits of Her Majesty, answering phones, collecting telexes, transferring important papers and vigorously opening and closing important-looking doors. A secretary summoned someone higher up the food chain to deal with our unexpected arrival. A disapproving woman with a monobrow appeared, identifying herself as the deputy governor.

'Hello, we're from the Australian Broadcasting Corporation,' I said, attempting not to sound too Australian. 'We've just arrived to shoot a story on the Falklands. I emailed last week about our visit, asking if we could arrange to meet the governor.'

She looked at me as if I'd farted, explaining brusquely that the governor was an extremely busy man and had more pressing matters. I persevered until she reluctantly agreed to let the governor know we were here.

Governor Howard Pearce, CVO, seemed equally unenthused by our arrival. A tall, slightly stout man in a pinstriped suit, he was the epitome of Foreign Office pomp and procedure, which did not regard television interviews with Australian reptiles as a priority. It took all my limited reserves of charm to persuade him to grant a 20-minute audience.

Governor Pearce began by restating Britain's line about its determination to defend the islands. 'The principle to which Falkland Islanders adhere is that they have the right to determine their own future. As I say, many families have been living here for four, five even six generations. This is their home, it's the place where they have all their economic stake and they feel that they have the right to decide where their future should lie.'

I ventured that the expenditure seemed somewhat out of proportion for a community that was smaller than a village.

'It is a small community. Two and a half thousand, two thousand, one thousand is a small community but that does not mean that those people don't have the same rights as larger communities.'

Britain had not always had such a noble commitment to its overseas dependants. In the late 1960s and early 70s, Britain unceremoniously expelled the entire population of the Chagos Islands, a British territory southwest of India. Some 1500 people, many of whom could trace their ancestry on the islands back to the 18th century, were coerced into leaving so the main island of Diego Garcia could be declared uninhabited and leased to the US for a giant military air base. (It might be noted in passing that the Chagossians, descended from Indian and Malay settlers and African slaves, are not white.) Despite several courts ruling the expulsions illegal, the British government still refuses to allow them to return. I asked Governor Pearce why those islanders had been treated so differently.

'Well we're here to talk about the Falkland Islands,' he said. 'And I think that's what we should focus on in this interview.'

'But why were they treated so differently from the Falklanders?'

'There were particular circumstances which applied in Diego Garcia. That's not an issue of which I'm an expert or in which I would wish to get involved. But if you like, if there was an exception, it was there.'

At the same time that Britain was turfing out the dark-skinned Chagossians, it appeared to be tiring of another colonial relic, the Falklands. In 1968 a Foreign Office delegation to the islands warned the islanders that the empire would not last forever. In the 1970s the British government secretly discussed leasing the islands back to Argentina. News of the planned betrayal leaked out to the Falkland Islanders and an embarrassed government rushed to assure them their future was safe.

'Back in the 1970s the UK and Argentine governments did hold a series of negotiations,' Governor Pearce conceded. 'But throughout that period, as today, the British government was committed to recognising the islanders' right to self-determination. And throughout those negotiations the British government said to the Argentines that there could be no solution to this dispute without the agreement of the islanders. And it's clear, I think it's clear to anybody who comes here, that islanders are at one in wishing to retain the status quos, in wishing to remain British and for the islands to remain British.'

Now the commitment was heartfelt and immoveable. Britain saw its victory in the Falklands as a defining moment of glory after decades of military defeat and imperial decline. The British military was here to stay.

The RAF Mount Pleasant base on East Falkland was costing the British taxpayers about A$250 million a year to maintain. There were about 1300 personnel with a naval port, a full-size military airport and an arsenal ranging from Tornado jets and Sea King helicopters to a frigate and patrol ship, reinforced by visiting submarines with Tomahawk missiles – all of it 14,000 kilometres from home.

Mount Pleasant is a 45-minute drive from Stanley, so it's rare to see soldiers in town, except on Saturday nights when they come into the pubs. We took a camera into the St Helenians' bar to try to talk to some, but the atmosphere wasn't conducive to filming. A drunken squaddie (a low-rank soldier, the British equivalent of a grunt) was doing naked cartwheels while his mates appeared to be eating their pint glasses.

Apart from a chance encounter with Scottish commandos training near the main highway, the naked fat man was the only soldier we'd seen in anything approaching action. I had sent a blizzard of emails requesting access to film military operations, including battle drills, Tornado flights and helicopter ship landings. But over the course of three days the PR office cited logistical problems, mechanical breakdowns, prior engagements, communications mix-ups, bad luck, poor weather, ill health, security regulations and lunch breaks as reasons why it wasn't possible to film a single moving thing.

The office did, however, allow us to drive to the other side of the island to film a memorial service with Britain's naval chief, Sir Alan West. He was on his last visit to the Falklands before retiring as First Sea Lord of the Admiralty. In 1982 he was part of the invasion force sent to repel the Argentines. The frigate he commanded, the HMS *Ardent*, was hit by enemy fire, and in the sturdy tradition of the British navy, he had been the last man off the burning ship, waiting until every survivor had been evacuated. Shortly after he stepped off the deck, the *Ardent* sank with 22 dead crewmen.

Now, 24 years later, grey-haired and distinguished, Sir Alan was standing on the hilltop overlooking the *Ardent*'s resting place to commemorate the loss of his men. A mournful bagpiper played as his entourage of naval officers and English vicars in regalia prayed for their souls.

'It brings back happy memories of a ship that was a wonderful ship and things like that, and then very sad memories at their loss,' he said after the service. 'But I'm very proud of what they achieved down here.'

'Given Britain's commitments in Iraq and Afghanistan, can it afford to keep this presence here?' I asked.

'Well I say this is important to us and that's why we keep it. I suppose we're very fortunate we're the fourth richest nation in the world.'

There's no doubting the courage and sacrifice of the servicemen who fought in the war. But it was extraordinary to see how little reconciliation there had been with Argentina in peace. Only a handful of Argentines lived on the islands, and most were only there because they had married islanders before the war.

The exception was Maria Peck, a beautiful young Argentine painter who had met her husband James in Buenos Aires in the 90s. James had grown up in Stanley, where his father was the policeman, but had moved to Argentina when he became an artist. They now divided their time between BA and Stanley where they were staying with James's mother.

Esteban took us around to meet them. They chatted in Spanish and sipped the Argentine national brew, maté, as the rain thundered on the cottage roof. James's bilingual six-year-old son sat playing with his toys. It was clear Maria hated the place. She didn't want to be interviewed in case it caused trouble with the islanders, many of whom strongly disapproved of James marrying an 'Argie'.

'It's an issue,' James said. 'If your wife was from China or North America or whatever, it wouldn't be an issue. You wouldn't feel people's suspicion, that, you know, you're messing with the enemy, which is how a lot of people consider it.'

He told us how he'd been abused at football games, heard mutterings as they walked down the street and even disparaging remarks when they had a baby.

'It's got a bit better the last couple of years,' he said. 'But it's still there. I'm still the person who married an Argentine. Because Maria is the only contact they have with Argentines. It's like if somebody's got a problem they see her as like being their way to say something. Because there's no like, there's no real contact. The only contact is through a newspaper article or headline, on the radio, and it's all third-hand stuff. But there's no people mixing. You know, it doesn't happen.'

I asked him if he thought things would improve.

'Maybe in 20 years, but I don't think so,' he said. 'I don't think it's going to be different. The issue is always going to be there unless the politicians get together one day.'

James felt many people didn't want to move on. 'A lot of people hang their problems on the war. You see that all the time. They blame the war for emotional problems, for insecurity. It's like they need a push. But because there's no contact there's no need to push themselves.'

'Would you like your son to grow up here?'

'For a while. I'd like him to witness some things, feel some things. But I don't know if it's for him, I really don't know, whatever. If an opportunity comes up for him somewhere else you know, then I'd be behind that definitely.'

As the trip wore on, Esteban grew increasingly despondent. Apart from James, nobody seemed interested in his face-saving proposals. Just as his Malvinitis had waned, his romance with the islanders was well and truly fading.

'I thought by now the Falklanders would be less obstinate, would be more prepared to talk to Arr-gentina, would understand that Arr-gentina can easily stop the claim if they are prr-epared to accept any imaginative, cosmetic solution that will save the face of Argentina. But no.'

Sergio was feeling reborn. For four days he had wandered the battlefields, facing his demons and laying them to rest. He seemed years younger, and for the first time in 24 years was at peace.

'I was very scared before I came back and when I was here in Mount Longdon, when I went back there I felt relieved, that a weight had been lifted from me, and it was like a dream for me,' he said. 'I don't know what really happened, but something happened inside of me that made me feel much better. I feel good, I feel much better, it's helped me a lot, I want to come back here.'

The shame was that he would never be able to return, and none of his friends would ever be able to experience that release. Neither side wanted such contact, clinging instead to the righteous certainty of the past. The conscripts would have to live and die with what they had suffered.

We flew out that afternoon. The weather had finally cleared into glorious bright sunshine. The plane taxied past the fighter jets and took off over green fields and sweeping coastline; a little patch of South American land that would be forever Britain, forever disputed and never completely at peace.

11. Jailhouse Rock

Cebu, October 2007

> I needed a place to put the dogs. The prisoners ruined
> the jail, so I put the prisoners in the tents and I had a
> nice place to put the dogs.
>
> Joe Arpaio, America's self-styled toughest sheriff

It was hard to know who was more excited, the homicidal ex-policeman or the dancing transvestites. News that the glamorous lady governor would be watching their next performance had swept through the prison faster than a dose of canteen botulism.

Gwen Garcia was Cebu's first female ruler in 400 years and was known to team history-making breakthroughs with stylish scarves and pantsuits. Hundreds of inmates were now busily practising their dance steps while the transvestites experimented frantically with different makeup.

Wenjiel Resane, the willowy lead dancer and self-appointed head girl of the 16 transvestites in her cell, felt honoured to be dancing for the governor. 'We love Mum Garcia!' she said.

'She is kind, loveable and caring.' (Wenjiel also explained that the drugs charges for which she was awaiting trial were just ridiculous.)

In his own quiet way the disgraced former police officer Leo Sucio was just as exhilarated as Wenjiel. A thick-set, no-nonsense father of three, he had somewhat blotted his police copybook by carrying out a series of (alleged) murders for which he'd already spent six years awaiting trial. But as the appointed head of the prisoners' committee he had worked hard to instil values of discipline and clean living in his fellow inmates. And he felt he'd played a small but significant role in turning the prison into an international dance sensation.

'We are not forced to dance here, we love to dance,' he told me. 'Dancing is one of the ways we bring discipline here. Because we could not coordinate almost a thousand people here without it.'

For the past few months the internet had been abuzz over clips of mass dance numbers posted from this provincial Filipino detention centre. Hundreds of inmates in prison uniform took part in tightly choreographed dance numbers to soundtracks of 80s classics like Michael Jackson's 'Thriller'. In the early days of YouTube, it was one of the world's first viral sensations, the prison performances garnering more than six million hits.

'We are proud to be called the Dancing Inmates in the Philippines and around the world,' Leo Sucio said. 'Even if we are prisoners we can still do good.'

But as proud as he was of his own contribution, he felt the main credit lay with the prison warden, Byron Garcia. He took off his shirt to reveal a handmade tattoo of the warden's chubby face on his chest.

'He's my idol,' the alleged multiple murderer said.

'He's the bad boy in this jail?' I said, trying to go with the 80s riff.

'There are no bad boys in this jail,' he answered coolly.

Byron Garcia had achieved his global triumph without any prior experience in running a prison. In fact, it was the first time he'd even worked in a prison. To be completely blunt, he didn't appear to have the slightest qualification to administer anything in a prison. He'd been given the job by his big sister Gwen, Cebu's first female governor.

'Actually I first appointed him as security consultant because that is his expertise,' Gwen Garcia explained to me when we first met. 'As far as my security was concerned, I needed somebody I could fully trust.'

Depending on your viewpoint, the Philippines combines either the best or worst of Asian and US culture. The country can certainly boast a wonderful community and family spirit along with can-do business attitudes and some tremendous adaptations of Broadway hits. On the downside, it can be prone to nepotism, corruption and violence mixed with more tackiness than Las Vegas.

In short, Filipinos can make an art form out of overdoing things, nowhere more so than on the island of Cebu.

I flew into Cebu with Mavourneen Dineen, another of our producers for whom complex shoots were a welcome break from organising teenage sons. Our cameraman was Dave Anderson, on loan from the ABC's Jakarta bureau. We had intended to shoot a quick 'postcard' story on the prison as part of a longer shoot in the region. But the more we looked into the dancing, the more twists and turns we discovered.

Cebu is one of the Philippine's oldest, most crowded and most developed provinces, with teeming cities, impoverished villages, frenetic ports and ship-building docks, dangerous coalmines, highly polluting heavy industry, seedy girlie bars and idyllic white sandy beaches full of tourist resorts, all of which adds up to a relatively vibrant economy which is unsurprisingly marketed as 'Ceboom!'

The island was one of the first ports of call for the explorer Ferdinand Magellan in 1519, became one of the first Spanish settlements, started one of the first universities in the archipelago, was even the first capital of the Philippines, and certainly had the first prison in the Philippines to become famous for something other than overcrowding.

My idea was to head straight for the jail, known as the Cebu Provincial Detention and Rehabilitation Center (CPDRC). But Mavourneen (Mav) had been intrigued by what she'd read about Cebu's glamorous governor.

Gwen Garcia had made it one of her first priorities to tackle the gangs that were effectively running Cebu's tough maximum-security remand centre. She had not only faced down the most violent elements but laid the way for it to become a centre for camp dance numbers.

So our first stop was an early morning rendezvous in her gubernatorial office.

We arrived to find her having a tense meeting with military top brass who seemed strangely terrified of the slim middle-aged woman in front of them. She asked us if we wouldn't mind waiting a few minutes. I asked if we could film and she nodded.

One of the three, a general, cleared his throat and meekly offered her a CD of nationalist songs, saying they hoped she would find it enjoyable listening.

Gwen Garcia accepted it with a smile that would freeze petrol, then resumed her attack, accusing them of stalling on the promised return of army land to the provincial government.

'I cannot see why there is so much foot-dragging on this matter!' she snapped.

'I don't think there is any foot-dragging, ma'am,' the general protested.

Her voice dropped to a whisper, sounding even more frightening. 'I am telling you very, very clearly, very, very specifically that this must all revert back to the province. So I want an update by 5.30 this afternoon.'

Military commanders in the coup-prone Philippines aren't used to being scolded by politicians, let alone a woman. But they sat quietly like chastened schoolboys, glancing nervously at our camera recording their humiliation.

'The President will be here on October 12, my birthday,' she concluded. 'We intend for that memorandum of agreement to be signed or else I'm going to raise a lot of noise.'

As the generals slunk out she turned to us with a gracious smile under immaculate makeup and hair and invited us to take their seats. This was not a woman to be messed with lightly.

'Would it be too much to say you've just had three generals for breakfast?' I asked.

She laughed. 'Well, I just had a very interesting courtesy call from the head of the army and the head of the central command here together with one colonel. Very interesting.'

She explained that the province had given land to the army on condition it be used for military purposes, only to find senior officers were illegally developing it for commercial real estate and building the most expensive houses for themselves. And she was not going to let them get away with it.

'I'm not a politician and I don't follow the traditional rules of politics,' she said. 'I do what I think is right. It's also good strategy because my political opponents never know what I'm going to do.'

Gwen Garcia was certainly breaking the masculine mould of Filipino politics. The wall in her office was covered with photographs of her skiing, riding horses and accepting a Best Dressed Women of the Philippines award. At barely five feet tall, and looking much younger than her 51 years, she was both charmingly feminine and intimidatingly tough.

Three years earlier she had decided to close the old detention centre, a violent, overcrowded relic effectively run by gang bosses. The idea was to move them to another facility where her brother Byron had installed security systems.

'Between the jail guards and the inmates there was a very lucrative business going on with smuggling of weapons, cigarettes and contraband items. They did not want to transfer and neither did the guards, I think, to the new facility which is equipped with CCTV cameras, with automatic door-locking systems.'

When the prisoners staged a sit-down strike, she called in the SWAT team.

'They were made to lie in the quadrangle. I went up here and told them, "From here on don't ever do this to me again! You will learn discipline here in this new facility. You will follow my rules and unless you learn to do that, you will be kept in chains." And they were chained, you know.'

Gwen put her brother Byron in charge of the new facility, with authority to sack any guards he didn't trust (dozens were summarily fired) and to separate gang members into different cells. But the main crackdown was on suspected sympathisers of the New People's Army, a long-running Marxist insurgency. They were transferred to other prisons to avoid stirring up trouble.

'These political detainees, when they are out there on the run in the mountains, could hardly conduct teach-ins without fear of being captured by the military. But here they had free board and lodging and a captive audience. They practically incited these other prisoners to rebel. So we went to court and said I don't think we should mix these political inmates with our own prisoners who were charged with normal crimes.'

Getting rid of the leftists had also eased the problem of overcrowding, which she blamed on the Philippines revoking the death penalty. (It had the bothersome side effect of ensuring prisoners who in the past would have been executed continued to stay alive and take up space.) Gwen's politician father had tried to reinstate capital punishment when he was in the congress but the government rejected his bill.

'I fully supported his belief that the death penalty must be imposed,' she said. 'Although there are other ways that we can also improve the situation in our jails.'

It was her brother Byron who hit on the idea of getting the prisoners to dance.

'He's an artist. In his younger days he used to sing and he accompanies himself on guitar. That was really his idea, that aside from just making them march to get physical exercise, he'd make it more interesting to bring in a choreographer and teach them to dance. My favourite is Sister Act, but they are preparing a new one for my birthday.'

Not everyone was enamoured with the governor's iron fist in a designer glove.

We left the salubrious governor's palace and drove to a cramped, dilapidated legal office in town. A dozen clients were squeezed into the dimly lit foyer waiting to see Rex Fernandez, a low-paid, bespectacled human rights lawyer struggling to represent scores of prisoners and their families.

His clients alleged communists who he said were bashed in Byron Garcia's new prison before they were transferred to worse facilities. 'They were given hell,' he said. 'They were beaten up, they were in solitary confinement which is a violation of the minimum treatment of detainees. They were punished for speaking out, which is their right. Communism is not a crime in the Philippines. Marxism is not a crime in the Philippines.'

He wasn't a fan of the dancing either. 'It was forced upon them, and this is not rehabilitative. Yes, they have their fame, but is fame rehabilitative? No, it is not. This is involuntary servitude. They are made to dance. They are robots.'

Rex's clients began hovering outside the door, impatient with us monopolising his limited time. It was time to leave anyway. We had an appointment with Byron.

The giant iron prison gate rolled back to reveal a recently built complex that looked more like an office block than a prison. Once inside, we saw the elaborate security and surveillance cameras.

A guard gave us a quick guided tour of the facility. There were both men's and women's sections, separated by chain fences and locked gates. On the second floor were 'rehabilitation' rooms where prisoners were sewing prison uniforms. But the most striking section was a huge central courtyard where the dances were staged. A group of prisoners in the corner had set up a karaoke machine and were happily belting out 'Feelings' and 'Touch My Body'. Other prisoners lay sunbathing while a group chatted with their families on a regular visit. The former police officer and alleged mass murderer Leo Sucio was playing with his children.

Byron Garcia sat above it all in his office, the prison's command centre and creative hub. He looked remarkably like the tribute tattoo on Leo Sucio's chest, with a pudgy face that matched his small fat fingers covered in expensive rings. They were busily sorting through music tracks on his computer as we were ushered in. He seemed relaxed and enjoying himself.

'Last night I tried to mix a song but I found out this morning it's too long so I have to shorten it,' he explained.

I started the interview asking whether he or his sister had thought up the idea of mass dances.

'I thought of it last year,' he said. 'I asked myself, what if these people dance in unison? That would be great. It would be good to look at. And if they learn unison, if they learn how to synchronise, I think this will aid in their rehabilitation. It changed their behaviour. Now they don't seek gangs any more. They think as one. So for one year and a half now we don't have a single case of violence.'

He had hired a professional choreographer to teach dance steps but selected all the music himself.

'I chose the music from the eighties,' he said.

'The golden era?'

'Yeah, the golden era. They are pretty nice song. You know, I've been accused of forcing them to dance. Nobody forces them. They dance because they want to dance. They want to get their exercise hourly, their daily exercise.'

He boasted that he had ended gang activity, charging anyone who tried to recruit members. To maintain discipline, he'd put ex-policemen and soldiers like Leo Sucio in charge of their fellow inmates.

I couldn't help thinking that police and soldiers imprisoned for corruption or murder might be a tad inclined to abuse prisoners, but Byron would have none of it. Nobody had been beaten, and the leftists Rex Fernandez represented had only been transferred to a military jail after they were caught 'spreading propaganda' by his surveillance cameras.

'They always complain. They want to rule the jail. It is a recruitment ground for them,' he said. Then he laughed. 'They always want to argue their rights and they always want to apply international laws!'

Apparently that last part was just ridiculously funny.

Down in the courtyard, prisoners assembled to rehearse the performance they would be staging for Gwen Garcia's birthday in two days' time. All wore plastic open-toed sandals, orange pants and T-shirts with a large P on the back. A woman choreographer drilled them on their steps, with Wenjiel standing in the front as lead dancer. Byron watched proudly, offering occasional suggestions to the choreographer. Even with the music continually stopping for choreographer's instructions, it was obvious this was a pretty tight unit. I estimated there were about 600 dancers. For some numbers, there could be more than a thousand.

Prison activists had been critical of the dancing, saying it was no substitute for vocational training. But it was more than you would usually see in Filipino prisons, many of which were hellholes. A federal prison in Cebu, which had just been closed, had been so crowded the prisoners had to sleep in shifts and guards lowered down food to them in buckets as if they were animals. In comparison, this seemed more like a holiday camp.

Byron boasted they slept only 16 to a cell, which was positive luxury by Filipino standards. In the absence of the death penalty, he kept numbers low by refusing to obey court orders to accept more prisoners.

'In the Philippines they're trying to find ways on how to decongest the jails,' he said. 'Well my approach is simple – no, we're full. We don't accept. Fully booked. No vacancy.'

Watching Byron clapping along to the music, I wasn't sure if he was a tough but fair visionary or a man-child playing with a giant toy from his sister.

Appointing a family member to such a position might raise eyebrows in Western countries, but in the Philippines it was standard. While Gwen Garcia had broken the gender mould of politics, she was firmly in the traditional mould of political dynasties. Her father, Pablo Garcia, had been governor of Cebu from 1995 to 2004 before moving to the congress and becoming deputy speaker. Gwen won the election to succeed him as governor.

'Of course it helped that he was not a bad governor,' she said. 'The people loved him and when they found out his daughter was running they were willing to listen to me, at least to hear me out.'

The people were similarly willing to listen when her father retired from congress, electing her youngest brother Pablo Jnr to his seat.

Political dynasties had dominated the Philippines since the US granted independence in 1946. At first they were the old land-owning elite. Then the uber-corrupt president Ferdinand Marcos imposed martial law in 1972 and marginalised some of the old families. They got their revenge when he was overthrown in the so-called People Power Revolution in 1986, led by the most powerful landed family the Aquinos. Cory Aquino, whose senator husband Benigno Jnr had been assassinated on the orders of Marcos, was elected president.

Remarkably, the new government brought in a new constitution to stamp out political dynasties, section 26 stating: 'The State shall guarantee equal access to opportunities for public service and prohibit political dynasties as may be defined by law.'

Yeah, right.

A 2012 study by New York University found the majority of congressmen were still related to people who had previously served in the congress. In 40 per cent of the 79 provinces, the governor and congressmen were related. (By amazing coincidence, Cory Aquino's son Benigno the Third had become president and Marcos's son Bongbong was a senator. What are the chances?)

Perhaps more important than the constitution was the entrenched *padrino* system of patronage in Filipino society. It meant nobody got any job in government, even the lowliest rank of officialdom, without a family connection or a friend in higher places.

Once in power, it was easy to ensure your family name was associated with largesse. Senators and congressmen enjoyed control of political slush funds of up to US$4.5 million each. They were called Priority Development Assistance Funds to pay for local infrastructure and development. Most people called them Pork Barrels. The politician not only decided how much money went where, but ensured their name was attached to the project.

Driving around Cebu, we saw countless billboards thanking the Garcia family for their good deeds. Any public building site, road project or even drain repair had a sign making clear it was all thanks to Governor Garcia or her congressman brother. There was nothing unusual in this. You could see it on any of the 2000 inhabited islands that make up the archipelago of the Philippines. And it ensured politicians with the right surname had a jump on their rivals. (Fortunately, this only happens in extremely rare cases in Western countries like the US, where fathers and sons and husbands and wives only occasionally take turns to run for president or use their children as presidential advisers).

The next day we joined the governor on a meet-the-people tour of her island to work that Garcia magic.

Dressed in high heels, tight jeans and a patterned T-shirt, she swept out of the capitol building into her official car, stopping only to kiss a baby a passing woman was holding, then sped off to her first engagement at an electricity project. Large crowds were waiting for her arrival and as the car approached them she leaned out and sat on the front window, holding onto the roof with one hand as she waved excitedly with the other. The crowd roared!

More kissing and hand-shaking followed as she proceeded to the microphone, talking up the benefits and jobs that were flowing from the project, then she swept back to the motorcade for the next stop, an irrigation project. More waving, kissing, cheering and extolling before sweeping back to the motorcade for the next engagement, a school.

This time crowds of children formed a line from the car park to the podium, holding out their hands to be touched by Mum Gwen as she charged up the steps to a crowd that couldn't have been more excited by a Pussycat Dolls concert.

'The pretty and handsome students are all here!' she shouted. The crowd went wild. 'It is true you are all good-looking because you clapped. Pretty girls clap!'

All the girls clapped.

'Same for the boys!'

The boys all clapped.

'Everyone who thinks I'm pretty, clap! It's important everybody claps.'

Everyone did.

'I love you with all my heart,' she cried. The crowd cheered, clapped, some even wept.

'For all of us, long live one Cebu!'

As she mingled with the students, teachers, priests and officials it was hard to imagine she could meet a more appreciative audience – until the next day, when she went to the prison.

Sixteen hundred inmates stood in the hot sun in complete silence, nervously waiting for her. She walked out to the balcony above them, wearing a smart white pantsuit and gave them a snappy salute. They burst into applause.

'Good morning, everybody. How are you? Is everybody okay? Is everybody okay?

The inmates cheered. They seemed to have completely forgotten that unfortunate incident when she put them in chains and made them lie on the ground until they said sorry.

'I visited you because I missed all of you!' They burst into applause.

'Do you know you are very popular around the world? Give yourselves a big hand! I thank all of you for believing that the CPDRD will put Cebu on the map.'

Then it was time for the dance number. It was not the standard crowd pleasers 'Thriller' or Van McCoy's 'Do the Hustle', but a new, bold experimental number they were performing for the first time.

It was the 1990 classic 'Sadeness Part 1' by Enigma, voted consistently as one of the top 10 songs to make love to.

En masse, the inmates began tightly choreographed movements to the sensual soundtrack celebrating the ambiguous sexuality of the Marquis de Sade, slowly moving into a perfect human crucifix to the French and Latin lyrics.

Procedamus in pace

In nomine Christi, Amen

Gwen and Byron funked up their own moves in time to the music as the song approached its steamy climax.

At the end of it, Wenjiel collapsed in a dramatic stage faint. This time it was Gwen and Byron's turn to applaud.

With the dance over, Governor Garcia walked down alone into the courtyard to shake hands with the entire prison population. It took more than an hour, exchanging a greeting with every one of them and planting a kiss on Wenjiel, who blushed and pouted and nearly cried.

'Governor, you've just shaken hands with 1600 people who can't vote,' I said when she'd finished.

'Well I shake hands not for the votes. I shake hands because I want to touch each and every person and perhaps by doing so I'm able to touch their hearts as well.'

Byron came over to us with a prisoner who had tattooed 'GOV GWEN GARCIA' on his forehead.

'Did you see this?' he asked.

'Wow, he's a fan,' I said.

Gwen laughed. 'This is until death!'

The prisoner smiled awkwardly.

Unfortunately for him, the tattoo was out of date by 2013 when Gwen succeeded her brother in the congress and won election to the position her father had held – deputy speaker.

Things took a slightly worrying turn in April 2016 when she was charged with corruption over the construction of the Cebu International Convention Center. Shortly after, her cousin the mayor of Cebu was also charged with graft over a social housing project. (In a political setback for the family, her third brother, Winston, then narrowly lost the election to take her old job as governor. On the plus side, a close ally named Rodrigo Duterte was elected president.)

Gwen strongly denied the charges that could theoretically send her to prison. It's for the courts to decide, of course. And I wouldn't suggest Filipino courts were anything other than rigorously independent. But I'm sure Gwen Garcia won't be having to dance to any 80s classics any time soon.

12. The New Vikings

Iceland, August 2009

> **What has destroyed Iceland has been rampant corruption, stupidity and greed.**
>
> Georg Brynjarsson, Icelandic economist, 2009

> **Iceland should be a model to the world.**
>
> Arthur Laffer, neo-liberal economist, 2007

The blonde-haired, blue-eyed, red-lipstick-wearing hipster seemed momentarily interested in the sight of a television camera and boom microphone.

'Where are you from?' she asked in perfect Standard English over the slightly avant-garde, edgy doof-doof music.

'Australian television,' I said. 'We're doing a story on the crisis and we'd like to ...'

But at the word 'Australian' she turned back to her equally aloof friends, effectively dismissing my existence. We were not from Europe, New York or *Monocle* magazine; just some hicks from Down Under.

As an Australian foreign correspondent you get used to being treated as a provincial, but rarely in a country with a smaller population than Wollongong (320,000 to be precise; mainly fishermen or sheep farmers). In a small-town nightclub on a remote island at 2 am it was more than usually stinging. We hadn't even been able to start filming the sophisticated-young-Icelanders sequence until after midnight because that's when they start to go out, after pre-fuelling on Absolut vodka at their homes. The capital Reykjavik prides itself on having New York-style nightlife, despite having only slightly more people than Toowoomba (119,000 to be precise; mostly fishermen or independent filmmakers).

Surrounded by chiselled-jawed Viking clones and Nordic beauties, I just wanted to go back to my hotel room next door and cover my ears against the sounds of Arctic Monkeys, Metronomy, MGMT and breaking vodka bottles that I knew would punctuate the rest of the night. (Young Icelanders like to drink spirits almost as much as they like being written up in London magazines as the new innovative arts centre or hot travel destination.)

The island hadn't always seen itself as so superior. On my first visit in May 1999, I just happened to arrive on the day of the parliamentary elections, perhaps the least reported ballot in Europe. The Prime Minister, Davíð Oddsson, somehow got wind of a foreign television crew visiting and sent word to the airport that we should head straight to his house. Minutes later my long-time cameraman Dave Martin and I were shepherded past the Icelandic media waiting outside for his victory speech.

The Prime Minister greeted us effusively (Me: 'This is my cameraman David.' PM: 'Hi David, I'm David too.') and, ignoring his own media, ushered us in for a drink and a one-hour chat.

A small, avuncular man with a mop of greying fair hair, Davíð Oddsson seemed more like an affable alderman than a prime minister. In fact his previous job had been mayor of Reykjavik. He proudly showed us photos of him posing with Ronald Reagan and Mikhail Gorbachev in 1986, when he'd helped host a summit between the leaders of the rival superpowers. Tiny Iceland had been chosen as the venue presumably for its symbolic location (it's halfway between Europe and the US, which is why it's been a member of NATO since 1949 despite having no army) but also for its relative lack of importance, avoiding any risk of the host country overshadowing the meeting of giants.

Fast forward a decade and everything had changed. Iceland had not only come to see itself as a major world player, it had even kick-started the catastrophe known as the GFC, the global financial crisis. Under Davíð Oddsson, first as prime minister and then as head of the Central Bank, this remote volcanic island community had embarked on perhaps the dumbest campaign in the history of Stupid. It had decided to become the new Wall Street.

That took some chutzpah. Remember, Iceland has just 310,000 people, give or take a touring experimental art group. Secondly, it's in the middle of the North Atlantic, not close to anywhere in particular except those other economic giants Greenland and the Faroe Islands. Thirdly, it has only four significant resources: sheep, fish, aluminium smelting and volcanoes, none of which lend themselves to global domination. (It would be churlish to add that many people believe they share the island with elf-like *huldulfólk*, so I won't, except to say that in 2004 Alcoa had to certify a site was free of archaeological sites related to *huldulfólk* folklore before they could build a smelter.)

In short, there was absolutely no reason for anyone over the age of 12 to think Iceland could be the next big player in global finance. But as the new millennium dawned that's exactly what this remote island decided to do, privatising and deregulating its stodgy state-owned banks and letting them loose on an unsuspecting world. Even more amazingly, it looked for a time as though they could pull it off.

An orgy of reckless borrowing and lending created an asset and debt bubble and a small class of international tycoons dubbed 'The New Vikings'. They snapped up everything they could get their hands on in Iceland then moved on to Europe, buying everything from department store chains to a premier league football club. As the Icelandic currency, the króna, soared, ordinary Icelanders cashed in, borrowing small fortunes in cheap foreign currencies to buy luxury items and big new cars and houses they'd never realised they needed.

Soon the *Wall Street Journal* was running articles like 'Miracle on Iceland' stating: 'Now, after a radical and comprehensive course of liberalization that mirrors similar reforms in Thatcher's Britain, New Zealand and Chile, Iceland has emerged as one of the world's most prosperous countries. Much of the credit goes to Prime Minister Davíð Oddsson.'

But in October 2008 the three main banks went bust within a few days, leaving a ruined economy and debts that Icelanders could spend a lifetime repaying. Relative to population, it was the biggest banking collapse in history. Iceland became the first developed country in 30 years to seek a bailout from the IMF. These days Davíð Oddsson wasn't meeting foreign TV crews. He wasn't even answering his phone.

Looking around the nightclub at now impoverished hipsters sporting the last expensive outfits they might ever own, apparently unaware the party was well and truly over, I wondered how this country could have forgotten that binges always end in hangovers.

By morning, once you sidestepped the broken vodka bottles and scattered glass from smashed showroom windows, you could gaze over the folly of debt-fuelled madness. There were gleaming waterfront office blocks without a single tenant, massive SUVs parked outside closed businesses, a giant half-built performance space that would never be completed, even an I-told-you-so-nyy-nya-nya-nya-nya visiting economist who'd agreed to meet us for breakfast.

Robert Wade was an Australian-born professor at the London School of Economics who'd made a study of the 1997 Asian financial crisis. In the summer of 2007, after observing Iceland's near-identical debt-fuelled boom, he warned publicly that the economy was 'dynamite waiting to explode'.

'They just politely dismissed what I was saying,' he told me over *Hafragrautur* oatmeal in a designer chic cafe. 'They had the line that they had these young Vikings, they were operating fully in line with European regulations and they had just discovered some secret, these young Vikings, which the rest of the world didn't know about.'

He wasn't just ignored. He was publicly attacked for daring to question the Icelandic miracle. A British economics consultant Professor Richard Portes, and an Icelandic professor Fridrik Már Baldursson, excoriated Wade in an article in the *Financial Times*, accusing him of carelessness and 'rumour-mongering'.

Robert Wade was a measured, quietly spoken man. But now that he'd been proven completely correct and 'experts' like Professor Portes were looking decidedly stupid, he couldn't completely conceal a shit-eating grin.

'It has subsequently come out that these people were paid huge amounts of money by the Icelandic Chamber of Commerce to say these things.' (Portes received £58,000 British pounds for 'research'.)

Wade hadn't been the only one to sound a warning. In June 2007 another visiting expert on financial crises, Robert Aliber, counted the number of building cranes then gave a lecture at the University of Iceland predicting a major crisis within a year.

More seriously, the International Monetary Fund (IMF) had given a scathing critique of Iceland's banking boom in August 2006. Its warnings included:

The banking system seems highly vulnerable to materialization of credit risk ...

Very high credit growth in an already deep market exposes Icelandic banks to credit risks when the cycle turns ...

Banks own stakes in each other. An economy-wide shock could have domino effects from banks to companies and vice versa.

Even beneath the diplomatic bureaucratic language, the message was obvious. Iceland was rooted.

'The IMF's report on Iceland in 2006 rang the alarm bell as loudly as the IMF ever rings the alarm bell,' Robert Wade continued over the hum of hungover hipsters ordering macchiato with cardamom. 'There was plenty of time in which the government could have begun to restrain these banks. But the point is the government bought into it and probably government ministers had lots of money invested in these ventures as well, so they were not about to cut off their noses, so to speak.'

I wandered around Reykjavik wondering how the rest of the world could have fallen for it. Beyond the funky bars and cafes of the centre, it looked more like a conservative small country town than New York or Singapore. There were neat cottages with brightly coloured roofs, small artisan shops and simple Lutheran churches. Yet organisations that set global opinion had swallowed the line that Iceland was the new international finance centre rather than a remote Atlantic bubble waiting to pop. A few days before the IMF released its scathing report, the international ratings agency Moody's had renewed Iceland's AAA credit rating. Even more bizarre was the response of the corruption rating agency, Transparency International, long a scourge of kleptocracies like Nigeria. In 2006, at the height of the bubble, it rated Iceland as the world's *least* corrupt country. Because as everyone knows, small communities never ever, ever, indulge in nepotism or cronyism ... especially when they get hundreds of billions of dollars to play with.

My first trip to Iceland 10 years earlier had been to report on just how cosily interconnected this small community was. With almost zero immigration since it was settled by Norse farmers in the ninth and tenth centuries, it was now the most homogenous society in Europe. A medical research company called Decode had digitised the genealogy of nearly the entire population and was compiling family medical histories to isolate the genes linked to serious illnesses.

The company's digital officer, Tórður Kristjánsson, delighted in showing his computer program, where he could type anyone's name and show their family links back through 508,000 people to Viking settlement. Almost everyone seemed related to Kettil Flatnose, born in 805. The medical records were being crosschecked with the DNA of 10,000 volunteers.

Decode's CEO, Kári Stefánsson, a tall bearded blond who looked like he had just stepped off a longship, believed his project would revolutionise the treatment of diseases like multiple sclerosis, diabetes, Alzheimer's and osteoarthritis. 'It's an absolutely miraculous instrument to use in the study of genetics of human disease.'

Ten years later the world was still waiting for the promised breakthroughs, but that first visit had left me with an indelible impression: Icelanders took their Viking heritage very seriously. Some of them were seriously starting to think they could once again conquer the world.

In such a tight-knit community it was inevitable that a small number of families would come to dominate. In a much-read critique of the crisis, Robert Wade wrote that a bloc of 14 families, popularly known as the 'Octopus', effectively ran the economy in the second half of the 20th century. They made their money from fishing, transport, oil importing, provisioning the NATO base and from insurance and banking. They also ran the government. 'This establishment provided the leaders of the two political parties which formed most of the coalition governments since the 1930s, and which divided up the spoils of office between core supporters.'

Iceland's Parliament House, just around the corner from the main banks, has an air of grandeur thanks to its building blocks of grey hewn stone. But the two-storey building is about the size of a suburban council chamber. It represents fewer people than some Australian shires and shares the small-town characteristics of any local council – people with big personalities tend to dominate proceedings.

Davíð Oddsson had been by far the biggest fish in this small pond. As a young man, he became an enthusiastic convert to neo-liberalism, the radical Thatcherite/Reaganite philosophy of small government and rampant corporate deregulation. It was the antithesis of the traditional Scandinavian mentality of a social democratic welfare state. As Robert Wade explained it, Davíð Oddsson was 'the chieftain' of a dozen or so like-minded ideologues studying law or business administration at the University of Iceland, who took over the editorship of a journal called *The Locomotive*.

'As they moved into positions of influence and power they remained a network of mutually promoting friends, more loyal to each other than to the organisations for which they worked. Known as the Locomotive group, they constituted a segment of Iceland's shadow elite,' he wrote. 'Several of them stepped out of the shadows into the limelight, taking the top political and juridical positions.'

Oddsson rose quickly through the ranks of the ruling Independence Party, vigorously persuading his conservative colleagues of the merits of deregulation and promoting opportunities for his like-minded friends. As prime minister from 1991 to 2004, he was able to put his theories into practice on an entire country, making Iceland a beacon of inspiration for right-wing think tanks and oil and tobacco companies around the world.

But I was here to meet a very different type of Icelandic politician – a hippie anarchist.

Birgitta Jónsdóttir greeted us at the parliament entrance just after we passed through security. Checks had been tightened since the previous winter's protests when as many as 6000 people besieged the building, banging pots and pans to register their disgust with the government's handling of the crisis. Birgitta had been one of the leaders of the protests, braving the dark cold every day to vent her fury. Now she was on the inside, elected to parliament in a wave of protest votes.

Pointing out the window to the empty forecourt, Birgitta reminisced on those simpler days. 'On Saturdays we had the van over there with the speaker system and we always got more and more people,' she said wistfully. 'It was completely packed everywhere.'

With straggly dark hair and loose organic cotton clothing, she looked nothing like the politicians whose photographs adorned a wall by the entrance. Well-groomed in neat suits, they were, to a man (and occasional woman), respectable, church-going, conservative middle-class citizens.

Birgitta pointed to some of the photos with disdain, detailing who had gone to school with whom, who had done business with whom, who owed money to whom, and even who had slept with whom.

'Some of the ministers from the government had very close ties with these banks and this was never really revealed properly. How is it possible that they allowed the Icelandic banking system to grow 10 times the size of our GDP? I mean how is that possible unless you have somebody looking the other way in order to make money out of it?'

Birgitta had never imagined herself as a politician. She'd once lived in the hippie hub of Mullumbimby on Australia's east coast and had been struggling to get by in Reykjavik as a single mother when the protests began. With no training in economics, she was now looking at how to rescue Iceland from destruction at the hands of financial experts.

'I'm hoping that people will sort of get back into the values of what's real in life. I mean material things are nice but they're not real.'

Birgitta said she also wanted to make Iceland a legal safe haven for whistleblowers so in future the dirty dealings of governments and corporations could be exposed. She had started working with an Australian I'd never heard of called Julian Assange on a new project called Wikileaks. A few days earlier, Wikileaks had released one of its first big tranches of leaked documents. More than 200 pages of loan agreements, emails and letters revealed how Iceland's largest bank, Kaupthing, had grown so big so fast. Essentially the bank owners had loaned themselves other people's money to buy mountains of stuff, leaving the debts to be paid by some other suckers well into the future.

'It's one of the greatest sort of Ponzi schemes in history,' Birgitta said.

Here's how it worked.

Kaupthing gave its biggest loans to its biggest shareholders and executives to buy more shares in the bank, artificially inflating the share price. Then the shareholders used those shares as collateral to take out even bigger loans to buy assets. For example, the Wikileaks documents revealed that 1.8 billion Euros were lent to companies linked to a board member Lydur Gudmundsson. Nearly 800 million Euros went to a company called Exista that owned 22 per cent of the bank. A note detailing the loan stated: 'bulk of the loans are unsecured with no covenants'. Soon the bankers were actual billionaires without having earned any actual money. And they could be confident they could take their time paying back the loans because, hell, they owned the bank.

It wasn't financial genius, just the kind of scam wise guys could have dreamed up in a Brooklyn bar. But Kaupthing and its fellow Icelandic banks took it further. They started lending money to each other. As Robert Wade explained it in his 2010 analysis 'Lessons from Iceland', Bank A would loan a billion to Bank B which would then loan a billion to Bank A. No money actually changed hands, but it allowed banks A and B to go to real banks in other countries like Luxembourg and borrow actual cash using the notional loans as collateral. Neat!

Now the banks were cashed up, bank salesmen were able to hit the phones offering predatory loans throughout Iceland.

Kaupthing used some of its chump change to hire John Cleese to present its television promotions, the actor apparently unaware he was fronting a Ponzi scheme more absurd than Monty Python. In one of them he looks to camera and says: 'Hi, I'm John Cleese, a very famous actor here in Hollywood. So famous that I can pick any company whatsoever to work for. And I certainly don't need to do advertising. But the fact is that I want to represent the magnificent company of Kapaflingfling.' (Voice off camera: 'No, Kaupthing.' Cleese: 'What?') Talk about laugh!

Kaupthing also produced slick corporate advertisements for discerning investors. Under shots of athletes and general high achievers a voiceover deep in gravitas declared: 'We thought we could double in size, and we did — every year for eight years. We thought we could increase our balance sheet — and we did. Kaupthinking is beyond normal thinking.'

The only problem was the banks had to keep money coming in to service their ever increasing commitments. But like any good pyramid scheme, there were always more bunnies wanting in. The higher the banks' share prices rose, the more people wanted to buy shares in them, even borrowing money from the banks to buy the shares. When money from Iceland ran dry, the banks turned to the ancient Viking tradition of raiding overseas.

One bank, Landsbanki, launched an internet deposit scheme called Icesave to hoover up money from the UK and the Netherlands. Icesave offered unbelievably high returns and the money poured in, from mum and dad investors to the London Metropolitan Police Authority, Cambridge University, several large city councils and even the UK Audit Commission, the body responsible for auditing the finances of city councils. In total, Icesave managed to suck in around 400,000 depositors.

By 2006 Iceland's once tiny banks were now listed in the world's top 300 banks, their assets nearly 10 times the size of Iceland's GDP. The banks' owners were not only leading billionaire lifestyles – flying private jets from Reykjavik to London to buy ever more assets like Marks and Spencer or West Ham United Football Club – they were also giving generous loans to the politicians who were supposed to oversee them and buying shares in Icelandic media that were supposed to scrutinise them. Most media coverage had been unquestioningly fawning, always calling the bankers 'New Vikings'.

(To visualise the absurdity of this, I hit on the idea of hiring actors to fight a Viking battle, then shooting the same scene with them wearing suits and constantly stopping the battle to answer their phones. But we had to scale back our plans when it turned out only two members of the local Viking re-enactment club had suits.)

Not all Icelanders pride themselves on their Viking heritage. Guðni Jóhannesson describes himself as 'a boring historian', largely because he's constantly having to bore everyone with the fact that Iceland doesn't actually have much of a Viking heritage.

'People are proud of their Icelandic heritage and they [the bankers] wanted to sell themselves as different so they connected to the so-called Viking heritage. But when you actually look at it, the Vikings were not the people settling Iceland in the old days. The people arriving from Scandinavian countries and the British Isles were mostly farmers, poor farmers who were not raping and pillaging and having glorious stories written about them.'

We met Guðni at his house with his Canadian-born wife Eliza Reid and two small children. As well as teaching at the University of Iceland, he had just published a book about the crisis. In a market as small as Iceland, it was a labour of love. He just wanted to put on record what had really happened and dispel some myths, including the idea that dodgy bankers were somehow intrepid conquerors.

'It's just their misunderstanding and our misfortune that we had to suffer for it. Some of the bankers were plain idiots as it turns out. Others were more unlucky than stupid. But the sad fact is that a few dozen people did this tremendous damage to the rest of us.'

He believed the reason they were able to get that far wasn't their warrior blood but Iceland's small-town provincialism.

'Everyone knows everyone and that's actually the problem. The surveillance authorities, the bankers, the politicians. You could always find someone who'd been in the same class as that person, or the wife was in the same club as the other wife, so the firewalls that should have existed and the regulations that should have been adhered to weren't. And that's down to the small-town atmosphere that inevitably exists in a nation of 300,000 souls. We were just too small to be a financial centre.'

Thanks to Davíð Oddsson, the Central Bank failed absolutely in regulating the banks. As prime minister, he split off many of its powers to a small Financial Supervisory Authority. In practice that meant young public servants, usually in their twenties, would visit the banks on their own to inquire nervously about their operations. Billionaire New Vikings with phalanxes of high-priced lawyers and mountains of documents would assure them everything was fine. (After meeting some of the authority's employees, the economist Robert Aliber described them as having roughly the level of competence of people picked randomly from the phone book.)

The Central Bank itself was even less of a problem for the 'Vikings'. After he resigned as prime minister in 2004, Davíð Oddsson became its chairman. So the man responsible for deregulation became the man in charge of regulation. What could go wrong?

Despite all this, Transparency International rated Iceland as the world's least corrupt country and international ratings agencies hailed it as a model of good economic management. That's why international finance analysts get the big bucks and the comfy chairs. They're just so good at what they do. It's worth quoting Moody's 2006 report at length, if only to marvel at the wisdom and expertise of an agency that can still make governments tremble before it.

> Iceland is a wealthy, advanced industrialized country that is also in the midst of a major economic diversification initiative that is enhancing the wealth and development of the economy.
>
> We feel market concerns about a banking crisis were exaggerated. In Iceland, the external debt buildup has financed high-quality external foreign investments and the banks' foreign assets and liabilities are very closely matched.
>
> [Iceland's financial system is] well-managed, well-capitalized, and adequately liquid, and capable of withstanding sizeable and simultaneous shocks from sharp adjustments in the exchange rate, asset prices, and asset quality.

Three years on, Icelanders had a dimmer view of their bankers than Moody's analyst Joan Feldbaum-Vidra, author of the report.

On my third day in Reykjavik I woke to an early morning phone message that something interesting was happening at a banker's house. We raced around to the address to see it had been daubed in red paint. Some people had arrived at dawn and spattered paint all over the front of the house. An elderly man named Sigardur was attempting to hose it off.

'It's a horrible thing to do,' he told me. 'I can't know what reason people are doing things like that.'

He explained the house belonged to his son Július Hreiðarsson, who had worked at Landsbanki. Fortunately, he was consulting in Luxembourg so didn't have to witness the damage.

'It's the second time it's happened,' he said, shaking his head in disbelief, wondering what could possibly have made people so upset.

Most of the New Vikings had fled Iceland. A bar in Reykjavik plastered their photographs onto its urinals so drinkers could pay their nightly respects. Bankers who remained in this small community were ostracised. There were cases of bankers sitting down in restaurants with their families only to see the other patrons stand up and leave.

Iceland's new social democratic government had already taken the decision to let the banks fail. There was no US-style bailout. Every investor took a hit. But taxpayers would still be burdened with a US$2.1 billion loan from the IMF.

Gunnar Sigurdsson was leading a campaign to make the bankers pay for their crimes. The 50-year-old theatre director invited us around to his small apartment that was about to be repossessed. He told us he had never been to a demonstration in his life until the crisis hit.

'Nobody was telling us anything. We had to read foreign newspapers to find out what was going on in Iceland and that got people very angry. They wanted to know what was going on, why this was happening.'

So he started organising televised public forums, demanding that politicians turn up to answer people's questions. Now he was leading a campaign to have the bankers prosecuted. Being Icelandic, he was also making an independent film about the crisis, with the working title *Crashland*. He was just finding financing for the film a bit of a challenge as nobody had any money.

'I'm living a very insecure life at the moment. I'm going to lose my flat, which is not a very big flat. I'm going to lose my car. I'm going to get bankrupt. Not because I was a stupid guy and I wasn't trying to do my deeds, because of the way things were handled in Iceland. So excuse me!'

Like many Icelanders, he had bought himself a new home and car in foreign currency, only to find the repayments doubled after the króna collapsed. He couldn't afford the repayments but he couldn't sell the assets because everybody else was in the same boat.

'Can you imagine that you have your house living in Australia or wherever you live, and suddenly your mortgage has doubled, just over one night? You know, we were doing okay. We were doing fine. Why be so greedy?'

Gunnar showed us some of the footage of the public forums. What was most striking was the discomfort of the old establishment politicians having to answer questions from the public.

'That was kind of a new thing for them,' Gunnar said. 'It was also a new thing for us as the common people.'

At one meeting the former foreign minister berated the booing crowd for daring to question her, shouting: 'Many people sitting here in this room want us out, but I'm not sure if everyone in this room is necessarily in a position to speak on behalf of the nation.'

Gunnar snorted as he watched the tape. 'That's what you call political suicide, live on television.'

He'd also managed to track down one of the formerly high profile New Vikings, a 42-year-old billionaire Thor Björgólfsson now living in London. It was an exclusive interview cut short when Gunnar asked him if he was a crook.

Gunnar Sigurdsson: 'So what would you like to say to those Icelanders who see you as criminals – they call you criminals?'

Thor Björgólfsson: 'Of course I have nothing to say.'

Gunnar Sigurdsson: 'So you cannot answer it?'

Thor Björgólfsson: 'I have nothing to say. I'm not a criminal. I've never been one. There's nothing to say. Right, I'm late – I have to run. [Abruptly leaves interview]

(Björgólfsson was never prosecuted and claimed to have become a billionaire again by 2015 when he published the inspirational classic *Billions to Bust and Back: How I made, lost and rebuilt a fortune*.) I asked Gunnar how he thought Iceland could have got things so horribly wrong.

'I think it's the corruption. We gave a couple of guys permission to use all their force to actually sell Iceland, to sell it! To make a fortune out of it. And leave the bill with the common public.'

We drove back to the town centre to find the forecourt of Parliament House was again full of protestors. Musicians on an impromptu stage were belting out anti-banker songs like 'You should count your fingers, one, two, three, those smiles of the wolves can be very expensive,' which sounds much better in Icelandic.

A rumour raced through the crowd that Davíð Oddsson had just wandered over to have a look, but by the time we reached the spot where he'd been sighted he and his bodyguards had disappeared. Instead we found Birgitta Jónsdóttir, who'd helped organise the protest. She told us it was giving a message to the British government. 'Icelanders are not going to pay for the money the banks lost.'

Britain was demanding Iceland repay billions of dollars that naive and helpless institutions like the Metropolitan Police had deposited in Icesave. Now that Landsbanki was in receivership (i.e. bankrupt) there seemed little money to return. Britain had already seized all the bank's assets in London. (Bizarrely, the British government briefly declared it to be a terrorist organisation so it could recover funds under legislation aimed at al-Qaeda.)

The British and Dutch governments had taken it upon themselves to pay out the bank's minimum insurance guarantees of up to 20,000 Euros per depositor. That worked out to 2.7 billion Euros for British depositors and 1.3 billion Euros for Dutch losses. They were demanding Iceland reimburse them for the payouts, which would have worked out to an average of 13,000 Euros for every man, woman and child in Iceland.

Birgitta's considered response as a member of parliament was to tell the UK to get stuffed. 'We want the people who stole the money to be held accountable.'

Amazingly, she managed to pull it off. When the government tried to negotiate repayment, she campaigned successfully in a referendum to block it. (This was in defiance of a stern warning from Moody's that it would downgrade Iceland's credit rating!) The bottom line was that the public would not contribute a cent until everything possible was recovered from the failed bank's assets and what Birgitta called 'its white-collar criminals' who still had shares in businesses all around Iceland and the world. After years of negotiations, Iceland finally agreed to repay an amount it considered fair. The cost to taxpayers was less than 10 per cent of what Britain and the Netherlands had demanded.

The decision to let the banks fail had an unexpected effect on the economy. By 2011 Iceland had returned to growth, years earlier than anyone had dared hope. By 2015 it was one of Europe's top performers.

Iceland also did what Britain and the US didn't dare or didn't want to do. It jailed the bankers. By 2016, 29 New Vikings had been banged up in an admittedly comfortable minimum-security prison, Kviabryggja, with a spectacular view of Iceland's magnificent volcanic rocks and fjords. But still.

(The inmates included the former chairman and CEO of Kaupthing, the bank John Cleese couldn't pronounce but had been happy to promote. One hopes he was paid upfront.)

Birgitta went on to found the Pirate Party, which by 2016 was outpolling Davíð Oddsson's Independence Party by two to one. She was even being touted as a future prime minister.

And when the same year, Prime Minister Sigmundur Davíð Gunnlaugsson was implicated in the Panama Papers for putting his money into offshore accounts, 30,000 people besieged the parliament and forced his resignation.

In the wave of anti-establishment sentiment that followed, Iceland elected a total outsider as president: Guðni Jóhannesson, the cleanskin historian who had punctured the Viking myth for us. The next day, in a sign the country was on a roll, Iceland beat England in the World Cup.

And on 2 December, after inconclusive parliamentary elections, our talent President Guðni Jóhannesson asked our talent Birgitta Jónsdóttir to try to form a government. (It didn't work out, as a minor left-wing party wouldn't agree to a coalition. But still. Being interviewed by *Foreign Correspondent* can change your life!) In just eight years Iceland had turned from a country ruled by bankers and crony politicians to one where banks and politicians were at the mercy of the common people.

For a tiny community, Icelanders do really amazing things. They're annoying that way.

13. Race to the Bottom

Ireland, February 2013

> **Sell the cow, buy the sheep, but never be without the horse.**
>
> Old Irish saying

Pat Hyland loved his horses, especially if they were properly cooked. He trotted out the fine qualities of his horseflesh as his Lithuanian assistant laboured mightily to set up the cooker.

'*Odalish. Vrehelfee. Sverhiprotee!*' he enthused.

(Our fixer Roisin would later decipher this as: 'Oh delicious. Very healthy. It's very high in protein!')

Pat, who went by the name Paddy Jack for its showman appeal, was the only man in Ireland who'd hit on the idea of running a horsemeat stall. He'd been doing it every Saturday for six weeks in Dublin's trendy Temple Bar market, positioning himself between organic vegetable carts and homemade jam stalls. It seemed a bold move in a country that revered horses almost as highly as children. But as Pat mumbled an explanation in one of the thickest Irish accents I'd ever heard, I had trouble following his reasoning.

'*Awlditahleenanaspanshanafrunshareetinit,*' he explained. (All the Italians and the Spanish and the French are eating it.)

'*Annahdaoirshareetinit!*' he continued. (And now the Irish are eating it!)

Pat was a fleshy man with a whisky-infused face and an obvious eye for a quick deal. As soon as his low-paid Lithuanian finished the hard work of setting up the mobile stall, Pat went into showman mode, slapping slices on the cooker and sighing with pleasure as he inhaled the fragrances.

'*Slovlimi. Yecantaysaysilf. Wanabitasalton?*' he offered. (It's lovely meat. You can have a taste yourself. Want to put a bit of salt on?)

I nodded enthusiastically, rather like a dog trying to please an owner who assumes pets speak English. When he passed me a steak I started munching.

'Hussabuckindaorrsna,' he continued. (That's the back end of the horse now). '*Thafrunensabitufayano?*' (The front end is a bit tougher you know?)

'Mm that's very good,' I said. And I meant it. I'd once spent a week stuck in Kazakhstan where horse was the main dish at the local restaurant and I'd learned to relish it. But in Dublin I was in a tiny minority.

'What kind of meat is that?' a woman asked as she noticed the unusual smell.

'Beef,' said Pat with a straight face and something approaching intelligible English.

'Horse,' he added after she tasted it. She looked at him as if he'd made a joke in bad taste.

Pat explained to me (as I understood hours later after Roisin explained what he'd been saying) that he sometimes only told people it was horse after they'd already sampled it so as not to scare them off. Best to let curiosity take its course.

The reactions of passers-by ranged from disgust to embarrassed amusement to morbid curiosity. Some even began gathering their friends around, daring them to try it. To their surprise, they found it remarkably tasty.

'It's nice,' one woman said. 'The flavour of the chargrill is very nice. It's nice and lean.'

At first Pat mainly sold his horse burgers to foreign tourists. But his trade with adventurous Dubliners had actually picked up in recent weeks amid all the controversy. While he was the only one selling horsemeat (relatively) openly, the Irish had just discovered almost every major supermarket had been doing it on the sly.

'*YewesiItortIwadafirsttodohorsindubla*,' Pat said. (Yeah well see I thought I was the first to do horse in Dublin.) '*Budoidinraly-thareetinudenwey*'. (But I didn't realise they were eating it anyway.)

It was the height of a meat substitution scandal that had spread across the globe. A chance discovery of horsemeat in processed food in Dublin had prompted investigations in dozens of countries, each with the same disturbing finding: almost every packet of frozen food contained traces of nag DNA. Horse had even been found in IKEA meatballs.

All the food corporations, abattoirs, meat transporters and farms had professed utter shock and complete ignorance as to how it had happened. Traces of colt, filly, mare, stallion, bronco or foal had somehow made their way onto every supermarket shelf and it seemed absolutely nobody was responsible.

So Dave Martin and I had come to Ireland to try to solve the mystery. Just how did an international horsemeat scandal start in the one country where nobody ate horse? (Apart from the odd customer charmed by Paddy Jack, of course.)

Our first stop was the unassuming office of Ireland's Food Safety Authority, where random tests uncovered the illicit horsemeat. The mild-mannered chief executive, Professor Alan Reilly, appeared slightly shocked by what had unfolded.

'We looked at a whole range of different products, those products that consumers wouldn't quite know what they're buying,' he explained. 'Products that are covered in pastry, products with something like a potato topping on them, and also beef burgers because the meat is minced. You've no idea really what's in a beef burger.'

The finding of the first test was so revolting they assumed it was a mistake. 'We found one product with about one-third horse DNA in it, which was just an incredible finding. We double-checked and triple-checked because we understood that if we were to go out public it was going to have quite an effect, certainly here in Ireland. At the time we thought it was an Irish problem.'

But the problem had already, as it were, bolted. Ireland's tests prompted other European authorities to check processed food samples. It seemed everybody was unwittingly caught up in the scam. Supermarket chains across the Continent had to withdraw big brand products, from Findus to Birds Eye. Burger King said it managed to spot horsemeat in its supplies just before it reached its burgers.

'It's turned out to be a European problem now, in fact nearly a global problem,' Professor Reilly said. 'There's over 26 countries in Europe who are now involved in this scandal and products have been withdrawn from shelves in places like Singapore, Hong Kong and some of the Caribbean countries, so really we are looking at what has developed into a massive fraud.'

As anyone who's ever been stuck in Kazakhstan could point out, there's nothing inherently wrong with horsemeat. In fact it's quite healthy: high in iron, low in fat and cheaper than beef or pork. In France and Belgium it's considered a delicacy. And compared to the organs, entrails, nose fragments and chemical additives in some processed meat, it's not the worst thing you could munch on. The problem as Alan Reilly saw it was that consumers could no longer trust what they were buying.

'Well it's difficult to speculate on exactly how long this scam has been going on,' he said. 'But what we do know is that manufacturers have been drip-feeding horsemeat into the food chain and they've been doing that at the expense of the consumer. It's a blatant fraud. If you are bidding for a contract and you're undercutting your competitors by adding horsemeat instead of beef, that is going to impact hugely on industry. And it's something that we have to stamp out very quickly because what you will have here is a race to the bottom and that's really not where we want to go.'

The scandal had provoked revulsion in every country it struck. It wasn't just that many found the idea of horsemeat to be disgusting. There were fears people were unwittingly ingesting the dangerous chemicals that racehorses were regularly dosed with. Muslims and Jews were particularly alarmed. If horse could be slipped in, why not pig?

But the biggest reaction was in the country where it started. The Irish public has a genuine affection for horses, explained in part by a long tradition of village life and close work with animals. We filmed an afternoon hunt outside Dublin, a local group of enthusiasts dressed in black coats and riding caps on beautifully groomed steeds, chasing a scent that had been dragged around the course rather than an actual fox.

'It's slightly different but it's good fun,' hunt master Mary Fedenberg told me. 'A drag hunt is also quicker than a fox hunt because the fox is very clever and can go to ground. You can be sitting around all day waiting.'

She said she was confident she had never eaten horsemeat because 'being a country person' she only bought meat fresh from the butcher.

'I mean we don't want to eat horses, even though that might be in the news at the moment. The horse is loved by all in Ireland really. We do love our horses and we use them. The horses here are bred to be hardy, to jump, to hunt. We're not going to eat them, just like you're not going to eat your dog.'

But like so much else here, the attitude to horses was also coloured by Ireland's troubled history with the large island to the east.

Since the 16th century Tudor invasion, England had occupied its Celtic neighbour and treated the Catholic inhabitants as inferiors, settling Scottish Protestants in the north to help tame the rebellious natives. In 1695 the English Parliament enacted the Penal Laws against Catholics that targeted, among other things, the right to own a horse. Specifically, it outlawed a Catholic possessing a horse valued at more than five pounds. In practice, it meant a Protestant could seize any horse that took his fancy and pay no more than five quid for it. Like every mean and stupid English law, it encouraged the exact opposite of what it was meant to do long after it had passed from memory. Even as the Irish moved into cities and lost all connection with the land, the dream of owning a horse persisted.

The day after our tryst with Paddy Jack at Temple Bar market, Roisin took us to see the most striking manifestation of urban horse love, the Smithfield Horse Fair. Traditionally held on the first Sunday of each month, it was an open-air market on a cobbled road in the centre of Dublin where small farmers and itinerant traders would haggle with mainly working-class customers.

The market had long been famous for the spectacle of horses and unkempt ponies suddenly appearing in the centre of a large city to tempt men living in council estates. Quite often buyers lacked the means to stable the horses, so they could end up in parks or even tiny apartments. (Alan Parker's 1991 film *The Commitments* celebrated the tradition with a scene of a boy taking a horse into a lift, explaining: 'We have to. The stairs will kill him.')

Smithfield had lately become infamous for the lack of care and safety standards, with animal rights groups decrying the sight of horses being trotted or even galloped around the plaza. It was a throwback to a rougher Dublin that was now at odds with the city's more gentrified image and the Dublin Society for the Prevention of Cruelty to Animals had petitioned the city council to close the fair down for good.

By chance, we'd arrived at the first market day in 273 years where authorities had decided to tame it. A new Dublin City Council by-law had just mandated trading licences and outlawed riding. A large police contingent was on hand to enforce the regulations and stop any lad trying to show off his equestrian skills. A few dozen men and youths stood around holding their horses and looking sullen.

'You've come to the wrong place,' a man whispered to me when he saw our camera. He was a Traveller, an intriguing sector of Irish society (sometimes derided as 'gypsies') who continued a nomadic tradition of living in caravans. 'We had a proper market yesterday out in the countryside. No police to spoil things.'

The urban dream of owning a horse hadn't always been matched by an awareness of what caring for a horse involved. And in recent years more Irish than ever had become horse owners. From the mid-90s Ireland went through the most atypical decade in Celtic history: an economic boom. A country synonymous with poverty began experiencing growth rates averaging 10 per cent a year. Within a few years it was one of the richest countries in Europe. The sudden wealth kicked off a building boom, with new estates and flash suburbs springing up around the cities and holiday McMansions sprouting along the scenic coastline. It was as if Shanghai was creeping towards the Cliffs of Moher.

The boom started not long after Ireland joined the European Single Market, but that in itself couldn't explain Ireland's astonishing transformation from loveable old economic punchline into what commentators were calling 'the Celtic Tiger'.

Some thought it was the inevitable outcome of decades of wise governance. A strong education system, growing female participation in the workforce and model cooperation between management and unions had laid the groundwork for Ireland to release its long suppressed potential. A few grudgingly conceded the orgy of easy money and predatory lending sweeping the world from a dangerously deregulated international financial system could also have slightly overhyped things.

But perhaps the single most important factor was Ireland's decision to slash its corporate tax rate to just 12.5 per cent, lower than Hong Kong or even Singapore. Multinational corporations started flocking in and white-collar professionals began emigrating *to* Ireland rather than *from* it. (After the EU took in half of Eastern Europe in 2004, eager Poles, Lithuanians, Hungarians and Czechs also arrived hungry for work, leading this nation of emigrants to start complaining about being swamped by migrants.)

It was a fine old time while it lasted, with cashed-up young people in renovated boutique pubs discussing which distant country they would go to on holidays rather than forever. Even Ireland's richest rock group, U2, whose passion for helping the world's poor was matched only by their obsession with minimising tax, kept most of their commercial operations at home. (Patriotic sentiment has its limits of course. In 2006 U2 started moving operations offshore to the Netherlands where the tax regime was even lower.)

More importantly, every half-decent builder suddenly had the means to pursue the great Irish dream of owning a racehorse, or at least a share in one, by buying into a racing syndicate. It became quite the thing to cover your plumber's crack with a flash suit and invite all your friends to watch your horse race. So when the global financial crisis hit in 2008 and Ireland's economy went down the toilet, there were two striking legacies: a nationwide eyesore of half-finished housing estates and a bevy of builders with unwanted horses.

Most of the thoroughbreds, quarter horses, Appaloosas and Appalachians were sold. Some were euthanised. Astonishingly, many were simply dumped in public parks and vacant lots, the owners presumably imagining they could fend for themselves like wild horses of old. They couldn't. Raised in stables, fed high-protein meal and tended with medicine, they were ill equipped for the shock of winters in the open, abandoned and trying to survive on patches of park grass.

It's not known how many were dumped, but more than four years after the crash we could still spot scores of horses as we drove around Dublin. Small groups stood listlessly in large parks and half-completed estates. All looked sick and emaciated.

Occasionally we would see one lying dead on the ground. Animal welfare groups had been doing what they could to help, rescuing horses and trying to find new owners.

Now that Ireland was back to its traditional state of economic struggle, fewer were able to take on the responsibility of stabling a horse. Young people were once more looking at emigrating. Our hotel foyer was hosting a Canadian government exhibition touting employment opportunities in North America's most boring province, Saskatchewan. Queues of unemployed Irish stretched out onto the street. Stingy employers appeared to be relying even more on low-paid, overworked Lithuanians and Poles. Fast food cafes tended to have a staff of one: a young Slavic girl taking the orders then running out the back to cook them.

Belonging to a racing syndicate was now a burden, not a lark. We filmed a local race for some television colour. A ruddy-faced owner, John Seery, told us he had bought into a syndicate in the good times and was struggling to hang on to his share post-crash. To his dismay, others had simply abandoned their steeds.

'There was a lot of people involved in syndicates who just had money and it became a prestige thing you know? They thought like "This is great!" A lot of them horses were put down I suppose you know or they were sold off. A lot of them were sold off to England, a lot of trainers were left with a load of horses on their hands cause people just walked away, you know?'

He was horrified to think they may have ended up on his dinner plate.

'Oh when they were eating the horses oh it was terrible really. You know when we heard this it really puts you know a dampener on everything.'

It seemed obvious the economic crash had created a pool of abandoned horses for unscrupulous traders to slip into the food chain. The mystery was who had done it and how?

Fortunately for us, one man in the island's north had spent nearly two years trying to solve that mystery and was now willing to talk.

Dave and I drove to the frontier town of Newry, just the other side of what is now an invisible border between the Republic of Ireland and Northern Ireland. I hadn't been there since 'the Troubles' when British military checkpoints controlled the frontier and Belfast and Newry were effectively partitioned into Catholic and Protestant sectors. The checkpoints were lifted after the 1998 Good Friday peace accords and the only sign now that you've crossed from south to north is that speed limits switch from kilometres to miles and Euros are no longer accepted. Northern Island, being an autonomous province of Britain, has its own banknotes equal to the British pound.

We'd come here to meet Stephen Philpott, perhaps the most frightening animal rights activist any animal abuser could have the misfortune to cross. He was head of the Ulster Society for the Prevention of Cruelty to Animals (USPCA) and had all the nuggety scrappiness of that once conflict-riven province. As we walked into the office we could hear him barking into his phone about his plan to prosecute a top barrister and hunt organiser for neglecting foxes. He had already humiliated the man on Belfast television, releasing video he'd recorded of the animals' conditions.

Years later Philpott would himself be humiliated for defrauding the animal charity, casting a pall across his formidable legacy. In his time as chief executive he forged a fearsome reputation as an animal rights defender, not to mention a shameless self-promoter. Long before the horsemeat scandal broke he became suspicious that something was seriously out of order with the horse population and decided he was the man to do something about it.

'Come for a drive, I'll show you how it started,' he said brusquely.

He took us down a rain-spattered country road to a field where he'd had his lightbulb moment 21 months earlier.

'There was thousands of horses in the open, you know. This field here, I counted 38 horses. And they disappeared overnight! Well once that got onto our radar we made it our business to find out what was happening to these Irish horses.'

Philpott organised video surveillance of fields where there were large numbers of horses. It wasn't long before they spotted a large truck being driven into one of the fields. Three shifty-looking men climbed out, lowered the back and led the entire herd into the truck.

They kept spotting similar daytime harvesting of abandoned horses. USPCA officers and private investigators followed the trucks to remote properties where the horses were unloaded into crowded pens. Once they followed a truck to the Belfast port where it was loaded onto a ferry to France.

'There was a huge systematic hoovering up of horses going on. Horses like that were everywhere in Ireland. They were on the sides of roads, they were in fields, they were all over Ireland. Those animals systematically started to disappear.'

Philpott took us back to his house to watch some of the surveillance footage. A police car with two officers was parked in his driveway. He nodded a curt greeting and continued inside.

'I've had a lot of threats,' he said. 'These fellas come round now and then to keep an eye on things.'

He flipped open a laptop and played some of the raw footage. I was astonished by how thoroughly he'd followed through. As well as following trucks, his staff had secretly filmed an auction where the same characters they had seen collecting horses were buying more.

'We saw some very bizarre behaviour. We couldn't give an animal away, yet certain individuals were falling over themselves up at sale yards to acquire the same animals that we couldn't give away. Now to us that just did not make any commercial sense whatsoever and you would need to have been in the whole horsey world to actually understand what was actually going on.'

Philpott was fairly certain that what was happening in the whole 'horsey world' was a massive criminal conspiracy to substitute cheaper horsemeat for beef and foist it onto unsuspecting consumers. The problem was how to prove it.

He explained to me that Irish racehorses and showjumpers were legally shipped to England and France every day without any need for inspection. But if they were being sent for slaughter, the transporters were meant to show horse passports containing records of any relevant medication the animal had been given and a statement that the animal was intended for slaughter for human consumption. The idea was to keep dangerous drugs out of the food chain, such as anti-inflammatory drugs like Bute that are often given to racehorses but are harmful to humans. Since 2009 horses had been injected with microchips to prevent passports being switched.

Philpott knew the system was widely rorted. There simply weren't enough inspectors, particularly on night crossings, to check passports. Scores had been retrenched in the post-GFC recession.

He said the rewards for cheating were potentially huge. If you could pass off cheap horses that were unfit for eating as fit to be butchered for meat, a lorry load that cost 1000 Euros could be sold for 4000.

Philpott kept digging and finally, as the horsemeat scandal was breaking, found the key to exposing what was happening: an informant.

'When the USPCA developed their own source from with inside this criminal conspiracy, it became very apparent from him that in over a three-year period he'd never been stopped once, he'd never been checked on a boat, he'd never had his passports checked and he told us that on many occasions all that was ever done was a head count at the abattoir. No one ever checked the individual passports for the horses – and we believe him.'

The USPCA was still trying to gather enough evidence to launch a prosecution. But Philpott agreed to let me meet the informant. Late at night a private investigator he'd hired arrived at our hotel with a nondescript northern Irishman he introduced by the codename Green Grass. He'd been in hiding for weeks in fear of his life. We agreed we would not show his face and use an actor to repeat his words for broadcast so his voice could not be identified.

Dave had set up a mini-studio in his hotel room, with cameras arranged behind Green Grass's head and pointed at his hands, which were concealed with gloves. He was nervous at first, but eventually told us how easily the outfit he worked for had beaten the system. They had forged passports in case they were checked. But with cash-strapped governments on both sides of the Irish Sea cutting back on inspectors, they needn't have bothered.

'Some horses had passports,' he said. 'Any horses that needed passports – there was duplicate passports or whatever you want to call them – homemade passports sitting there to do the job.'

'Did anyone ever check these passports?'

'Never.'

'The whole time you were doing this, you were never stopped by officials?'

'Never. Not at the boat anyhow.'

For three years he'd helped transport thousands of horses out of the Belfast port to abattoirs in England. Officials barely glanced at the consignments. Some of the horses were so weak the gang dosed them with cortisone and Bute to survive the journey.

'So was there any horse you wouldn't take?' I asked.

'No. If it could walk up the ramp, if you could get it up the ramp, it would be on.'

He said the abattoirs never checked the condition of the horses or the passports.

'They'd take the passports, but they'd usually hand you back a bundle of passports.'

'Did you ever see any officials at the abattoirs?'

'Never.'

'All the abattoirs say they had no idea that they were using meat that shouldn't be used for human consumption.'

'They knew.'

Green Grass was cagey about who he was working with, but the private investigator told me later that some of the gang members were former paramilitaries from both the IRA and the Protestant Ulster Volunteer Force. 'Now there's no fighting they've been getting more into crime. Doesn't matter which side they were on. It's all about money. The worse thing that happened to them was peace. Now there's no border so they can't smuggle like they used to.'

Some of the substitution happened in Ireland. The most startling surveillance video was of an abattoir in the south. Philpott's men had followed horse lorries to the site and waited in the darkness as they were unloaded.

'You're now in the dead of night, and as if by magic, out of the darkness you see vehicle after vehicle starting to appear stuffed full of valueless Irish horses,' Philpott said. 'The next morning when we got back there, it was as if it had never happened. The abattoir was locked up. There were no horses there. All that was left was their hooves and their heads and their guts and the horsemeat had gone. So that was when we worked out what was actually happening. This was all to do with horsemeat. These animals were being spirited away in the middle of the night and the reason for that was their meat.'

The surveillance tapes hadn't been shown publicly before. Philpott had promised them to a local TV station first but said we could be the next to broadcast them. I was surprised he would give us such an international scoop. But I sensed there was a lot of embarrassment in Ireland about the substitution racket and some would rather not see how their own country had started it.

Philpott believed the authorities had deliberately ignored what was happening. 'In one fell swoop we have neglected an entire species of animal and we really all as welfarists, as a developed country, we should all be ashamed of that. Nobody cared. And that's the bottom line in this whole story. Nobody cared. Nobody bothered asking the question we asked: where are all the Irish horses going? In the situation that the Irish economy found itself, we loved money more. Money was more loved than the horses.'

We drove back to Dublin to fly out but unexpectedly there was one last thing to shoot. Pat Hyland, the only Irishman openly making a living serving horsemeat, had just got himself a racehorse.

He rang my hotel and from what I could glean over the course of 10 minutes of asking him to repeat himself, he had discovered that a horse he was planning to butcher was a thoroughbred. He was thinking of giving it a reprieve if it could win a race the next day.

'That sounds great, Paddy, we'd love to film it. Where's the race going to be?'

'*Poyndapoyn.*'

'Sorry?'

'*Poyndapoyn.*'

'Where is that?'

'*Poyndapoyn! POYNDAPOYN!!!!*'

'I'll get Roisin to call you.'

The race was a 'point to point', an Irish institution where young horses belonging to amateur trainers get a chance to compete in a steeplechase across farmland, riding from steeple to steeple or point to point. It's something of a nursery for future stars, or in the case of Pat's horse, a chance to avoid the chopping block.

We arrived at the race meeting to find hundreds gathering around the improvised course and dozens of bookies chalking up odds and taking bets. Pat was leading his horse out of a trailer to loosen it up for its make-or-break dash.

My ear was adjusting to his accent by now and I could almost understand as he explained he'd bought the horse for its meat but then discovered a French racehorse had sired him.

'It's just we were coming home along the road and we had his book you know and he had a very good breed of pedigree on him. But when the recession came a lot of lads didn't want their horses so they sold them cheap. We were going to kill him and then we changed our mind. My daughter said we'll give him a chance, and here it is.'

'So instead of becoming a horsemeat sandwich, he's a racehorse again?'

'That's right.'

'And what's his name?'

'Do Or Die Sullivan.'

The name didn't appear to be inspiring much confidence in the punters. Do Or Die's odds remained ominously long at five to one on the bookies' stand.

The bell sounded and Do Or Die Sullivan was off to a good start in his first ever race, pulling ahead to the front of the pack. Pat sucked in his breath with excitement then fairly ran to the other side of the field to watch him finish. I caught up with him just as the horses barrelled past the finish line. Perhaps it was first-time nerves or the steeples, but he'd finished a disappointing seventh. Pat exhaled deeply, his breath whistling between his teeth.

'Is it horse burgers for Do Or Die?' I asked.

'Nah, we'll give him another go,' he said. 'He had a big day.'

Lucky for Do Or Die Sullivan, the Irish still love their horses.

14. Reef Madness

The Spratly Islands, April 2014

> Go to their graves like beds, fight for a plot
> Whereon the numbers cannot try the cause,
> Which is not tomb enough and continent
> To hide the slain.

Fortinbras in *Hamlet*, Act 4, Scene 4

Philosophers have long despaired at senseless wars over random plots of land — in Fortinbras's case a tiny island. But not even Shakespeare could have imagined the 21st century variation: a multinational conflict over an underwater reef.

I wasn't pondering the philosophical ramifications as I hid in the bow of a Filipino fishing boat. I was more concerned about the three China Coast Guard ships bearing down on us.

We were trying to reach a rusting Filipino navy ship that had been scuttled on the reef. It was manned by a detachment of marines with the job of stopping China claiming the reef for itself. So China had laid on a siege to starve them out.

The China Coast Guard ships used water cannon to blast any boats trying to bring supplies from the Filipino mainland. Just the wake of the Chinese ships could sink smaller boats.

We'd spent days sailing around the South China Sea trying to sneak in from behind, but now their radar has spotted us they were coming at full speed around the reef to block us. My cameraman Wayne McAllister had packed and waterproofed the gear as best he could in case we were water-cannoned.

We ducked down in the hope they'd take us for a lost fishing boat rather than a charter carrying a foreign television crew. But the Chinese ships were racing towards us and the reef was agonisingly distant.

I was starting to wonder if this was a good idea.

*

The Spratly Islands are not the first place people think of as a flashpoint for the next big war.

Until recently, Western governments paid little attention to them and few Westerners had even heard of them. For the most part, they're not even proper islands, just submerged reefs and small islets without fresh water at the southeast of the South China Sea. But for decades Asian countries have been tussling over every rock and sandbar.

The Philippines, Vietnam, Malaysia and Brunei each claim large slices of the area. China and Taiwan claim the lot. The fight isn't so much for the reefs and islets but the vast oilfields around them. If China wins, it will be in prime position to start drilling. It could also become the gatekeeper to one of the world's most plentiful fishing grounds and busiest shipping routes, with more than US$5 trillion worth of goods transported through the South China Sea each year.

After 9/11 China took advantage of America's distraction with the War on Terror to start occupying the area, building artificial islands on top of submerged atolls, the dredging destroying the coral reefs around them. Troop garrisons, anti-aircraft guns and even runways followed, with China making clear it intended to occupy the entire island chain.

I'd been trying to cover this unseen, bizarre conflict for more than a decade. But no country had been willing to risk China's wrath by taking foreign journalists into the area. In 2007 the Philippine's Defence Minister agreed to fly us out to a military base on its main Spratly island of Pagasa. We could tour the base and explore a small civilian village next door. But as I was driving to Sydney airport the office rang to say the trip was off. The Chinese Foreign Ministry had learned about the trip and pressured the Philippines to cancel.

By 2014 the mood among rival claimants had changed. Diplomacy was going nowhere and China was using coast guard ships to try to seize Filipino territory. We applied to the Defence Ministry again and the answer was yes, we could go to Pagasa and had full permission to film the stranded marines … if we could get to them.

I flew into the Philippines resort island Palawan, with *Foreign Correspondent*'s staff cameraman Dave Martin to start the journey. Palawan is famous for its beaches and coral dives but it's also the main base for the Filipino navy to patrol the Spratly Islands. Stretching from the country's southwest to the coast of Malaysia, Palawan's entire western coast fronts the South China Sea or, as the Philippines call it, the West Philippine Sea.

The local Defence public affairs officer, a woman with the beguiling moniker of Lieutenant Cherry Tindog, explained what lay ahead. We could travel the next day on a ferry taking supplies out to Pagasa. After that it was up to us to try to reach the besieged ship. We'd have to run the blockade on our own.

The local authorities helped us hire a small fishing boat to follow the ferry to Pagasa then attempt to take us to the reef. We arrived at the port to find the ferry being loaded with provisions for the island's village: electrical appliances, canned food, bottled water and palettes of live goats and chickens.

The ferry looked well used and spartan. There were no facilities for passengers except a handful of tiny cabins and one toilet. But it was our only way to reach Pagasa. The first of more than 100 passengers were already bringing their belongings on to claim sleeping space on the wooden deck for the three-night journey. They were a mix of civil servants, military personnel and island residents returning from a break on the mainland.

The ageing boat instantly brought to mind headlines like 300 DIE IN FILIPINO FERRY DISASTER. Even so, Dave seemed genuinely remorseful the next morning when he started passing blood due to a mystery illness and a doctor declared him unfit to travel. 'Don't worry, you've dodged a bullet,' I reassured him.

I scrambled to find another cameraman and the China correspondent, Stephen McDonnell, agreed to send down the bureau shooter, Wayne McAllister, on the next flight. He arrived blinking in the harsh sunlight with a hastily assembled kit and just a vague idea of what the assignment was. But he was keen. Wayne was much sought-after for his camerawork and had a great knack for charming people, even if he occasionally frightened small children. With an imposing build, wild eyebrows and a long dark beard, he looked like a pirate thinking of joining the Taliban.

The ferry pulled out that evening, packed to the gunwales with supplies and passengers. As special guests, Wayne and I were allowed to cram our gear into one of the open cabins and half stretch out on hard wooden bunks. Most of the passengers lay side by side on mats on the floor. Those with hammocks claimed every post and railing on the top deck. It was hard to walk through the bodies to join the long queue for the toilet.

I lay uncomfortably on my bunk with a novel I'd brought for the journey, the only thriller ever written about the Spratly Islands. It was called *SSN*, code for nuclear-powered submarines. The blurb on the back cover summarised the plot. 'China has invaded the oil-rich Spratly Islands. The American response has been swift and deadly and the Third World War has begun.'

The story was ridiculous. It followed a US nuclear submarine, the USS *Cheyenne*, as it single-handedly destroyed the entire Chinese submarine fleet to 'liberate' the islands. The publishers had even turned the story into a video game, allowing nerds to stalk and destroy commie subs.

The author of the 1996 novel was the American thriller writer and right-wing military nut, Tom Clancy (although one reviewer suggested unkindly that 'Some tool bag author supposedly co-wrote it and then Tom Clancy passed by, took a shit on the manuscript, and called it "co-written"').

The book and game reflected Clancy's trademark certainty that US might could save the day. In reality it had been left to the smaller nations around the South China Sea to try to stand up, unsuccessfully, to China's slow invasion.

The Philippines' method of defence was to try to colonise their claim. In the 1970s the government decided to settle civilians on the island of Pagasa next to its military base to bolster its assertion of sovereignty, somehow persuading civil servants and their families to move to the middle of nowhere and pretend to be villagers.

Having a village in the Spratlys allowed the Philippines to declare its holdings a municipality, which it called Kalayaan, meaning 'Freedom Land'. There was even a mayor, Eugenio Bito-Onon, representing not only the village on Pagasa but the islets, sandbars and reefs around it.

The next morning we found Mayor Eugenio in the bridge fussing over details of the journey with the crew. He greeted us warmly, extolling the importance of his 'oil-rich' municipality to his impoverished country. 'We call Kalayaan the submerged Saudi Arabia of the Philippines,' he beamed.

Thin, bespectacled and poorly dressed, the mayor seemed nothing like the brash politicians you typically find in the Philippines. Living in Palawan, he'd decided to run for office in frustration at how little was being done to develop Kalayaan. His reward was the Philippines' poorest municipality and regular trips on one of its most uncomfortable ferries. He seemed an honest man in a country where politics was an entrepreneurial activity.

His main frustration was that politicians were giving him hardly any money to develop Pagasa, while every other country was pouring a fortune into bolstering its holdings. He flipped open his laptop to show us satellite photos he'd downloaded from Google Earth.

'This is Mischief Reef and it's an atoll. It's not even an island,' he said, pointing at a photo of a Chinese base being built on a reef the Philippines once claimed. 'The Chinese constructed first this fishermen's shelter. Later on, a three-storey-high garrison with a basketball court. There's already a wind generator!'

Malaysia and Vietnam had followed China's lead, building reef bases that would look at home in a James Bond film. One Malaysian installation even had luxury accommodation for diving. 'You see the premises of the hotel and you see the swimming pool and a jetty port?' he asked, pointing at another satellite photo.

'You don't have that on your islands, do you?'

'We just envy.'

The aerial photo of the mayor's island showed a dirt runway, an army barracks and a tiny village.

'This is Pagasa, our pristine, beautiful island waiting for development.'

On the ferry time passed slowly, with only the occasional dolphin pack breaking the monotony. Men squatted at the back of the boat playing cards or watching a small portable TV while their wives sweated over electric rice cookers as their children lay listlessly on the deck. The lower deck was like a crowded sauna. Even the Filipinos, accustomed to humidity and close-quarter living, were starting to despair. The top deck was almost as bad, the relief of a strong breeze tempered by the stench of fumes from the funnel. Some passengers had managed to switch to the small fishing boat we'd hired to follow us. It was now almost as crowded as the ferry.

By the third day we were approaching contested territory and a Filipino navy frigate arrived to escort us. At this end of the Spratlys the duelling parties were the Philippines and Vietnam. Mayor Eugenio offered to take us to a small marine base on the island of Parola, right next to a Vietnamese-controlled island. It was a relief to get off the boat into a rubber duck and motor in to the beach. A small detachment of marines greeted us on shore.

It seemed an awful place to be posted. The marines lived in primitive huts in total isolation and had a ration of six glasses of drinking water a day. But the mayor told us it was better than another base we could see on the horizon where marines lived in a hut on stilts on a sandbar.

Three kilometres away, on the island of Pugad, Vietnam had put in serious investment. Looking across the azure sea we could make out multistorey structures and a working harbour. The Philippines had once claimed that island too, but in 1975, when the marines left for a patrol, Vietnamese troops moved in and seized it.

Mayor Eugenio stared wistfully at the contrast between what Vietnam and the Philippines were spending. 'We belong to the poorest municipality. I'm not a national government chief executive. I believe that the national government should exist to support the local government. That's what I'm doing now, just really asking them to help me because my vision for Kalayaan is to develop this for marine fisheries, a special zone for marine fisheries and tourism.'

The marines staged a short drill for our benefit, firing at an imaginary enemy and even suffering imaginary wounds. Despite the proximity, the supposed foe wasn't Vietnam. One marine told me they were planning a goodwill lunch with their neighbours.

'So who is the enemy?' I asked.

'China.'

In the late afternoon we reached Pagasa, the largest island in the Spratlys chain and the 'capital' of Mayor Eugenio's municipality. Everyone climbed down ladders into small boats taking passengers to shore, mothers passing down babies and small children, Wayne passing down cameras, tripod and battery chargers.

The island seemed part tropical paradise and part rusting graveyard. We motored towards the beach past the hulks of old ships as I scanned for the jetty. There wasn't one.

'There's supposed to be a jetty, where you see here there's a causeway,' Mayor Eugenio said. 'Never finished. Since 1997!'

The shore water was too shallow for the boats to come in so we had to wade the last 20 metres carrying all our gear as crewmen and passengers lugged supplies and electrical appliances.

We walked down a bush track to the village administrative centre, a simple building with a meeting room, office and primitive shower. There was no guest accommodation but Wayne had thought to bring two one-man tents. After a dinner of rice and seafood, I set up my mosquito-proof tent on the grass verge outside and had my first good sleep in four nights.

The thud of disco music shattered the early morning stillness. Young council workers who'd come out on the ferry were starting the day with an aerobics class. Mayor Eugenio was already up organising an official ceremony. Two hours later a delegation from the adjoining military base and all 180 villagers assembled to raise the Filipino flag, sing the national anthem and hear his address.

The mayor had brought good news. The council workers would be installing a mobile phone tower. And they'd brought a very special guest.

'We have a visitor here with us. A doctor doing a medical mission for all in the village!' The villagers cheered.

Next to the gathering was a statue of the man who had started the Philippines' occupation of the Spratlys, Tomas Cloma. He was a 1950s fishing magnate who decided the uninhabited islands could be put to commercial use. So in 1956 he sailed out with 40 men into the 'West Philippine Sea' and took formal possession of seven islands. His original intention was to build a cannery to save his fishing boats having to waste time heading back to the mainland. But in an apparent Napoleonic moment he decided instead to become a sovereign. Four days later he issued a public notice declaring unwavering possession of the territory, which he named Freedom Land, with him as leader. He even issued postage stamps.

Taiwan and Vietnam went ballistic, claiming the unoccupied islands belonged to them. Cloma stuck to his guns, later renaming his kingdom Colonia. But things ended badly for him in 1972 when the Filipino dictator Ferdinand Marcos jailed him for impersonating an admiral.

His claim to the islands was never really taken seriously, but it did spur the Philippines on to start occupying the islands with soldiers and later civilians.

Nobody had taken much notice of the Spratlys at all until World War Two when Japan used some of the islands as forward bases. After the war it was a free for all. In 1947 the Nationalist government of China claimed ancient sovereignty of 80 per cent of the South China Sea, producing a map with 11 dashes along the coasts of Vietnam, the Philippines, Brunei and Malaysia. The Chinese Communists followed the same line after defeating the Nationalists and driving them to Taiwan. (For some reason the Communist map had only nine dashes, becoming known as the Nine-Dash-Line).

All this put China on a collision course with Vietnam, which argued that as the islands had been claimed by the French as terra nullius they were passed on after independence in 1954. Over the following decades there were frequent skirmishes between the Chinese and Vietnamese over the islands, some of them deadly. In 1998 the Chinese navy machine-gunned scores of Vietnamese soldiers occupying a sandbar called Johnson South Reef, even filming the massacre for propaganda purposes. While China claims the Vietnamese opened fire first, the film shows Chinese marines using anti-aircraft guns to mow down the Vietnamese standing in waist-high water as a voiceover proclaims: 'History will remember this moment forever!' (Vietnamese supporters keep posting the clip on YouTube to ensure just that.)

Just days before we left Palawan, a more restrained battle was taking place in the Paracel Islands north of the Spratlys. China was attempting to install an oil rig and its coast guard ships were using water cannon and ramming boats to keep the Vietnamese at bay.

The Philippines hoped its civilian settlement on Pagasa would help keep China at bay, but after 40 years it still looked like a Potemkin village. There were a few dozen simple huts on sandy tracks. In one of them we found the village schoolteacher, Jacqueline Morales, handwashing clothes after the gruelling journey.

'I'm so glad we are here in our home today,' she said. 'We can do what we want to do, unlike on the ship. It's so hot you get dizzy.'

Jacqueline told me she and her husband had moved here as a patriotic duty as much as for work. Having civilians here meant it was harder for China to seize the island. 'But I worry about what might happen,' she said. 'We know how interested they are in the island. Of course they can do whatever they want to do. And even if there are people here … well, I'll leave it in God's hands.'

Her two young daughters knew nothing of this. For them, Pagasa was paradise. We found them down on the beach swimming and giggling with friends. At the end of the beach was an old bunker the military had built in the 1970s when the base was established.

Mayor Eugenio appeared and showed us inside. Pointing to the thick wall he said: 'If you have one like this and you get hit by an M-16, you will not be hurt, because it's so thick.'

But the whole structure was lopsided, literally sinking into the sand. It was as outdated as all the other island defences.

We could hear a distant rumble from the outer reef. Mayor Eugenio said it was Chinese dredges. 'They crush the coral into powder and then use that as fillers for boats or something,' he said sadly. 'If you go there, there's no more rocks. It's just become turned into sand.'

It was clear that the Philippines was losing its battle to hang on to its holdings. While other nations were pouring money into their claimed territory, greedy Filipino politicians were spending as little as possible. Even money earmarked for development disappeared into officials' pockets.

'If I compare our development to the rest of the islands in the South China Sea I think the site for the west Philippines here is the least developed and sometimes you know that gives us frustration. Great frustration.'

It was time to start our journey to the besieged navy ship.

That night, under a full moon, Wayne and I waded into the water with our gear and piled into the ferry's small tender boat. It took us across the bay to the fishing boat we'd hired for the most dangerous part of the trip.

It was about 12 metres long, with a crew of six and a suspiciously well-dressed passenger I took to be a navy spook.

It was a simple wooden workboat with no creature comforts, not even a toilet. 'Just stick your arse over the side,' Wayne said helpfully.

I wondered why the crew would take the risk of confronting the Chinese coast guard. The Chinese had stopped the last three attempts to supply the ship, threatening to ram and sink the boats. But it was soon clear the crew saw it as a patriotic duty. They joined arms and began praying for a successful mission.

The captain told me the boat was fast and he was confident we could reach the ship before the Chinese saw us.

'They will not hurt us if we keep going, we don't stop.'

We headed out past the lights of Chinese dredges, working round the clock to strip the outer reef. I lay down on the deck using my backpack as a pillow but couldn't sleep. Next morning we caught sight of our destination – Ayungin Shoal.

In 1999, in a desperate bid to stop approaching Chinese ships from seizing the reef, the Philippine Navy scuttled the ship on top of it. Small detachments of marines had been manning it ever since. Now the Chinese had surrounded them.

We could see the old ship on the horizon. Further on were three Chinese coast guard vessels watching for supply runs from the mainland. We thought our plan had worked until the ships began turning in our direction. They moved quickly around the reef but our boat was at full throttle powering towards it. The coast guard ships were billowing exhaust as they tried to close the gap. It was going to be close.

Then suddenly we were in shallow water, the coral and rocks of the reef visible underneath us. The boat slowed down. The crew cheered. The Chinese ships pulled back. And we sailed up to one of the strangest things I've ever seen.

The ship, called BRP *Sierra Madre*, was an utter wreck, a decrepit hulk that looked like it could split in two at any moment. There were huge holes all over the side, where parts of the ship had just dropped off into the sea. There weren't just pockets of rust. The entire ship was rusted. It was like something from a post-apocalyptic movie.

The marines were ecstatic to see us, the first and only visitors since they'd arrived a month earlier. Most of them seemed to be in their early 20s, enduring what must be the worst posting in the military. But they were making the most of it. They brought us into the mess room where they'd prepared a banquet of fresh fish they had caught that morning.

The commander, Second Lieutenant Earl Pama, looked to be as young as his men. He apologised for the state of the ship. 'The government has plans to repair the ship,' he explained. 'They sent supplies and equipment for repair but were unable to get through because they were stopped by the Chinese coast guards.'

He showed us around the deck, warning us to walk on the rivets that covered iron beams. Everywhere else were huge holes. He said there had been bad accidents with men falling to the bottom deck.

The ship's interior was little better. There was no electricity for refrigeration or air-conditioning and it felt like the inside of a furnace. There were also clouds of mosquitoes and the constant scurry of rats. I thanked them for the offer of a cabin but told them I'd be sleeping on our boat.

The Chinese coast guard ships had now moved as close as possible to the reef, circling us like sharks and coming to within 200 metres of the ship. In contrast to the *Sierra Madre*, they looked new and comfortable, their closed windows suggesting air-conditioning throughout. Looking into his camera lens, Wayne could make out men with binoculars and cameras pointed towards us. I gave them a cheery wave but Wayne looked tense. He worked in Beijing and knew how Foreign Ministry officials could react if they saw a photo of him in this restricted area.

'At least I can say I had a Chinese visa,' he said.

The *Sierra Madre* had been a relic even before it had been scuttled. The US had used it to transport tanks in World War Two and the Vietnam War before gifting it to the Philippines. The ship's guns were now completely rusted and useless. The only thing that seemed to work was the radio. Two marines occupied themselves in the radio room but the others had little to do except find food. One asked if we'd like to see him shoot fish with his M-16. Lieutenant Pama intervened before Wayne could get the shot.

It was obviously hard to keep discipline on the ship. The men wore their uniforms loosely and were usually shirtless. One marine had shaved his hair into a mohawk. But there seemed little point in enforcing regulations on a stationary, rusting wreck. The men's role wasn't to prepare for battle with the Chinese, it was simply to be a part of an endless waiting game, the marines serving as human shields until the Chinese lost patience and went away. That didn't seem likely. China seemed confident of driving them out.

Lieutenant Pama showed me a video he'd shot on his phone as they came in to relieve the last detachment. The coast guard ships continually cut across the boat they were in, creating a wake that threatened to sink them.

'They moved close to us, about 20 metres, so we couldn't get in. They stop us by fronting the bow of our boat. The problem was, if we got hit, probably our boat would be damaged and the lives of my men would be in danger.'

The next morning the marines donned snorkels and masks and swam out across the reef to spear fish as a stationary Chinese coast guard ship watched. They came back with an impressive haul. But fish was losing its novelty as a meal.

'Every day we have fish!' a chubby marine named Staff Sergeant Alan Sisteros complained. 'I need something else on my tongue.'

His chance was about to come. The military had arranged a relief drop for that morning to coincide with our visit. A small plane appeared overhead and after circling dropped two large crates on the deck. One toppled over the side and Sergeant Sisteros was dispatched to collect it. I joined him on a raft as he paddled out to the booty, marvelling at the state of the ship as we moved around it, wondering how it hadn't already fallen apart.

Sergeant Sisteros hauled the box up on the raft, already savouring what it might contain. 'Maybe inside this box there's meat or beef!'

'Do you ever wish the Philippines would give you a slightly better ship to live on?'

He laughed. 'Ha! I cannot answer you, sir.'

Up on deck, knives came out to slice open the box. The contents seemed aimed more at morale boosting than blockade busting. Along with a case of drinking water there were boxes of Jollibee fried chicken, the Filipino equivalent of KFC. And cans of spam.

Sergeant Sisteros was soon ripping into the cans in unbridled joy. 'Spam bacon! This Spam bacon good!'

There was also a bag of letters from schoolchildren in Palawan, illustrated with crayon drawings of the ship.

One marine read a letter aloud and his voice began to choke. '"My dear soldiers. Thank you for heroically guarding our territory. You are our inspiration. We love you all."'

Everyone went silent and stopped eating.

'I feel sad and lonely,' he said through tears. 'But I'm proud to be here to defend our territory.'

We left at dawn, with our footage carefully downloaded onto USB drives and hidden in the boat's crevices. But the Chinese made no move to stop us. We passed them as they resumed their daily encirclement of the ship.

Two days later anti-Chinese riots broke out across Vietnam in protest at China's actions in the Paracel Islands. Factories with Chinese characters were burned to the ground. One man reportedly died when a Taiwanese-owned bicycle factory was torched.

As the months passed, China intensified its occupation, dredging around every reef it seized to build ever-larger military bases. China claimed it was merely building facilities for search and rescue operations. The US claimed satellite photos revealed it was installing surface-to-air missiles. By 2015 the US and Australia were flying military aircraft over them to challenge China's assertion of exclusion. Each time the bases warned them they were violating Chinese airspace.

In July 2016 the Permanent Court of Arbitration in the Hague shot down China's claim to the South China Sea, ruling there was neither an historic nor legal basis to the Nine-Dash-Line. China simply ignored the ruling.

By now the Philippines was losing the will to oppose Beijing anyway. The new President, Rodrigo Duterte, was more concerned with fighting his own citizens, encouraging police to execute suspected drug dealers and users. Stung by US criticism of the killing spree, Duterte announced he would tear up the US defence alliance and look for friends elsewhere. China was happy to oblige with promises of non-judgmental assistance. All it asked was that the Philippines negotiate directly with it on the Spratlys rather than side with the other claimants and the US.

China has emerged more determined than ever to occupy the South China Sea, while the US is just as determined to stop it. The new US President, Donald Trump, already threatening a trade war with China, has talked of a massive military build-up.

If China decides to seize any territory, the easiest target will be the rusting ship on Ayungin Shoal, a move that would trigger surrounding nations to go onto military high alert. The US response would be critical, but for the first time it has a leader who at best seems reckless and at worst unhinged. More than ever, the world could conceivably face war over tiny islands, islets, sandbars, rocks and underwater reefs.

15. I Am the Walrus

King George Island, January 2015

> **Whether it's in relation to the walrus population, whether it's in relation to penguins, you can have iconic species which can attract community interest.**
>
> Greg Hunt, then Australian Minister for the Environment, announcing new measures to crowd-fund Antarctic research, 11 October 2014

> **That f------ Greg Hunt thinks there are walruses in Antarctica. Er ... there are none south of Finland, Greggie.**
>
> @MikeCarlton01, Twitter

In fairness to Greg Hunt, any walrus that managed to make its way from the Arctic across the equator through the Southern Ocean to Antarctica would indeed attract community interest.

Critics might wonder why the minister named an alien species in support of his proposal. His staff might have been grateful he didn't nominate polar bears. But Antarctica has always been a confounding and confusing place.

While the Arctic was settled many centuries ago, it wasn't until the 19th century that people were even sure the Antarctic existed, let alone knew what kind of creatures lived there.

Numerous expeditions sallied south in the 18th century, led by formidable navigators like Captain James Cook, but all were defeated by storms and icepacks. It wasn't until 1819 that humans first set foot on the very tip of Antarctica, at a rather manky landfall that would later be named King George Island after the British monarch. At the time the ship's captain, William Smith, imagined he had sighted the mysterious Great Southern Continent. In fact, continental Antarctica was a further 120 kilometres south through ice-packed ocean. The island was at the tip of what's now called the Antarctic Peninsula, a finger of land, rocks and islands pointing up towards South America like a rude gesture. But with the discovery of King George Island, the door to the mysterious southern land had been opened.

A year later a Russian expedition led by Fabian Gottlieb von Bellingshausen stopped over on the island before heading south to claim First Sighting of Continent rights. The following year a sealing ship spent the winter on King George Island, clubbing and shooting seals for their skins while incidentally becoming the first humans to stay in Antarctica. Other hunters followed and by 1829 the entire seal population on the island had been wiped out.

It was not an auspicious start to humanity's relationship with Antarctica. But it set the pattern for the next century or so: claim territory and kill things while trying to avoid being stuck in ice. In 1819 Britain claimed sovereignty over King George and its neighbouring islands, naming them the South Shetland Islands and rolling them into its Falkland Islands dependency. Chile and Argentina claimed King George too, on the basis they were closest to it.

But nobody settled there. It was unthinkable. There was nothing to live off except the odd visiting seal. You couldn't even find a walrus.

I didn't hear of King George Island until 2014, when, like William Smith 195 years earlier, I stumbled across it. I was desperate to find a story in Antarctica, mainly because I'd never been there. (This, contrary to what journalists say when collecting awards, is by far the greatest motivation for travel.) There seemed to be only two ways to visit. I could go on a tourist cruise ship from South America to the Antarctic Peninsula to look at whales and icebergs, but that would be a marginal story far beyond the ABC budget. Alternatively I could get in line and wait years for a media spot on an icebreaker trip to a science base and do the same stories everyone else has done. Antarctica simply doesn't allow independent travel. You can't just catch a plane and stay in a hotel. It's just not possible. Or so I thought.

Then I read in Wikipedia that Antarctica had a town with an airport on an island called King George. Best of all, it had 'a small hostel capable of holding a maximum occupancy of 20 guests'.

On the spot I decided I was going there and it seemed there was a story waiting to be done. The island had once again become the gateway to Antarctica, but for science rather than seal slaughter. Thanks to its proximity to South America,

14 countries had set up science stations on the island. I had visions of crazy Russians popping over to the Chilean bases for pisco sours while Koreans cooked hotpot watching Germans count penguins. If Wikipedia was right, I just needed to book flights and hotel rooms.

Wikipedia is a trusted source for many influential people, including the aforementioned former Environment Minister and walrus enthusiast Greg Hunt. In a 2012 interview with the BBC, during a period of extreme bushfires, he reassured listeners that bushfires were a naturally occurring phenomenon and shouldn't be linked to global warming. His knowledge had not come from his department, which had advised the opposite. It had come from Wikipedia.

'I looked up what Wikipedia said for example just to see what the rest of the world thought,' he said. 'And it opens up with the fact that bushfires in Australia are frequently occurring events during the hotter months of the year, large areas of land are ravaged every year by bushfires, and that's the Australian experience.'

His comments were in response to the executive secretary of the UN Framework Convention on Climate Change, Christiana Figueres, suggesting climate change was causing intensified bushfires, prompting Prime Minister Tony Abbott to accuse her of 'talking through her hat'. (The insult missed its mark. When I later interviewed the Costa Rican diplomat she told me she hadn't understood what hat-talking meant.)

Whoever wrote the Wikipedia article on King George Island was talking through more elaborate headwear. It took some days of phone calls to tour companies and late-night calls to South America to establish that there was no hotel on King George Island or anywhere else in Antarctica. While there were regular commercial flights to the island during summer, they were only available for accredited science station personnel or to organised tour groups. And tour groups could spend a maximum of one night on the island (camping on ice) before transferring to a cruise ship. What I had in mind was technically impossible.

It would have ended there except my girlfriend, Brietta Hague, a new producer on the program, spoke fluent Spanish. Night after night she rang Antarctic institutes from Argentina, Chile and Uruguay before finally charming a particularly oily public affairs officer from Chile to agree to formally sponsor our visit, allowing us to apply for a spot on the plane. The one rider was the Chilean base would be full over summer and we'd have to find somewhere else to stay.

Night after more nights we rang Antarctic institutes in Moscow, Seoul, Brasilia, Lima, Warsaw, Beijing and Berlin, begging for accommodation so we could publicise their uniquely important scientific work. Germany told us we'd have to wait a year, while Brazil and Peru never answered. Russia, South Korea and China promised us a night or two, while the Polish said we could stay as long as we wanted, provided we could reach their base on an isolated bay on the other side of the island. (Doubtful.) It wasn't much but it was enough to present a dodgy itinerary to the airline to convince it we weren't going to freeze to death. I figured once we got there someone would have to let us sleep on the floor rather than turf us out in the snow.

And so, on a crisp summer's day at Punta Arenas at the bottom of Chile, in a triumph of hope over caution, we boarded a commercial jet with scores of scientists from a dozen countries to fly to Antarctica.

Accounts of the first trips to Antarctica told of unimaginable hardship: ships frozen in ice, slow deaths from exposure, and vague hints of cannibalism by survivors. Our trip had in-flight service. I tucked into the foil-covered airline meal with a choice of bad red or white wine as the plane flew over the Drake Passage. Just two hours later we were starting our descent.

The island looked like a giant black rock with patches of ice. We flew in low over the water towards the gravel runway then gasped as the plane aborted the landing at the last moment and pulled up sharply into the air. The pilot adjusted the plane's direction for the second attempt and the plane thudded onto the landing strip, bouncing past the wreckage of a military aircraft that weeks earlier had crashed on take-off.

A man stood beside the plane saying, 'Welcome to Antarctica,' as each passenger climbed down the steps. Brietta had come as producer, with Dave Martin shooting. We stood in awe on the runway, each holding the maximum luggage allowance of 20 kilograms, marvelling at the glaciers and ice-covered hills around us. We had finally made it. It was the height of summer and in the bright sunlight the temperature was just below freezing. I shivered with excitement as much as with cold.

A bearded, stressed-looking Russian, Valery Lukin, greeted us briskly and helped us with our luggage to his van. He was chief of the nearby Russian base, Bellingshausen, named after the great Russian explorer who first sighted the continent. He'd agreed to put us up for the first two nights for a modest fee to be paid in Euros. Antarctica is a cashless continent but as we pulled into the base I could see why the Russians needed the money.

Bellingshausen was a relic of a once glorious Soviet past. The USSR had been one of the main players in Antarctica, setting up large bases as Cold War footholds on the continent as much as for research. Investment in science had plummeted since the end of the Soviet Union. The base was shabby and underfunded, with few resources for scientists. But that meant it had plenty of spare rooms. We were given a small room each, with a single bed, a cupboard and desk. Valery said we could stay as long as we wished.

He took us to a dingy mess room in another building on the base to meet the other residents. About 20 men sat at laminex tables watching a fuzzy satellite feed of Russian television. The kitchen was on the side, with trays of unappetising stodge featuring an abundance of tinned cabbage, potatoes and spam. A few fat-covered cold cutlets sat unwanted on the side. Remarkably for Russia, there was no alcohol, just tea and instant coffee with powdered milk.

The men, mainly technicians rather than scientists, greeted me and Dave with marginal interest but paid close attention to Brietta, a phenomenon that would be repeated throughout our stay. Antarctica had a chronic shortage of women.

There was only one other female in the mess, a young German student named Marie Rümmler sitting with three colleagues from the University of Jena in Germany's east. The oldest of them, Dr Hans Ulrich-Peter, spoke fluent Russian. He explained he had been coming to the base to study penguins since 1983. Back then, his university was part of communist East Germany and the base belonged to the communist USSR, complete with resident KGB spies. With the end of the Cold War both countries had disappeared. East Germany had been absorbed into West Germany and the new capitalist Russia had inherited the former Soviet Union's bases. But the penguin program had continued.

'One reason is we have many friends here,' he said. 'And of course the culture is similar. It's a big difference to South America and China.'

The main South American base, belonging to Chile, was just a five-minute walk away. It was the hub for all the scientific missions as the Chilean air force ran the airport alongside it. The base was much larger and more comfortable than Bellingshausen and even had showers and wi-fi. But it was absolutely packed with scientists for the summer season, sleeping in shifts on bunks or crashing on the couches.

The base had been set up in 1969, a year after Bellingshausen opened. That was just before the Marxist Salvador Allende came to power in Chile and for a few years the base enjoyed fraternal socialist relations with Bellingshausen. The friendship continued even after the right-wing dictator Augusto Pinochet seized power. The brutal Antarctic environment dictated that neighbours put politics aside and cooperated if they wanted to survive.

Even today, with regular flights, constant supplies and more comfortable conditions, there was an unwritten law that different countries' bases helped each without question. As we arrived at the Chilean base there was a flurry of activity on the waterfront as a barge arrived with a container. Minutes later a mobile crane trundled down from the nearby Chinese base to unload it. Chinese officials in matching red parkas chatted to the Chileans through an English interpreter as the container was hauled onto shore.

Among the Chileans was a palaeontologist, Dr Marcelo Lepe, starting a stint as the base leader. Every month Chile rotated through a different scientist to coordinate research. 'You don't need an agreement at a high level to ask the Chinese for the crane to move your container,' he told me. 'With the Antarctic community something very special is happening. I really believe that we all feel under a different flag on this continent.'

It hadn't always been so cooperative. For much of the 20th century Western powers had scrambled to claim the continent with the same ruthless enthusiasm they'd shown carving up Africa in the 19th century. Bizarrely, Australia had the biggest of the overlapping claims, asserting sovereignty over 42 per cent of the continent, an area three-quarters the size of mainland Australia. But with no means of developing their territories or exploiting the minerals beneath them, the claims were essentially meaningless.

In 1959 the competing powers bowed to the inevitable and agreed to put their claims on ice. Under the Antarctic Treaty the continent was opened to all countries for scientific research. Aggressive military activity was banned and a moratorium was put on mining until 2041. But by 2015 the Antarctic Treaty was starting to strain. New technologies had in theory now made mining economically viable. China was rumoured to be mapping vast mineral deposits in anticipation of the moratorium's review. Even Marcelo Lepe had his doubts the spirit of friendship and pure scientific research would last forever. 'I worry about that. If just one country decides to exploit something, every country will try to exploit that resource. This will probably be the end of the Antarctic Treaty.'

While Chinese institutions are generally reticent to host foreign journalists, and I'd had a troubled relationship with the Chinese Foreign Ministry while I was a correspondent in Beijing, the Polar Research Institute couldn't have been more helpful. They were happy to let Dave and me visit the base as long as we were happy to sleep on a mezzanine above the dining room. Every bed would be taken.

The Great Wall station was the first Chinese base in Antarctica when it opened in 1985. Now there were six more across the continent. It seemed communist China was taking up the mantle dropped by the USSR.

A car arrived to take Dave and me the short distance along the bay to the base while Brietta stayed behind to organise the rest of our trip. The Chinese base was even better than the Chileans'. There were comfortable three-storey buildings with modern laboratories and a half-size basketball court. Chilean soldiers were playing a friendly match with the Chinese.

The food hall was a revelation after the Russian spam. It was like a gourmet Chinese restaurant with copious amounts of Great Wall wine.

The station chief, Ning Xu, was keen to be interviewed, explaining how good relations were with the other bases. 'It is very much like a community,' he said. 'We help each other. We live peacefully and harmoniously here for the purpose of scientific research.'

Things got a little frosty when I asked him about rumours of China mapping mineral deposits. 'We are not searching for minerals. We are mostly searching for animals and plants.'

When I tried to press the issue, he quickly changed the subject. 'You look very handsome and you are very approachable,' he said.

Now I knew he was lying.

We returned to Bellingshausen to find Brietta had organised for us to join a sea elephant hunt.

The Chilean Antarctic agency had been reluctant to offer us opportunities to film but Brietta had befriended some of the lower orders, who agreed to take us on something normally off-limits to cameras.

We headed out early morning with six scientists and a soldier named Luis Torres Molino who was in full commando gear. Luis was a diver with the Chilean Gendarmerie seconded to Antarctica to bring muscle to the scientists' work. Trailing behind him was a camera-shy hunter with a crossbow.

Luis explained the hunter would be shooting elephant seals with darts to get skin and blood samples. Then Luis would go into the herd to retrieve the samples. 'Don't worry, it won't hurt them,' he assured us. 'It's just like a pinprick.'

After a 15-minute trudge through the snow Luis spotted a herd in the distance and shouted excitedly. They looked like gigantic sea slugs, weighing up to three tonnes each. The hunter raised his crossbow and fired a dart straight into one of the biggest. It roared in anger as the others started snapping their huge jaws. Luis crept gingerly among them, ready to jump back if any lunged at him. Step by step he moved towards the dart, then grabbed it as one of them turned on him. He slipped on the ice as the seal snapped at him, recovering just in time to regain his footing and leap out of the way. A bite could have severed a leg, or at the very least given him a potentially fatal infection. But he came up smiling.

'A good sample, a very good sample. Nice!' he beamed.

They repeated the process until he'd recovered four darts with blood-filled vials.

A young Chilean scientist, Jolange Sara, began sorting the samples into test tubes to analyse in the laboratory. 'Here we have a sample of tissue, skin and fat which is used to check for contaminants,' she explained. 'An example of contaminants is pesticides and heavy metals.'

Even this far south, industrial pollution was making its way into the food chain. Rather than being a pristine natural laboratory, Antarctica was becoming an indicator of how humanity was damaging the planet. The most serious effect was climate change, or as Murdoch newspaper columnists would call it, 'so-called climate change'. You could see it all around the island. The Antarctic Peninsula was warming faster than anywhere in the southern hemisphere. The average annual air temperature had risen 2.8°C since the first bases were set up 60 years ago.

Luis took us out into the bay where they were collecting marine samples. It was stunningly beautiful. Two humpback whales surfaced in front of us followed by rafts of penguins. But the look of an ice paradise was deceptive. In the distance we could see Collins Glacier. It had retreated almost two kilometres since the 1960s. Where we were sailing had been solid ice when I was a boy.

That night, as we checked emails at the Chilean base, Solange whispered to Brietta in Spanish that a *científico muy importante* was sitting in the corner. That 'very important scientist', who looked like a spry Father Christmas, was Dr Peter Convey, the senior research scientist for the British Antarctic Survey. 'You should ask him about climate change,' Solange suggested.

Dr Convey was obviously something of a rock star to the other researchers, who flocked around him talking of their projects and asking his opinions. He was on his 17th trip to Antarctica, during which time he'd won the UK Polar Medal and founded the chief advisory body on climate change in the continent. He was happy to give us an interview. Unlike many scientists who had been cowed by denialist media, Dr Convey didn't hold back about what was happening.

'We have a very complicated system and we've pushed it beyond the bounds of what it's done naturally in at least several million years,' he said. 'We have essentially knocked the global climate system out of kilter. And I would say, rightly we should be scared about what's going to happen to humans.'

Dr Convey had little time for so-called sceptics, including an Australian columnist he said he'd heard of named Andrew Bolt.

'They're saying something that a government or a politician can pick up on a sound bite and could use to justify a vote-winning action like supporting a coal industry or not supporting the development of technologies that don't cause so much damage.'

While that was happening, the Antarctic ice sheets were breaking up, threatening to raise global sea levels by a metre within decades. 'Sea level is rising and whether or not you accept everything the IPCC [Intergovernmental Panel on Climate Change] says, the current rate of sea level rise is at the very top end of their probability ranges. You can question the contribution of the different possible causes, but sea level is going up.'

That became a theme over the coming days as we talked to scientists doing the painstaking, often dull work of measuring temperatures, ice cores, glacial retreat, pollution levels and animal populations. Whatever we'd heard about climate change, things were actually far worse. And nobody could tell how bad the future was going to be.

'Even if we stop now,' Peter Convey said, 'even if we miraculously could remove all of the CO_2 from the atmosphere and go back to square one, it's not automatic that the system would return to the original state. We've pushed this out of stability and in many ways we don't know where it's going. If that's not a serious problem, I don't know what is.'

It wasn't all gloom though. As we found the first Saturday night, Antarctic scientists like to party.

Normally the bases were dry, but as we sat watching a movie in the Chilean common room, word came that a shipment of alcohol had arrived. Within moments the movie was abandoned and cups of pisco and Coca-Cola were being passed around. Someone found a USB file of Latino dance music and the half-dozen women present were dragged up to salsa. A group of Russians and South Koreans appeared out of nowhere along with the German penguin researchers. The pisco flowed freely without any thought of rationing it for coming days. After an hour, the party moved next door to the Chilean Air Force base where scores of young airmen and soldiers began competing for the women's attention.

Brietta had insisted we keep our relationship a secret so the macho Latinos would accept her as the boss and not my *mujer*. An increasing number of Chileans began sidling up to me to ask if 'the beautiful woman' was single. 'Sure,' I said lamely. 'I'm sure she'd love to dance.'

Then that moment came when things pass from friendly to disturbing. Soldiers were hitting on Brietta and friendly gestures were suddenly drunken handling. I grabbed her and apologised that we had an early start. Three men tried to come out with us, one insisting he was too drunk to stand and Brietta should support him. We eased him off and kept walking to the Russian base. We had to push the door behind us to keep the most persistent admirer outside.

Early the next morning, with a pisco hangover, we went to church.

While the Russian base had been starved of funding for science, some rich businessmen had poured in money for salvation. On a hill above Bellingshausen stood the last thing you'd expect to see in Antarctica – a traditional wooden Russian Orthodox church.

It had been built in Siberia in 2002 from private donations, disassembled into logs and transported on the icebreaker that brings down the Russian base staff each year. The Church had even sent a full-time priest, Father Sophrony Kirilov, who lived in a container shed behind the church and ate at the base mess.

He was 38 and took his job seriously, conducting regular liturgies with the help of two believers from Bellingshausen. It was an extraordinary sight. The interior was decorated with icons and Father Kirilov was in full clerical garb, chanting and waving incense as he performed the Eucharist. All that was missing was a congregation.

None of the other Russian staff came to worship. The scientists were mainly atheists and the technicians and workers didn't bother. So Father Kirilov's main visitors were the odd daytripping tour group that came out of curiosity before returning to their cruise ships.

'Building a church is a quick job,' Father Kirillov told me sadly. 'It's educating the souls to love God and their neighbour that is a lengthy process'.

The Germans spent their days chasing penguins. We joined them on a long hike to a colony of Gentoos and Adélies. Adélies are the classic Antarctic penguin with black and white faces, while Gentoos have brightly coloured beaks. Dr Ulrich-Peter explained that rising temperatures were having a dramatic effect on their numbers. Adélies feed mainly on shrimp-like krill, which in turn feed on organisms under ice. As the ice retreated they were moving further south in search of food.

'It means less ice in winter, it means less diatoms, less krill and less penguins.'

Large Gentoo penguins, which feed mainly on fish, were taking their place. 'Gentoos hate ice. It means if there if less ice, it is an advantage.'

You could see the different diets from the different coloured penguin poo, or guano, that carpeted the colony. Swathes of foul-smelling red poo meant krill. But there was far more stinky white poo, which meant fish.

To find out exactly what the penguins were eating involved taking blood samples from several penguins. The method was even more startling than shooting darts into elephant seals. Dr Ulrich-Peter and his students raced after penguins with large butterfly-style nets, catching and collecting them while the captured penguins tried to peck the humans or beat them with their wings.

The pecks were manageable but the wings could hurt. Made of solid muscle and bone, they packed a serious punch. 'Gentoos are the worst,' Dr Ulrich-Peter grimaced as one pounded his side.

They held each penguin tight as the young student, Marie Rümmler, injected a needle in the feet to draw blood, trying not to gag on the stench.

Such is the glamorous world of Antarctic science.

I was starting to think of the scientists as unsung heroes, sacrificing all on the ice to collect real evidence while right-wing nut-job columnists sat on their fat arses in newsrooms googling denialist websites to produce drivel taken as gospel by equally thick politicians.

And there did seem to be a genuine spirit of cooperation surpassing any political or national differences.

We were keen to cross the bay to visit the South Korean base where we'd been promised accommodation. But even Antarctica has doofuses. On King George Island his name was Alejo Contreras.

Contreras was 53 and looked about 70, with white hair, a surly, grizzled face and a Robinson Crusoe-length beard. He was employed by the Chilean airline to arrange transportation for tour groups but seemed to have a pathological aversion to journalists, particularly women.

Brietta had tried to charm him into hiring us a boat to visit the South Koreans. His response had been to sneer and walk away. We tracked him down to the Russian base and I tried to persuade him to help us. Instead he called us troublemakers.

'You're not supposed to be here, you are breaking the Antarctic Treaty!' he snapped. 'Who invited you?'

I told him we were sponsored by the Chilean Antarctic agency, INACH. He would have none of it.

'I will call the Australian Antarctic Division and have you fired,' he shouted.

I had no idea what the man's problem was, perhaps extreme sexual frustration from years in Antarctica or haemorrhoids.

Brietta asked him what was wrong and he turned to me. 'You are not real men, you Australians. You hide behind a woman!'

As Brietta steamed at his insult I asked the Russians if they could help us out. As luck would have it, they were sending their barge to the South Koreans the next day to drop some supplies.

Dr Ulrich-Peter warned against it. 'The barge is in terrible condition and the driver is a drinker,' he said.

We decided to chance it.

The next afternoon we stood on the rusting barge as it chugged over the bay. The weather started to turn but we were used to constant changes and confident it would improve for the return journey.

The Korean director, a forty-something woman called Dr In-Young Ahn, met us at the base wharf and showed us around the base. It was even nicer than the Chinese station with heated toilet seats, a hydroponic room to grow fresh vegetables and perhaps the best mess room in Antarctica. We wolfed down chicken hotpot, tofu stew and kimchi.

Dr Ahn obviously took great care of the welfare of staff. There were even small bottles of shampoo in each hot shower. About a third of the scientists were women. That was a big change from the early 90s when Dr Ahn spent six months at the King Sejong base and there wasn't even a ladies toilet. She hadn't just been the only woman there. She was the first Korean woman on the continent. Now she had become the first Asian woman to be running a station.

'So yes, it's definitely unusual,' she laughed.

She loved Antarctica but said it could sometimes feel like a prison. On this side of the bay they were often trapped for days by bad weather.

'Of course it depends on how you think that this place is. It depends on your mind. You could be happy or you could be very depressed.'

We were about to find out. The Koreans offered to take us back in a Zodiac inflatable but the weather suddenly closed in. High winds whipped up whitecaps in the bay, making it too dangerous to cross. The Koreans had good reason to be cautious. A few years earlier one of their boats flipped over in a storm and two staff died in the freezing water.

We were stuck in the base along with all the other staff, killing time playing pool or hitting balls at the base's indoor golf range and sleeping on couches in the rec room. We soon began to wonder if we'd make it back in time for the return flight to South America.

Some scientists call it the A-factor, meaning the Antarctica factor. Whatever plans you make, Antarctica will change them. It's a philosophy of acceptance and patience. But after three days trapped in the base I was starting to feel stir-crazy.

Eventually the weather cleared enough for Dr Ahn to nervously give clearance for a boat to take us across the bay. I was excited to be back at Bellingshausen, right up until the dinner of spam and cabbage.

By chance it was *banya* night, the weekly traditional Russian sauna. In a shed behind the base the Russians had rigged up a diesel heater to steam up a small wooden cubicle. In groups of two and three they went in naked to sweat out the week's dirt and beat each other with birch branches to get the circulation pumping. It can feel like being in a bad prison movie but I was used to it from my time as Moscow correspondent. What I wasn't used to was the next step: a compulsory dive into a large outdoor tank of freezing water. Not wanting to look a complete wimp, I took a dive-bomb ... into an outdoor pool in Antarctica. I fought back the urge to scream in pain. What came out instead was: 'Beam me up, Scotty!'

It was three days more before we could leave. Fog rolled in and the scheduled plane couldn't land, twice turning back after leaving Punta Arenas. When it finally arrived, I was ready to leave. The Russians would be there another four months before an icebreaker arrived for the long trip home.

I was grateful to have come to Antarctica but realised it took a special person to live there. It's a hard, demanding and often thankless place to work. I still think of the scientists as heroes.

And of climate change denialists as morons.

16. Neighbours

Cuba, July 2015

> I don't care if the polls show that 99 percent of
> people believe we should normalise relations in Cuba.
> Democracy has to come first.

Republican Senator Marco Rubio, December 2014

> It had to do with Cuba and missiles, I'm pretty sure.

White House Press Secretary Dana Perino, admitting she hadn't heard
of the Cuban Missile Crisis, 26 October 2007

Ralph Kaehler, a lanky slow-talking cattle breeder with one eye on the road and one on his watch, one hand on the steering wheel and another clutching a cellphone, was a man in a hurry.

'Okay, just let me know when the visas are approved. I know you're trying real hard. We sure appreciate your efforts. Toodaloo!'

The clock was ticking on Ralph's plan to fly to Havana and the Cuban Foreign Ministry was processing his application slower than the corn grew in the fields around him.

'I'm still pretty sure we're going to be able to join you in Cuba,' he told me as we drove through rural Minnesota to one of his endless business meetings. 'The folks in the trade section are doing their best and it takes time, but we always get there in the end.'

'Ya got that right!' I said, mimicking the slow drawl of the country bumpkin characters from the film *Fargo*.

'Aww, now I told you that was our neighbours in North Dakota,' he laughed. 'We don't talk like that round these parts.'

Ralph did a good line in folksy hayseed but it masked a razor-sharp business mind that had seen him challenge the US trade embargo on Cuba.

In 2002, at the height of a periodic clampdown on contact, he joined a Minnesota trade delegation to Havana. The then governor, former world wrestling champion Jesse Ventura, defied the State Department to take down a group of farmers and agribusiness leaders to meet the Cuban dictator, Fidel Castro. Ralph brought one of his top breeders on the plane – a shorthorn cow called Minnesota Red – and presented it personally to Castro at the trade show.

El Jefe took an immediate shine to Ralph and his two sons Seth and Cliff, aged eleven and thirteen. So began a bizarre friendship between a geriatric Marxist revolutionary and a devout Minnesota farming family.

'We've met with President Castro probably five or six times,' Ralph said proudly.

'What's he like?'

'Well, to have that level of leadership that long, he does have a natural presence about him. He is very dominating in a conversation because he's quite confident.'

Then he added: 'You know, there's a real good chance we could all meet him in Havana.'

I'd come here to meet Ralph and his wife Mena at the start of a planned shoot in Cuba with the loose working title 'Ralph goes to Havana'. President Obama had just announced an historic breakthrough in relations and the Kaehlers were keen to take advantage of it.

That night at their farmhouse, they played me a VHS tape of their first meeting with El Jefe.

It showed Ralph and his young sons displaying Minnesota Red to Castro, who questioned them through a translator about feed and costs for the cow.

'Castro was a farmer so he's very interested in the nitty-gritty,' Ralph whispered to me.

Governor Ventura and corporate executives waited in frustration in the background, as Castro continued to chat with the Kaehlers. He gently patted the boys' heads and invited them to the official table as he signed the first US cattle import deal since the revolution.

Most remarkably, Castro deviated from one of his marathon orations to include the boys in his speech, declaring it a turning point in history. 'They are proof of the fact that our relations will be lasting relations,' he announced. 'And our trade will continue to increase for we are already negotiating with the future generation of American farmers.'

Ralph fast-forwarded to other highlights of the trip: Castro letting the boys sit in the back of his official car, sending them to a water park to swim with dolphins, and even having them sit next to him at a concert by the Buena Vista Social Club.

Watching the tape, Mena's eyes filled with tears of maternal pride. Even Ralph started choking up.

'It's changing our national policy,' he said. 'You know it helped push it. He's the coolest world leader we've met with.' Then he laughed at the strangeness of it all. 'Cos there's so many of them that we've sat down with, ya know?'

Ralph began a brisk trade with Havana, sending animal feed and embryos to improve the quality of Cuba's cattle, all the time navigating the US State Department's interference and tortuous export restrictions. Almost every time he flew down, Castro made time to meet him, once summoning him from his hotel after midnight.

Ralph had to stop exporting in 2008 after the global financial crisis crippled Cuba's tourism industry, leaving the government unable to pay.

Now, in 2015, he was planning to restart the trade, all thanks to President Obama's recent pledge to roll back the Cold War relic of the US embargo. On 1 July Obama announced the US would restore diplomatic relations and he would press Congress to relax the suffocating trade restrictions.

'Instead of supporting democracy and opportunity for the Cuban people, our efforts to isolate Cuba despite good intentions increasingly had the opposite effect, cementing the status quo and isolating the United States from our neighbors in this hemisphere,' Obama said in his address. 'The progress that we mark today is yet another demonstration that we don't have to be imprisoned by the past. When something isn't working, we can and will change.'

The embargo, known in Cuba as *el bloqueo* (the blockade), had started soon after Castro led the overthrow of the dictator Fulgencio Batista, whose brutal regime had been supported by the US government and bankrolled by the US mafia.

The 1962 Cuban Missile Crisis cemented Cuba as the enemy. The US nearly went to war over Soviet efforts to place nuclear missiles in Cuba.

The embargo continued, with some exemptions for food, agricultural commodities and medicine, even after the US opened trade with its old communist foes China and Vietnam. Right-wing Republicans refused to budge while an island 145 kilometres from Florida remained communist. Cuban exiles in Florida ensured any presidential candidate deviating from the embargo would face electoral slaughter in the state. And Ralph thought that was just plain stupid.

'If our kids acted like our governments with the embargo you would take them back in the room, give them a swat on their butt and tell them to straighten up and play better,' he said. 'Heck, even in a marriage you don't agree with your spouse on everything! But that doesn't mean you quit talking to them full-time. You have your days where you may not. But we need to normalise our relations, open up trade, be a good neighbour and keep things safe. I mean it's going to be better for both countries.'

If Obama was opening the door, Ralph wanted to be the first one in. 'As our trade opens up, Cuba will be in our top 20 trading partners quite easily,' he predicted. 'Potentially top 10 in many of the main food products. Anyway, I hope we see you next week in Havana.'

While Ralph waited on his visa, we flew down to Cuba to see how much was really changing.

*

I had last been to Cuba in 2000 when I was the ABC's Moscow correspondent. Russia ended all the Soviet subsidies after the breakup of the USSR, sending Cuba's economy into freefall. But there were still cheap weekly flights from Moscow to its former client state.

Fifteen years later, getting there from Cuba's next-door neighbour was more difficult. The US still had criminal sanctions against visiting as tourists, though thousands travel there anyway under 12 exemptions, including religious activity, humanitarian work, cultural interchange and visiting friends. (Tour agencies simply ask Americans which exemption they want to pretend they're travelling under.)

We chose to fly through Mexico, Brietta producing and Dave shooting.

Starry-eyed leftists often think of Cuba as the true socialist paradise, enduring economic hardship only thanks to the crippling US trade embargo. But any twit can see the stifling bureaucracy as soon as you reach the airport. There was a two-hour wait at customs as they inspected every centimetre of our gear, even photographing parts they found suspicious. Our drone camera was immediately confiscated with a promise we could pick it up when we flew out. (We would never see it again.) The only distraction in the sweltering heat was the unique uniform for female staff; short military skirts over lingerie-style patterned tights that looked like a bulk sale from a 90s Frederick's of Hollywood catalogue.

Our fixer Josue Lopez met us at the exit. As with any shoot, we'd depend on him to guide us around, translate for me and find people to interview. In an authoritarian regime like Cuba, fixers were under extra pressure, balancing the constant requests from journalists to speak to dissidents with safeguarding their own futures after the foreigners flew out and left them to face the consequences.

Josue was in his late thirties and looked like a skinny Josh Brolin. He had a goatee beard with a Marlboro Red permanently jammed in his lips. He'd been working non-stop for foreign media coming to see the 'new' Cuba and appeared exhausted. But he was keen to work on our story.

'This Ralph Kaehler seems like a cool guy,' he said.

And he was glad that for once his clients didn't want to spend all their time chasing dissidents.

'I don't think much of those guys,' he said. 'They're not sincere. They make a lot of money from America out of being critics.'

Josue told us Cubans weren't particularly upset about the lack of Western-style democracy. Their frustration was over how hard it was to get by. State wages paid barely enough to eat. People wanted opportunity. And young people in particular wanted to be connected with the outside world. 'Getting good internet here is a nightmare,' he said.

My main memory from 2000, apart from the amazing colour and vitality of Cuban people, was the sheer drabness of the service economy. Outside the restricted tourist resorts, it was a wasteland. Shop counters were empty. Meals in state-run restaurants consisted almost solely of rice and beans. One 'Chinese' restaurant served rice and beans with soy sauce.

That at least had changed. In 2008 Castro handed over power to his 'younger' brother Raul, now a mere slip at just 84 years of age. Raul agreed to loosen the socialist economy to encourage private farming, and farms were selling fresh produce to new private restaurants.

'I'm going to take you guys to one of the best restaurants in Havana,' Josue promised.

We checked into our hotel, the former mafia-run Capri where US mobsters partied right up until Castro's guerrillas stormed the foyer on New Year's Eve 1958. A European hotel chain had just refurbished the 1950s high-rise to cash in on a post-GFC tourist boom. As in almost every hotel and *casa particular* (private homestay), every room was taken.

Josue took us into the old city to hire a car for the night. There were scores of 1950s American cars queued up waiting for passengers. Left over from before the revolution, the classic cars had long been a fixture of Havana's tourist spots. Now they were all over the city. Josue explained that people were buying up old cars around the countryside to turn into private taxis for both tourists and locals. The owners somehow managed to turn the rusted bodies into gleaming classics but the engines were nearly always ripped from Russian Ladas or Zhigulis.

We cruised around in an open-top Buick along the sprawling Havana waterfront called the Malecón, past hundreds of people promenading or dancing in the twilight, then turned down potholed streets surrounded by beautiful but crumbling 19th century buildings. The old city seemed in even worse shape than I remembered. 'The problem's the bureaucracy,' Josue said. 'It takes forever for anything to be fixed.'

The driver took us down a narrow alleyway barely wide enough to pass through and dropped us at a new restaurant called O'Reilly 304 after its street address. Beans and rice weren't on the menu. The dishes were fabulous, inventive and made from fresh meat and vegetables. The ponytailed barman, Wilson Hernandez, was cranking out an array of cocktails from Cubanitos (rum and clamato juice with celery, coriander, lemon, pepper and celery bitters) to his own inventions like Havana London (cranberry pieces, lemon peel, gin, tonic, curacao, lime, rum and star fruit). 'This is our revolution,' he joked.

Josue then took us to the most amazing nightclub I've ever seen.

Called FAC (*Fabrica del Arte Cubano,* meaning Cuban Art Factory), it was a disused cooking-oil factory converted into an art and entertainment space. Models paraded new fashion designs, intellectuals pondered photo and painting exhibitions, bohemians gyrated to house music in the dance hall or watched old American silent films in a small cinema. The Saturday night crowd was almost exclusively local. There was hardly a tourist in sight.

Everyone I spoke to was excited about Obama's speech. We interviewed two music producers, Raidel Garcia and Tomas Hernandez, decked out like Newtown hipsters with gelled hair and oversized glasses.

'It's good that there are eyes on this new Cuban society,' Raidel said. 'This society is a bit different from the traditional one and a bit more open-minded. I tell you what. Cuban food is delicious, exquisite. Exquisite! I encourage all American tourists to come and delight themselves with Cuban food. There's no need for McDonald's. There's no need for Burger King. There's no need for Domino Pizza.'

Some tourists were flocking to Cuba to see it before it was ruined, thinking Obama's announcement would soon see Havana littered with American chain stores. But not even young people seemed to want that. And with the rigid socialist bureaucracy still in control, I thought it unlikely any opening, whenever it came, would see a flood of permits for McDonald's on the Malecón.

On the drive back to the hotel, we saw crowds of young people on a small hill peering into cellphones. 'The government's just started building public wi-fi spots in the last few months,' Josue explained. That was quite a change from 2000, when the only way to access the internet was to book a computer at the congress library. And you had to be a foreigner.

The regime was still nervous about the web. Many sites were blocked and home internet was almost unknown. But officials were cautiously freeing up access to appease public demand. Josue said the number of wi-fi spots was growing every week.

Some change was agonisingly slow. We had nothing planned to shoot the next day so Josue invited us to his farm outside Havana. As good as the money was from fixing, his real passion was to live on the land. He was raising goats and had just bought an Arabian horse. But developing the farm was a trial. Thanks to both the embargo and Cuba's byzantine import rules, there wasn't a single hardware story in Havana. Josue couldn't even buy fencing tools, and it was almost impossible to find basic items like fertiliser. Farming was organic by necessity, which meant it was incredibly labour-intensive. And Josue spent every Sunday labouring.

I wanted to know what the old guard thought of Obama's pledge, so Josue took us to meet a neighbour, an octogenarian called Niño Catalino, which strangely enough means 'cheery boy'. He lived in a simple dark house with ancient furniture. He'd spent the 1950s fighting the Batista regime and showed us a portrait of him as a handsome young revolutionary, posing for the camera like a matinée idol. He was now almost completely deaf but judging by his reaction to Brietta still had an eye for the ladies. 'Who is this lovely *chica*?' he schmoozed.

Before the interview Josue gestured to him that his fly was open. 'No matter,' he laughed. 'The cage is open but the bird is dead.'

'What do you think of Obama?' I asked.

'Hehh?'

Josue repeated the question, loudly.

'Hehh?'

The next day we drove three hours out of Havana to the tobacco-growing centre Viñales. Capital cities are rarely a true indicator of what's happening in society and I wanted to see the reality of life in the countryside. The roads were as bad I remembered, but one change was striking. There were few of the social realist billboards that used to ring the highways, and the ones that remained were old and fading. Perhaps the government had finally acknowledged that people were more interested in making money than revolution.

The town of Viñales was idyllically picturesque, with small brightly painted cottages and families sitting on verandahs smoking cigars and chatting as their children played. But it looked desperately poor, with horse-drawn carts rattling down the streets alongside Russian cars.

We moved into a small guesthouse run by local farmers. Our choice wasn't entirely random. An Australian journalism student, Libby Hogan, who was doing a stint on *Foreign Correspondent* as an intern, had stayed with them on holidays the previous year and said they were 'a beautiful family'.

Like everyone in town, they were trying to supplement their meagre income with tourist dollars. The family had scraped and borrowed to build a small house next to their home. They were slowly building a second house opposite, but lack of money meant they had only just finished the walls.

The women in the family clearly ran the show. The mother, Kenia Carriles, fussed over us while her daughters and niece brought us an array of home-cooked food grown on their farm.

For the equivalent of a Yankee dollar each, she made us mojitos. For an extra dollar, we could have a hand-rolled Cuban cigar that would cost $50 in Australia.

It was obviously an extremely close and loving family, the girls giggling and teasing each other before retreating to their house to look after Kenia's husband, who'd been stricken with sciatica, and his father who everyone called Abuelo, 'Grandpa'. Kenia seemed a devoted housewife but told us she was a trained biologist. The state still provided good education and free health care. But there was just no way to survive on the wages.

'The economy is always the same,' she said. 'We don't have rights, no matter how hard we work, because of the embargo and the lack of commerce with all these countries. The economy affects everything. It affects everyone, even the children.'

The next day they took us to their 60-acre farm. Unusually for Cuba, it had stayed in the family after the revolution rather than being joined into a large collective farm. We soon found out why. The land was completely isolated. It was a half-hour drive to the nearest road junction. Abuelo appeared with two bullocks and a cart to take us three kilometres into the bush.

We trundled along the dirt track, Kenia pointing out the different crops they grew. In the steamy heat, it felt and looked like farms I'd seen in South-East Asia. One of their main staples was rice. 'We harvest it every year,' Kenia said. 'We collect four to six hundred pounds of this rice. It's for our consumption. We don't sell it. It's for our tourist business.' Then she sighed. 'I would like to have a more modern way to farm.'

After the economy collapsed in the 1990s, Cuba started to run out of food. Now having to import most of the country's needs, the government was offering land grants to people to grow crops. It promised tools and fertiliser and animal medicine. They rarely came.

Like all *campesinos*, the Carriles improvised, making their own tools from scrap metal and wood. We watched Abuelo raise a long pole, with a machete tied on the end, to the treetops. 'This machete is to cut down foliage to feed the pigs because they don't have any other food,' Kenia explained.

At 79, Abuelo still worked up to 12 hours a day on the farm. He was a slight but strong man with a bald head and gentle eyes. He took immense pride in providing for his family.

'I don't have any money. I eat what I grow,' he said smiling. 'It's what I will always do. As well as help others.'

For all the hardship they were suffering, the Carriles were no dissidents. They revered Fidel Castro as the father of the revolution and were overwhelmed and slightly nervous when I told them we hoped to meet him.

Back at their home, Abuelo showed us medals he had earned in the revolution. He hadn't been a fighter but he had sheltered Castro's rebels, knowing he would be killed if they were discovered. He had hated the Batista regime since he was seven years old and his family was thrown off their land by the dictator's cronies.

'It was dangerous. You couldn't speak out. They would hang you from a tree. We had three friends who were dumped in the sewer in Tortuga.'

His eyes started to well with tears. 'I feel pain for those who could be alive and who are not. We have them in our thoughts always. What a great joy the revolution was! It was a great joy for the Cuban people.'

While the US had backed Batista, tried to invade Cuba to reinstate him and had spent half a century trying to destroy the Cuban economy, the Carriles felt absolutely no ill will towards Americans.

'Our problem is not with the American people,' Kenia said. 'They are welcome to come and discover Cuba. The issue is with the US government stopping trade so our farms and businesses can't prosper.'

We headed back to Havana the next day. Ralph and his family had finally been given their visas.

Standing at the airport to meet them, we came face to face with a socialist dickhead.

'You cannot film!' he shouted.

I showed him our filming permit.

'You cannot film here!'

'Yes we can.'

'No you cannot!'

Ralph came through the exit with Mena and their two sons, Cliff and Seth. The young boys who had befriended Castro were now 23 and 25 and had brought their girlfriends Shelby and Bailey.

'Well it sure is great to be here,' Ralph said. 'What do you want to do first?'

We wanted to film them driving into the city but their nervous guide wouldn't allow it. So we met them at the hotel and toasted with mojitos to a successful visit.

The government wouldn't let us film any of their meetings.

This was one of the strangest things about Cuba. It's an incredibly vibrant culture with the friendliest, most passionate people you could meet. But they're governed by dull, unimaginative communist bureaucrats who could fit seamlessly into the middle management of a Soviet tractor factory.

Finally, the minders agreed to let us film the Kaehlers at a stud farm, after they finished a meeting with trade officials.

It was a special moment. To Ralph's surprise, Minnesota Red, the cow they had presented to Castro, was alive and well and living there.

'That's the one that was in the video with Cliff and Seth,' Ralph said excitedly. 'And that's her daughter and that's her son. So you can see they've adapted to the Cuban environment. Most cows don't make it to be 13 years old. We're quite surprised that she's still going. For us it makes us feel good. It shows our cattle can adapt, but to have this longevity, it shows it was the right selection genetically for Cuba to help them improve their animals.'

Ralph was still passionate about transforming Cuba's stock. But despite his best efforts, little had come from his trip. Even with the tourist dollars the Cuban government simply didn't have the money, and for all Obama's rhetoric, the embargo was still firmly in place. US exporters were even forbidden to make direct payments to Cuba. Everything had to go through a third country.

'We've had some great meetings and we've definitely got interest,' Ralph said. 'We heard from the Cubans, they love the products we introduced to them. Unfortunately, they're not buying them right now and the Ministry of Foreign Development and Trade has made it very clear the lack of credit and the third country banking is being a huge barrier to them buying more.'

Despite Ralph's many hints, there was no sign of another meeting with Fidel. Now 88 and in poor health, he rarely appeared in public and never gave interviews. It was obvious the authorities weren't going to let a foreign camera crew shoot a spontaneous meeting. The era of the Castros was finally nearing an end.

But after a week in Cuba, that part of our story was no longer the focus. I wanted Ralph to meet the Carriles.

On their last day in Cuba, the Kaehlers agreed to make the long trip to Viñales to have lunch with a farming family that was so different to theirs yet uncannily similar.

We arrived to find the whole Carriles family waiting nervously outside their house to greet us. None of them spoke any English and Ralph's Spanish — 'just enough to get me into trouble and get me out again!' — was little better. It didn't matter. Within moments they were embracing, chatting and laughing with Josue and Brietta running between them doing simultaneous translations. Mena and Kenia were congratulating each other on their families and crying.

Abuelo had gone to the farm the day before to collect one of his prized pigs. It had been roasting on a stand over hot coals since dawn. Cigars and mojitos came out as he sliced off pieces for the guests.

'I love it!' Ralph cried. 'It doesn't get any better than home barbecue.'

Kenia proudly led them inside for a feast. 'Here we have a delicious meal for you. All the produce is from our farm.'

Lunch was epic, course after course of fresh food. I dreaded to think how much the family had spent and knew the worst insult I could give was to offer to pay.

Ralph sat contentedly, a farmer savouring another farmer's bounty. 'If we had US officials here having this meal, I know what they would say when they left – we need to end all the animosity – and the same with Cuban officials. If they were sitting at the tables of regular families, I think it would make it easier for both of them to get rid of, I don't know, for lack of a better word, some of the obnoxious rules.'

After lunch the girls produced an old music player to show their guests how to salsa, moving in the easy rhythm that seems part of the Cuban DNA. Ralph returned the favour teaching them Minnesota polka.

It was an awkward attempt at dancing, with two steps back for every step forward, rather like Obama's bid to end the embargo.

Eighteen months later Fidel Castro would be dead and the US would have a new president vowing to scrap Obama's rapprochement (though some wondered if it would depend on Havana's willingness to host a Trump casino).

But on that hot July afternoon there was an unmistakeable feeling of hope; the world's biggest superpower and its tiny island neighbour were at last on a journey to becoming friends.